Decolonising Indigenous Rights

Routledge Studies in Anthropology

1. Student Mobility and Narrative in Europe
The New Strangers
Elizabeth Murphy-Lejeune

2. The Question of the Gift
Essays across Disciplines
Edited by Mark Osteen

3. Decolonising Indigenous Rights
Edited by Adolfo de Oliveira

Decolonising Indigenous Rights

Edited by Adolfo de Oliveira

Routledge
Taylor & Francis Group
New York London

First published 2009
by Routledge
711 Third Avenue, New York, NY 10017

Simultaneously published in the UK
by Routledge
2 Park Square, Milton Park, Abingdon, Oxon OX14 4RN

Routledge is an imprint of the Taylor & Francis Group, an informa business

First published in paperback 2011

© 2009 selection and editorial matter the editor; individual chapters the contributors

Typeset in Sabon by IBT Global.

All rights reserved. No part of this book may be reprinted or reproduced or utilised in any form or by any electronic, mechanical, or other means, now known or hereafter invented, including photocopying and recording, or in any information storage or retrieval system, without permission in writing from the publishers.

Trademark Notice: Product or corporate names may be trademarks or registered trademarks, and are used only for identification and explanation without intent to infringe.

Library of Congress Cataloging in Publication Data
Decolonising indigenous rights / edited by Adolfo de Oliveira.
    p. cm.—(Routledge studies in anthropology ; 3)
    Includes bibliographical references and index.
    ISBN 978-0-415-33950-6
    1. Indigenous peoples—Land tenure. 2. Indigenous peoples Civil rights.
3. Indigenous peoples—Legal status, laws, etc. 4. Self-determination, National.
I. Oliveira, Adolfo de, 1964-
    GN380.D43 2008
    305.8—dc22
    2008000582

ISBN13: **978-0-415-33950-6** (hbk)
ISBN13: 978-0-415-80785-2 (pbk)
ISBN13: 978-0-203-44920-2 (ebk)

*This book is dedicated to the memory of my father,
Adolfo de Oliveira, Sr., attorney (1933–2005)*

Contents

Acknowledgments ix

Introduction: Decolonising Approaches to Indigenous Rights 1
ADOLFO DE OLIVEIRA

1 Indigenous Peoples and Their Territories 17
ANDREW GRAY

2 The Reconstruction of Waimiri-Atroari Territory 45
STEPHEN G. BAINES

3 Legal Process of Abolition of Collective Property:
The Mapuche Case 65
JORGE CALBUCURA

4 Religion, Belief and Action: The Case of Ngarrindjeri
"Women's Business" on Hindmarsh Island, South Australia,
1994–1996 79
JAMES F. WEINER

5 American Indian Sovereignty: Now You See It, Now You Don't 105
PETER D'ERRICO

6 A Possible Indigenism: The Limits of the Constitutional
Amendment in Argentina 122
GELIND

7 Strategies for Equities in Indigenous Education: A Canadian
First Nations Case Study 132
MARLENE R. ATLEO

8 Notes on the Role of the Teacher in Indigenous School Education   165
   EDMUNDO ANTÔNIO PEGGION

9 Disease Versus Genocide: The Debate Over Population   173
   PAULA SHERMAN

10 Indigenous Peoples, Civil Society, and the Environment:
   The Struggle for Sustainability   190
   MARIO BLASER

Contributors   211
Index   213

Acknowledgments

This volume grew out of the Virtual Seminar on Indigenous and Minority Rights (September 1998), organised by the Centre for Indigenous American Studies and Exchange (CIASE) of the University of St. Andrews, UK, and by the Study Group for Inter-Ethnic Relations (GERI) of the University of Brasilia, Brazil. I am grateful to all those that helped in its making, particularly to Helder Ferreira de Sousa, from the University of Brasilia, who did the first desktop editing, Alan Passes and Yoko Nitahara for the revision, and to Marlene Atleo, Peter d'Errico and James Weiner, for the support in the realisation of the seminar. I am grateful also to the Brazilian National Research Council (CNPq) and to the Wenner-Gren Foundation for Anthropological Research, whose grants I received while working on this volume.

Adolfo de Oliveira

Introduction
Decolonising Approaches to Indigenous Rights
Adolfo de Oliveira

THE SUBJECTS' REBELLION

March 16, 1997. It was a hot summer afternoon when a crowd gathered in front of a building of unconspicuous appearance in Carpina, Pernambuco, in the Brazilian Northeast region. Indians from Northeast Brazil and the Eastern states of Minas Gerais and Espirito Santo, regions that were among the first to be invaded by the Portuguese in the 16th century, made up the group. Indigenous societies have been subject to a centuries-long process of sociocultural blurring and "integration" with the colonial (and later national) society. One could not tell the difference, in terms of appearance, between any of those Indians present and the local non-Indians—except for the display of occasional feathers, in adornments dutifully copied from Amazonian models.

Northeastern and Eastern Indian peoples were exposed to the European invasion from its outset. They were deprived of their languages and customs by the imposition of religious "administrators" (and later lay ones) for the narrow strips of land that the Portuguese Crown "granted" to them. They were forced to adopt a European language, European attire and a European economy.[1] By the middle of the last century, Northeastern and Eastern Brazilian Indians were considered "non-Indians," and were deprived of the few pieces of land they still possessed. Scattered through the whole Brazilian Northeastern and Eastern regions, living in areas left unoccupied by the European and national expansion, they formed the "raw material" from which today's Indian peoples in the region have constituted themselves, mainly since the 1970s. Since then, a growing number of Indigenous peoples[2] in the region have asserted themselves as rightfully—and lawfully—entitled to Indian Lands and special rights as Indians.

Within the building the president of FUNAI[3] addressed the participants of the first workshop organised by the Indian agency to discuss and reformulate its policy towards indigenous peoples from Northeast and Eastern Brazil. Two representatives of the Indians, directors of APOINME,[4] were invited to attend the meeting. They refused. Now, the Indians were demanding full participation in the event. Between them and access to the workshop there was a short wall, one and a half metres high, two Federal Police agents in charge of the security of FUNAI's president, and the unwillingness of the Indian agency—in the pathetic figure of a thin, short officer with arms akimbo—to accept the Indians' participation in the event.

And now a tense altercation takes place under the sun between Indians and Indian agency officers at the entrance to the building, the point of physical convergence of all these elements. In the reigning antiphony, demands of access and peremptory refusals mingle with reasonings on the impropriety—and material impossibility—of trying to hinder access to the Indians. The latter, more pragmatically, illustrated the aforementioned impossibility by transposing, in a single chaotic movement, the short wall between them and the refreshing shadows beside the building. The first Indian to jump over the wall, a woman, re-enacted (probably inadvertently and maybe unconsciously) a famous passage of Brazilian national history attributed to the Duke of Caxias, a national hero: "I'm going to jump over, and those among you who are truly Indians[5] shall come with me!" In a few seconds the patio is taken over by a humorous mob trying to find shelter from the glaring afternoon sun—also taking over, in their own way, the space of the (official) discussion of indigenist policy in Northeast Brazil.

A general feeling of embarrassment gripped both anthropologists and indigenists,[6] then (almost) all "barricaded" inside the main auditorium, whose door was locked from the inside by the FUNAI president's Federal Police escorts. A few participants tried to articulate justifications for their presence within the improvised citadel. Others glanced nervously at the windows, where the Indians, visibly appreciating the comic side of the situation, pressed their faces and hands over the entire transparent surface, trying to get a glimpse of whatever was going on inside. Not only the windows but also the whole front of the building were full of curious Indians—even some children—who were also scattered along the gardens, refectory and other rooms of the building, so suddenly emptied of their "official" occupants.

The FUNAI workshop was initially proposed as the first of two conjugated events, intended to appraise indigenist policy for the region and elaborate new directives for Indian public policy. The purported aim was a discussion of the official indigenist practice—defined according to an idealised "Amazonian model"—and its adaptation to local reality. In the first instance, the discussion would centre on the Indian agency itself, its own identity relative to the new *fin-de-millénaire* Indian reality. The idea behind this was to define first and foremost the place of the Indian agency within the field of indigenism: the agency has been suffering from an "identity crisis" caused by the very presence of indigenous politics on the contemporary stage. This was a task that could not be undertaken in the presence of the Indians, the very agents of the "crisis," the organisers argued. A second instance would follow: the outlining of a new policy for Indian peoples would be the object of another meeting, this time centred around Indigenous peoples and organisations and their claims.

However, during the months that followed the organising meetings for the Carpina seminar, this second agenda began to lose its relevance in the institutional discourse, slipping into oblivion in the final stages of the organisation of the event. At the same time there was an appropriation by the Indian agency of the event's agenda, which was turned into a stage for the enactment of an administrative reform. So, when the Indians jumped that wall, they were intervening not in a "session of institutional psychoanalysis" (as the event was termed by one of its organisers), but in a policy-making gathering, one which—by common accord between Indian and non-Indian participants, with the exception of the FUNAI officers—did not undertake the task of reformulating the indigenist policy on account of the evident lack of Indian participation. The gathering called for a new meeting to define the new lines of Indigenist policy; this time, with the Indians themselves.

Needless to say, this second meeting never occurred. But the Indians' action—neither the first nor the last of its kind—succeeded in establishing a measure of "horizontality" in the relation between the state and Indigenous peoples, who are no longer "subjects" for national state's policies, in the sense of passive receptacles of its action. The little "subjects' rebellion" of Carpina placed the Indians as *Fin-de-milléhaire* in their relation to the State.

This may seem surprisingly little at this turn of the century, especially in the Americas, caught this between two "indigenous" events of great symbolic (and not only symbolic) importance. The northern extremity of the continent saw the handing over by the administration of the territory of Nunavut to the Inuit in Canada.[7] Its southern end saw the Mapuche rebellions in Chile.[8] Both the autonomy achieved by the Inuit and the politics of self-determination put forward by the Mapuche are facets of a changing reality, and one that is not limited to the Americas. Carpina is part of this reality. Only if one considers that most Indigenous peoples there did not even exist as such during the lives of most of the last generation, can the full implications of that event be understood. A mere generation ago, the very possibility of articulating an indigenous discourse would be denied to the actors of Carpina's little interethnic drama. Presently we witness the emergence of their voice (quite literally) imposing itself on the state as a legitimate part in a relation that is forcibly shaped as an inter-ethnic dialogue.

THE DIALOGICAL CHARACTER OF INDIGENOUS AUTONOMY

Although terms such as "autonomy" and 'self-determination" are not frequently used in Brazilian Indigenous politics, the event described above and the situations experienced by the Inuit and Mapuche are visibly of a kind. The issues of self-determination, autonomy, self-government, sovereignty, or any other denomination they can have[9] are certainly of growing importance in the international scenario. The diversity of perspectives concerning the position of indigenous peoples in relation to national states is phenomenal, both within particular countries and between them. One element, though, seems common to the "field" as a whole: the great concern over the relationship between Indian peoples and the national states they find themselves within. This is certainly related to the "universality" of the "Indian" situation as a colonial situation (Balandier 1963, 1966). Effectively, "Indians" only exist in relation to national states; if the latter are lacking, the whole idea of "Indigenous" loses its meaning. "Indigenous" is a category defined by a certain form of relationship with the national state, as the Mexican anthropologist Guillermo Bonfil Batalla has put it,[10] and thus possesses a generality derived from its lack, at this level, of substantive content. This same generality is the basis nowadays for the paradoxical "universality" of Indigenous politics as the achievement of a dialogical approach in Indigenous peoples' relationships with national states.

By "dialogical" I mean a form of relationship that takes into account the viewpoint of Indigenous peoples regarding their own existence as a valid argument in the process of the elaboration of public policies and, more generally, in the relationship with state's (and encompassing society's) institutions. And if this seems rather prosaic today, one has only to remember how, not more than thirty or forty years ago, Indian voices were taken only as laments of a fading reality, inexorably destined to vanish, to realise how their contemporary situation has changed. It is this (potentially) dialogical situation that permits one to say, with Deloria and Lyttle (1998 [1984]: 15), that a notion such as self-government is "an exceedingly useful concept for Indians to deploy when dealing with the larger government because it provides a context within which negotiations can take place." In the same vein, Myrna Cunningham, former rector of the University of the Autonomous Regions of the Caribbean Coast of Nicaragua (URACCAN) and one of the mentors of the regional autonomy of the Indian peoples of Nicaragua's Atlantic coast, says that among other things it means

> the space for negotiation, which Indigenous peoples and ethnic communities count on to reach stability in the exercise of local, integral self-development and the opportunity to exert their historic rights in their own region. (Cunningham, 1988: 275, my translation)

Mexican Zapoteco scholar Manoel Ríos, in his turn, talking about the planned political-administrative autonomy of the Zapotecos of the Mexican state of Oaxaca, depicts autonomy as the "horizontalisation" of the relationship with the Mexican state:

> The project of autonomy of indigenous peoples is a proposal of a new relationship for the Mexican state and its self-denominated policy of participation. It is a new way to reach concrete responses to old, unaccomplished demands without reiterating the 'poverty and dependence' model that characterises indigenous regions up to this day. The proposed autonomy cannot be conceived solely as a movement of ethnic-cultural affirmation; it is basically a project that seeks to obtain new answers and not a new dialogue, because the latter did not exist before; it seeks to establish a dialogue with indigenous communities and organisations themselves. It proposes to the state a new form of relationship, departing from a horizontal structure of relations. (Ríos, 1988: 453–454, my translation)

In these quotations are depicted some of the implications of the term "dialogy," as I use it here. The German philosopher Karl-Otto Apel (1980) calls "dialogy" an entering into a language-game communication with the "object" of understanding, no matter how reflectively detached this communication might be.[11] That is, dialogy does not need to be actual, concrete verbal dialogue: it is a metaphor for a kind of understanding that implies the "language-game communication"[12] mentioned by Apel. Thus one could speak of a dialogical practice[13] as one that establishes such language-game communication. This "communication" implies the adoption of an ethics of logic (Apel, ibid.: 259), to be found in the demands for mutual recognition put forward by persons as the subjects of logical argument. As Apel puts it,

> As potential 'claims' that can be communicated interpersonally, all human 'needs' are ethically relevant. They must be acknowledged if they can be justified interpersonally through arguments. (Apel, ibid.: 277)

The "need" for autonomy—here a real, not a potential, claim—is quite concrete among indigenous peoples. It is expressed and reaffirmed in indigenous peoples' dealings with "their" national states: in their self-determination. Indigenous politics can be appropriately described as the struggle to bring to the fore the acknowledgement to which Apel refers. Indigenous peoples' ethnopolitics have communicative competence (Apel, ibid.: 208): the capacity of "reflexive distancing and creative sovereignty" in relation to the language-game of their relationship with the nation-state.

This dialogy is, quite concretely, the "product" of the agency of the stance Apel (ibid.) calls the intermediate social sphere of actualisation of moral values. The relationship between the State and indigenous peoples falls within this sphere, which is marked by the presence of a juridical-administrative superstructure that regulates and formalises such relationships. Those who have reflected upon this point have remarked that this intermediate sphere has adopted a relativistic viewpoint (albeit not exactly willingly) in its relationship to Indigenous groups within state borders. This accomplishment has taken place following lobbying by international groups whose action has been marked by a relativistic approach characterised by the defence of social diversity (Apel's macro-sphere). This viewpoint has been formalised, in varying degrees, as part of the juridical-administrative structure of the states involved.

It cannot be said, of course, that this "dialogue" is free from hierarchical cleavages. As the Brazilian anthropologist Roberto Cardoso de Oliveira reminds us, the very setting of the "dialogue," usually the language of the encompassing non-Indian society, makes it difficult to consolidate a plea for the validity of the arguments of Indian interlocutors: the dialogue itself is committed to the rules of the hegemonic discourse (Cardoso de Oliveira 1998: 179–180). But, Cardoso de Oliveira himself adds, the overcoming of this state of affairs begins with the institutionalisation of new structures forged with the participation of indigenous peoples themselves. And this is precisely what has been happening throughout the globe. It could be said, again following Apel's argument, that the consolidation of ethnopolitics and its agents[14] in the international scenario involves the playing out of a dialogical capacity.

In the introduction to a recent book on human rights and anthropology, Wilson (1997: 8) places in an anthropological setting a known hermeneutic critique of relativism.[15] He starts from the problem posed by the "traditional" universalistic approach to the issue of human rights when applied to local settings foreign to the ideal of Western, individualistic society. The ideological grounding of the universalistic approach in the Western notion of the individual as the repository of rights renders it unsuitable to cross-cultural application. But, on the other hand, the relativistic approach conjured to solve this problem is itself plagued by an inherent contradiction, since it constitutes a meta-narrative with totalising claims that critiques the possibility of existence of meta-narratives and totalising claims, being a self-undermining discourse. Cultural relativism, Wilson contends, reifies "cultures" as bounded, internally homogeneous monads, a highly unlikely representation in a world that has the presence of agents and institutions of nation-states everywhere and where the notion of human rights has been thoroughly globalised (Wilson, ibid.: 13). The anthropological task should be one of describing the different contexts of materialisation of the issue:

> A diversity of normative orders may still prevail, and may even be exacerbated by global processes, but they are no longer predicated upon isolation. Rather, a sense of difference is constructed out of relatedness, opposition and an awareness of plurality. [...] Just because a cultural form is global, it does not mean that everyone relates to it in the same way—its interpretation depends on local and individual value distinctions.
>
> The universality of human rights (or otherwise) thus becomes a question of context, necessitating a situational analysis. It is possible to

have contextualisation without relativisation, since one can keep open the possibility [. . .] that contexts are interlinked through a variety of processes [. . .]. (Wilson, ibid.: 8–9)

Wilson's proposal for describing the contexts of materialisation of human rights is refreshing, especially when compared with approaches that seek to find "correspondences" between human rights and non-Western legal codes and traditions at the level of their "inner cultural logic."[16] But in my opinion his critique of relativism fails in distinguishing between relativism as ideology and the relativistic approach (Cardoso de Oliveira, 1998: 170) that informs anthropological reflection. Relativism *qua* ideology has been adopted as part of the meta-narrative of national governments opposed to the insertion of human rights in their polities (Wilson, 1997: 8). On the other hand, the relativistic approach to the issue permits one to apprehend it not as the actualisation of a fixed set of rights in specific contexts, but as creation: the sorting out of new categories of phenomena that may be construed as relevant in relation to the notion of rights involved, and as a reflection upon the notion itself. A subtle difference of emphasis that implies a critical approach to notions of Indigenous rights, in the sense of testing their adequacy in the face of the very diversity they seek to support.

Such an approach is the way chosen by most contributors to this volume. The chapters presented here take a relativistic turn by questioning the use of Western notions to describe/deal with the issue of Indigenous territories (Gray, Baines, Calbucura); the use of Western concepts of political autonomy and sovereignty to describe/construe indigenous political projects (d'Errico); the Western notion of development as applied to Indigenous peoples (Blaser); Western notions of education in its relation to Indigenous societies' educational practice (Atleo, Peggion); the broad Western historical understanding of the relationship with Indigenous societies (Sherman); and the adequacy of the legal notion of "belief" to depict Aboriginal religiosity (Weiner). On the other hand, all authors have either hinted at the "embeddedness" of local issues in the tissue of a translocal "system" or state of affairs, or have stated it explicitly (Weiner, Baines). What Weiner says about Australian Aborigines can be, I think, extended to the whole field of Indigenous rights:

> By accepting the terms and conditions of the beneficial legislation empowering their religion, culture and claims to land, Aborigines are already conjuncturally implicated [. . .] in Euro-Australian society. (Weiner, this volume)

This "conjunctural implication" is somewhat more complex than it looks, even though its relative "universality" lends it an air of homogeneity. The groupings taking part in the interethnic relation have become considerably more complex at this *fin-de-millénaire* juncture. Different agents are now on the stage. Supranational, non-State organisations (nongovernmental organisations, NGOs) play a part where before only national states/societies and their agents did. Furthermore, Indigenous peoples' relations to the national states have diversified as well, with the emergence of different organisations and stances of representation to deal with Indigenous issues in particular, individual ways. The contemporary "setting" provides a counterpoint to the "universality" of the indigenous situation, since this very same "diversification" of which Weiner speaks also implies diversity. Diversity of forms of relating to the state and the encompassing society at large, that is, a diversity in the ways the "Indigenous situation" is accomplished in different places.

If diversity is present in the "gaps" in the "universality" of the indigenous situation, it does not mean that national states do not exert a homogenising influence over Indigenous peoples. The "embeddedness" of Indigenous issues into wider, state society—even in states that recognise and support some measure of Indigenous rights—is inevitably carried out within a highly hierarchical and asymmetric context, which may even have the perverse effect of "domesticating difference" in the act of supporting it. Argentine anthropologist Claudia Briones, discussing Indigenous identities, remarks that:

> In the same way some may worry that land claims and self-determination may endanger the principle of state sovereignty and internationalise the discussions—generating transnational pressure which one cannot ignore—others are concerned that the dynamics of Indigenous identities may become hostage to a mere simulacrum of diversity [. . .], in a form of self-orientalisation that 'essentialises' culture [. . .], or in a 'pasteurisation' of difference [. . .] We are also concerned that these dynamics may be brought to accept rigid standards of authenticity, that are impossible to meet [. . .], or may be co-opted by state agencies apparently sympathetic [to Indigenous peoples] [. . .], or suffer the same fate as other ethnic, linguistic or religious minorities and subordinated sectors of society, especially when the achievement of a significant measure of self-determination seems to effect a conversion of rights into privileges [. . .]. (Briones, 1998: 14, my translation, references omitted)

The points enumerated above could comprise a list of impediments to inter-ethnic dialogue. In a general way, such impediments convey, reproduce and reify the constituent asymmetry of inter-ethnic relations. Even so, the establishment of real dialogue is possible,[17] or else it is made possible by the everyday discursive practice (and political practice in general) of Indigenous politics. By this I mean that within the parameters of the relationship between indigenous societies and national states there is the possibility that the difference between them is not overshadowed by the hierarchy that marks their relationship. Our times bear witness to the increase of a sort of dialogical action that assumes both Indigenous and State societies as subjects of a dialogue, thus breaking with the "objectifying" approach that has marked their relations throughout the first half of the 20th century.[18]

The foundations for such action are being laid through the agency of Indigenous organisations and other, pro-indigenous ones. Apel seeks to establish the grounds for a rationally based ethics of universal scope; if it is at all possible, it will be one that establishes the grounds for the possible coexistence of different ethics—of different worlds of meaning and agency. If the space of diversity is a dialogical space, dialogy itself must be assumed as diverse. The contributions to this volume provide "critical snapshots" of such diversity in different contexts and places, as well as expose actual instances of dialogue—and of impediments to dialogue. As fragments of the ethnography of a worldwide, ongoing "subjects' rebellion," the contributions to this volume bear testimony to the diversity of perspectives on Indigenous rights issues, as well as to the "family resemblance" between them.

On the issue of Indigenous lands Andrew Gray takes the notions of "territory," as they have been used in Indigenous peoples' land claims, showing their incompatibility with those held by state agencies, which identify "territory" with "State" and thus see in Indians" claims a threat to national states. His deconstruction (or "decolonising") of the latter shows its indebtedness to 19th-century evolutionist thinking. Stephen Baines, in his turn, describes the imposition of territorial notions—and borders—by the state on a particular indigenous people in Amazonia (the Waimiri-Atroari), and its consequences. His article provides a cogent analysis of the construction of "directed self-determination" among the Waimiri-Atroari by a mining company working in their territory. Baines shows the simulacrum quality of such policy, where a private company takes up the state's "colonial" role vis-à-vis the Indians, while incorporating their image in their own efforts to legitimise their presence in the area. In the same vein, Jorge Calbucura presents Chilean agrarian policy towards the Mapuche—the dismantling of their communal territories, which was seen by many as a "model policy"—as the biggest threat to their continued existence. The authors depict the peculiar tension between the "local" of Indigenous peoples' claims, based in their own perception of their geographical (and also social and spiritual) space, and the "universal" of state dominance. This forges a situation where Indigenous territories can only be understood as a particular set of relations to the State.

The issues of self-determination, autonomy, and the relation to the juridical-administrative structure of the state, addressed by Peter d'Errico and GELIND's chapters, reveal the (potential) dialogical character of the relation between state and non-state societies. D'Errico shows how Western political/legal notions like "sovereignty" may be deceptive when applied to Indigenous societies, while GELIND's chapter shows the limits of Argentine legislation concerning indigenous issues. The central concern here is the possibility of indigenous societies exercising their specific ways of living within national states, as expressed in the latter's legal superstructure. This visibility as autonomous groups with their own specific, self-determined future is probably a hallmark of the dialogical aspect of the relation being established between Indigenous societies and national states at this *fin-de-millénaire*. This departure from earlier, ethnocentric standpoints has been transforming Law itself, as related to Indigenous rights issues. There is a transition from the use of a monological judicial model to the adoption of pluralistic ones, as anthropologist Raquel Yrigoyen (1998) has analysed in the Guatemalan case. The very perception of this issue by state agencies is already a sign of the transformations that the sovereignty of national states is undergoing, marked by, among other things, the construction/awareness of alternatives "under" the state sphere. This seems to be a distinctive element of Indigenous rights in our times. Although limitations do exist in great number, especially in relation to the implementation of these juridical dispositions, the mere existence of the latter is in itself indicative of the possibility of the establishment of a dialogical relationship between Indigenous societies and national states.

On the issue of indigenous education, Marlene Atleo takes an explicitly dialogical standpoint to re-work the framework of the educational process and proposes a new education-as-communicative-action formula, destined to re-educate both First Nations people and non-native people in Canada to live in a pluriethnic society. Edmundo Peggion questions the place of the teacher among the Shavante people of Central Brazil, from his experience as member of the Tucum Project, a training programme for indigenous peoples. Paula Sherman, in her turn, deal with the wider issue of the presence of Indigenous peoples in the global system, reviewing critically the historiographical versions of "contact" with indigenous peoples, showing its genocidal character.

If a single issue were to be taken as the issue *par excellence*, the most representative of this "dialogical turn" in the relation between Indigenous peoples and the states they find themselves in, that would probably be the so-called "anthropological advocacy" (taken here in the literal sense), examined in the contribution of James Weiner. What are the characteristics of such activity, bringing together anthropologists (as well as other professionals), Indigenous peoples, national administrations and judicial systems? To understand this is to understand too the peculiar position of anthropologists vis-à-vis Indigenous peoples and, indirectly, vis-à-vis the ideologies of national states.

Anthropologists are frequently mystified when reflecting about their role in judicial matters as "scientific" expert witnesses. In Brazil, Aracy Lopes da Silva questions whether there is any anthropology at all in anthropological reports (for judicial/administrative purposes), since they are written to "answer" the queries of a non-anthropological "audience," which is not interested in the questions anthropology traditionally poses itself (Lopes da

Silva, 1994). In Canada, Ignatius La Rusic warns that the anthropologist as scientist has little control over the statement that is placed before the court, and is thus subjected to legal strategy and not scholarly argumentation (La Rusic 1998). In Australia, Kenneth Maddock sums up some of the perplexities involved in the awareness of the peculiarities of the "advocacy" field:

> [W]hen Aboriginal claims become embroiled in public controversy the accuracy and integrity of anthropological work can be questioned. In particular, the use to which anthropologists put information can, with some justification, be cynically regarded if they appear to be blurring the boundary between the anthropologist as expert and the anthropologist as partisan or advocate. (Maddock, 1998: 1)

This disconcerting dialectic between the "expert" and the "advocate" is not the only delicate issue at stake. There is also the issue of a supposed "objectivity" which anthropological knowledge arguably does not possess, but which is apparently required by the court and state agencies, being the very reason for the anthropologist's presence in the whole process. The anthropologist is supposed to possess "firsthand scientific knowledge," often based on fieldwork (or at least on his or her professional capacity for conducting fieldwork) about the sociocultural background of the issues dealt with by juridical/administrative spheres. This "scientific" position has its commitments, one of which is to a supposed "neutrality" in the exercise of the role of "expert witness" in the court. As Brazilian anthropologist João dal Poz (1994: 58–59) has remarked, this position involves a fundamental contradiction since the anthropological practice is marked by living in close association with, participation with, and commitment to the peoples studied—providing thereby the "local" knowledge for which anthropologists are called as witnesses in the first place:

> We are thus left with a deep contradiction between the profession of anthropologist, which is based in participation and in living in close association [with the peoples concerned], and the distancing imposed by judicial experts, which highlights negatively the involvement between anthropologists and the communities they do research with. A question could be posed: how to find specialists, researchers on a specific Indian community if anthropologists are held suspect from the outset? (Dal Poz, ibid.: 59, my translation)

It is ironic that the same concern with localism and particularity, which according to Wilson prevented anthropology from reflecting earlier on issues related to human rights, is the reason why anthropologists are now called to play their role as "experts" on Indigenous rights" issues. It is also, of course, the same reason why they are "placed under suspicion" by those who required the anthropologist's presence in the first place.

Anthropologists are needed for their commitment to localism (as "research object" and as theoretical bias) via the practice of fieldwork. But what endorses the knowledge they produce in the juridical context is the representation of the anthropologist's work as "technically correct," while other, non-"technical" aspects of the anthropologist's practice are downplayed. Different dialogical contexts, different knowledges. The "expert witness" role places anthropologists, ironically, in the position of providers of "hard" evidence for legal processes that are embedded in a highly dialogical, interpretative context. As La Rusic (1998) points out, lawyers have given up long ago any intention of bringing "the truth" to the fore, resigning themselves to put before the court the defendants' cases in the most favourable way. This ethical standpoint, while strange to anthropologists—who identify strongly with the issues they advocate—is revealing of the heavily argumentative nature of the juridical sphere. This approach poses interesting questions pertinent to the practice of a dialogical (applied) anthropology related to Indigenous issues. While some would try to set "more objective" standards for data gathering, hoping to "solve" in this way the contradiction described above, a dialogical approach would be centred on a discussion about the adequacy of the categories within the context of the judicial (administrative, etc.) argumentation community with which the anthropologist works. As Weiner (this volume) points out, we should concentrate on describing and analysing the conditions under which Indigenous peoples' claims are made to appear, including the peculiar judicial/administrative "environment" within which these claims acquire meaningfulness. Weiner's advice can also be properly applied to the role of the anthropologist as expert witness. If the anthropologists' role in judicial processes is one of informing the court about the transcultural aspects of claims involving Indigenous peoples (and other ethnic groups), then the aspect of informing the court on the appropriateness of the questions it poses should not be downplayed by anthropologists. "Transcultural" here can work both ways. Adapting Marlene Atleo's (this volume) definition, it could be said that a large part of the anthropologist's role as expert witness is to "re-educate" those participating in the (legal) process, promoting the awareness of sociocultural diversity.

Probably the two main differences between anthropology as it is practised in universities and anthropology as an applied discipline are the argumentation communities implied in each practice, and applied anthropology's character of symbolic production aimed at action. The efficacy of the applied anthropological argument depends on how these two aspects are correctly evaluated by the anthropologist involved. They are not to be regarded as external to anthropology; rather, they are a constituent part of the practice of the discipline. Overing (1985) contends that the moral and ethical aspects of knowledge cannot be isolated from its pursuit. Indeed, to take a dialogical standpoint in applied anthropology issues implies the adoption of the ethical as the privileged ground for the relationship between anthropologist,

Indigenous societies, and judicial (and administrative) systems. On the other hand, the adoption of an "objectifying" standpoint also implies the establishment of a particular ethical relationship, one that reduces indigenous societies to the passive role of "objects" in relation to the judicial system and to the state at large. To include the ethical (and the moral) dimension in the reflection concerning applied anthropology is to acknowledge its importance in the structuring of the "applied" field in itself.

A GROWING POLILOGUE

All these points show, first and foremost, the overwhelming presence of Indigenous voices in today's political scene, engaged in an active dialogue with nation-states and their manifold agencies. These voices in themselves are not a recent phenomenon. Indigenous peoples, in general, have always had a voice. The difference is that Indigenous peoples' claims to existence as societies differentiated from mainstream national societies are taken nowadays as valid arguments in the dialogue with the states, while in the recent past they were regarded as the sad laments of peoples destined to disappear within a fully Westernised planet. In this sense, it can be said that Indigenous peoples participate today in an argumentation community together with the agencies of national states. For as much as state and national culture domination is present everywhere, it does not have the monopoly of valid arguments anymore: the state is not inevitable, nor does it retain exclusivity as intermediary between Indigenous peoples and the encompassing society. Nowadays, there are alternatives to the state and its truth. I believe that this is the distinctive characteristic of the relationship between Indigenous societies and national states in our times. If we want to analyse, and deal with these relationships in any way, we must bear in mind this fundamental trait.

The dialogical character (as far as the state is concerned) of present-day ethnopolitics also demands changes in our ways of knowing Indigenous peoples, be it in social anthropology, sociology, economy, education, law, history, or any other area that, in one way or another, deals with Indigenous peoples' issues. The chapters in this volume have amply demonstrated this point. A sensible approach to the question today involves efforts towards the "decolonisation" not only of the relationship between Indigenous peoples and national states, but also of the concepts and analytical approaches we utilise to understand Indigenous peoples.

In his discussion of "postcoloniality" in Africa, Terence Ranger defines three main meanings for the term: (1) the coming of Third World identities and spokespeople into the first world; (2) the privileging of particular methods and problematics so as to subvert Western rationality and "imperial science"; and (3) a descriptive sense, "the contemporary state of ex-imperial societies in Africa and Asia and also the attempts being made to describe them in ways which have meaning" (Ranger, 1997: 72, 271). I believe we can talk of decolonising our approach to the relationship between Indigenous societies and nation-states in quite similar ways. National states' relations to Indigenous peoples are changing fast, and we must keep up with changes also in a theoretical level. The central change is, I believe, the consolidation of Indigenous peoples' voices as legitimate participants in inter-ethnic dialogues. This demands change in our very definitions and ways of approaching the issue of the relationship between Indigenous peoples and states—our "methods and problematic"—so as to describe in meaningful ways the field of ethnopolitics.

These objectives, as seen from the above, cannot be attained unless one is fully aware of the diversity of voices that compose the not-so-harmonic chorus of the field of ethnopolitics. This is why this volume has brought together different categories of "knowers" (anthropologists, jurists, educators, Indigenous activists/scholars, sociologists) to take up the theme of indigenous rights: the issue is no longer restricted to a single professional field, if it ever was. A multitude of voices is responsible for defining the meaning of the field. If the latter is to be appreciated (or dealt with) in its full dimension, it is necessary to bring together this multitude of voices in a polilogue. This volume is intended as a contribution to such a polilogue.

REFERENCES

Apel, K.O. 1980. *Towards a Transformation of Philosophy*. London and Boston: Routledge and Kegan Paul.
Balandier, G. 1963. *Sociologie Actuelle de l'Áfrique Noire*. Paris: Presses Universitaires de France.
Balandier, G. 1966. The Colonial Situation: A Theoretical Approach. In Wallerstein, E. (ed.): *Social Change. The Colonial Situation*. New York, John Wiley & Sons.
Bonfil Batalla, G. 1995 [1972]. El Concepto de Índio en America: Una Categoría de la Situación Colonial. In *Obras Escojidas, Tomo I*, pp. 337–357. Mexico DF: Instituto Nacional Indigenista.
Briones, C. 1998. (Meta) Cultura del Estado-Nación y Estado de la (Meta) Cultura. *Série Antropológica*, 244. Brasília: UnB.
Cardoso de Oliveira, R. 1998. *O Trabalho do Antropólogo*. São Paulo: Ed. da Unesp/Paralelo 15.
Cunningham, M. 1998. La Autonomía Regional Multiétnica en la Costa Atlántica de Nicaragua. In M. Bartolomé and A. Barabas (cood.), *Autonomías Étnicas Y Estados Nacionales*. Ciudad de Mexico: CONACULTA/INAH.
Dal Poz, J. 1994. Antropólogos, Peritos e Suspeitos: Questões sobre a Produção da Verdade Judicial. In O. Sampaio Silva, L. Luz and C. M. Helm (orgs.), *A Perícia Antropológica em Processos Judiciais*. Florianópolis: EDUFSC/ABA/CPI-SP.
Deloria, V., and C.M. Lyttle. 1998 [1984]. *The Nations Within: The Past and Future of American Indian Sovereignty*. Austin: University of Texas Press.
La Rusic, I. 1988. Reinventing the Advocacy Wheel? In R. Paine (ed.), *Advocacy and Anthropology: First Encounters*. St. John's, Canada: ISER/Memorial University of Newfoundland.
Lopes da Silva, A. 1994. Há Antropologia nos Laudos Antropológicos? In O. Silva, L. Luz, and C.M. Helm (orgs.), *A Perícia Antropológica em Processos Judiciais*. Florianópolis: EDUFSC/ABA/CPI-SP.

Maddock, K. 1998. The Dubious Pleasures of Commitment. *Anthropology Today*, Vol. 14 (5):1–2.
Overing, J. (ed.). 1995. *Reason and Morality*. ASA. Monographs. London: Tavistok.
Ranger, T. and R. Werbner (eds.). 1997. *Postcolonial Identities in Africa*. London: Zed Books.
Ríos, M. 1998. Los Zapotecos y la Autonomía Indígena. In Bartolomé, M., and A. Barabas (coord.), *Autonomías Étnicas Y Estados Nacionales*. Ciudad de Mexico: CONACULTA/INAH.
Sampaio Silva, O., L. Luz, and C. M. Helm (orgs.). 1994. *A Perícia Antropológica em Processos Judiciais*. Florianópolis: EDUFSC/ABA/CPI-SP.
Wilson, R. (ed.). 1997. *Human Rights, Culture and Context*. London: Pluto Press.
Yrigoyen, R. (ed.). 1998. Justicia y Pluralismo Legal en Guatemala. Paper presented at the *Virtual Seminar on Indigenous Rights*, The University of St. Andrews, Scotland, July 1998.

NOTES TO THE INTRODUCTION

1. Growing saleable products like cotton, mostly to buy clothes and other accoutrements of a European "life style," Indian version; and working as a cheap, occasional labour force, a position they still frequently find themselves in nowadays.
2. Legislation in Brazil rules that an Indian community is one that has a historical liaison with a pre-Colombian people, thus making room for the presence of many Indigenous communities like those in Northeastern Brazil.
3. Fundação Nacional do Indio (National Indian Foundation), the official Brazilian agency for indigenous affairs.
4. The Association of Indigenous Peoples of Northeast Brazil, Minas Gerais and Espírito Santo.
5. Actually the expression used in Portuguese ("Indios de verdade") may be translated also as "true (in the sense of "legitimate") Indians." This says a lot about Indian identity in Northeast and Eastern Brazil: most groups in the area are the "result" of relatively recent (mostly mid-forties on, with a dramatic increase during the last three decades) ethnogenetic processes, having their identity as "true Indians" strongly denied by their non-Indian neighbours.
6. "Indigenism" is originally the name of the "official lore" related to the state management of Indian peoples. Nowadays indigenists work not only for the National Indian Foundation (FUNAI) but also for many non-governmental organisations, which have "appropriated" the term.
7. On the Inuit and the Canadian territory of Nunavut, see http://npc.nunavut.ca/eng/index.html (available in English).
8. About the Mapuche rebellion, see http://linux.soc.uu.se/mapuche/news/anews00.html (available in Spanish).
9. I am not implying they all mean one and the same thing, or even that they all are related to claims put forward by ethnopolitics. See, for instance, Deloria and Lyttle's (1984) account of the trajectory of the notion of "self-government" in the United States, pictured by them as both "the subject of a wholly arbitrary bureaucratic action and very spontaneous Indian militant activities" (1984: 266).
10. "The category of Indian is actually a supra-ethnic category that does not denote any specific content of the groups [it encompasses] but a particular relation between them and other sectors of the global social system of which the

Indians are a part. The category of Indian denotes the condition of colonised and refers necessarily to the colonial relation" (Bonfil Batalla, 1995 [1972]: 342, my translation).

11. Apel (1980: 185). In this section Apel comments on the central question for social scientists, as Wittgenstein and P. Winch would put it: are the rules used by the scientist to describe behaviour really followed by those whose behaviour is being described? He continues: "The answer to such questions can only be derived from a language-game communication with the object, no matter how reflectively detached and indirect this might be. This implies a method of "interpretation" (*verstehen*)."

12. I follow here Apel's interpretation of Wittgenstein's notion: "[T]hese language-games can be characterised in their heuristic conception as units of linguistic usage, life-form and world (situational) interpretation that are constituted by a behavioural rule. [. . .] It is not only so-called "linguistic usage" in the traditional sense that belongs to the "language-game" but also all thought and action which is "interlaced" in some way with linguistic usage. The context of the Philosophical Investigations makes it clear that this includes all human behaviour which involves an "understanding" of "meaning" and is (therefore) itself intelligible. [. . .] the model of the language game implies both the immediate world (situational) understanding which is an aspect of "meaning something" and, in the narrower sense, the "hermeneutic" understanding of the intentions that reside in the immediate understanding of the world and are expressed in the actions and deeds of human beings" (Apel, 1980: 22–24).

13. The philosopher actually refers to the sphere of understanding, not of practice.

14. I refer here to wider, "generic" identities as Indians, Native Americans, First Nations peoples, Aboriginal peoples, Native peoples, Forest Peoples, Autochthonous peoples, etc., as opposed to particular, "tribal" affiliations.

15. "One frequently hears that they have reached the objectively valid factual judgement that the norms which human beings either recognise or follow in practice are, to a large degree, relative to the particular culture of the time, i. e., they are subjective" (Apel, 1980: 229).

16. Wilson (1997: 13). His critique of such approaches is definitive: "[S]imilarities may exist, but we can never know how they will articulate until the concepts are brought into a concrete relationship in a particular socio-historical context" (ibid.).

17. This possibility of the creation of a democratic discursive ethics in the inter-ethnic context is to be understood as a possibility—as a regulating idea, the reference for a praxis aimed at the empirical achievement of such a community of argumentation and communication (Cardoso de Oliveira, 1998: 191).

18. As Wilson (1997: 13) puts it, the debate "universalism vs. relativism" in the human rights field raises basically two issues: (a) what concept of human ontology (and rights derived from "human nature") is to be used; and (b) what significance is to be accorded to the notion of "culture" in the construction of a normative moral order. The dialogical approach advocated here to the field of Indigenous rights issues, on the other hand, focuses on the communication between different societies, i.e., between state and non-state (Indigenous) societies. In relation to the two issues mentioned above by Wilson, it could be said that the debate concerning Indigenous rights approaches should raise the issues of (a) what form of communication—one could almost say, what language-game—is to be used in order to bridge the "gap" between particular human societies.

1 Indigenous Peoples and Their Territories

Andrew Gray

TERRITORY, COLONIALISM AND DECOLONISATION

The concept of territory encompasses a broad range of connotations, which contain serious implications for the rights of indigenous peoples. The vagueness and breadth of a term such as territory provide ample scope for heated discussion when indigenous rights are under review. During the revision of ILO Convention 107 in Geneva between 1986 and 1989, for example, the indigenous representatives present were adamant about the importance of recognising their rights to territories. However there was vocal opposition on the part of some governments to any acknowledgement that indigenous peoples have territories (Gray 1990: 184–186).

The debate has continued at the current standard setting process for a United Nations Declaration on the Rights of Indigenous Peoples (Gray & Dahl 1991: 169–170). In 1994 the twenty-six experts of the UN Sub-Commission on the Prevention of Discrimination and the Protection of Minorities unanimously approved the Declaration, which declares in Article 26 that:

> Indigenous peoples have the right to own, develop, control and use the lands and territories, including the total environment of the lands, air, waters, coastal seas, sea-ice, flora and fauna and other resources which they have traditionally owned or otherwise occupied or used. This includes the right to the full recognition of their laws, traditions and customs, land-tenure systems and institutions for the development and management of resources, and the right to effective measures by States to prevent any interference with, alienation of or encroachment upon these rights.

In March 1995, the draft Declaration on the Rights of Indigenous Peoples was sent up by the United Nations Commission on Human Rights, which is a political body consisting of government representatives. The Commission formed a Working Group to discuss the draft and, in November 1995, the world's states began to make their comments. Not surprisingly, one of the terms that several governments objected to in the draft was "territories." Governments such as Brazil (followed by a few other Latin American countries as well as the United States, Bangladesh and Japan) all considered that the use of the term territory is solely a prerogative of states. Within an anthropological context this argument seems absurd. The idea that indigenous peoples do not have territories runs counter to the development of anthropological theory over the last 100 years.

Throughout the history of the discipline, anthropologists have both defended and undermined the rights of indigenous peoples: they have been expert witnesses on both sides of court cases (La Rusic 1985: 165–169); they have been thorns in the flesh of indigenous peoples (Deloria 1970); and they are regularly considered as parties to a discipline which is the "handmaiden of colonialism" (Gray,1987a: 482). At the same time, many have dedicated their lives to supporting specific indigenous peoples; others have founded support organisations for indigenous rights; and some have worked against the process of colonisation. In spite of this chequered history, anthropology in itself has not been influential in the process of forming international standards for indigenous rights, and the views of anthropologists (where they exist) are usually eclipsed by the more mundane but immediate concerns of state power politics.

Indigenous peoples themselves have their own way of perceiving their territorial rights, which broadly consists of a package comprising the collective rights to self-determination as peoples, control over the development of their resources and recognition of their own political institutions. Any way of trying to relate an international concept to indigenous peoples will encounter some philosophical difficulties. The complicated spectrum of between five and ten thousand indigenous languages and cultures throughout the world means that trying to use a universal term to define indigenous territories will be somewhat problematic. However, over the last twenty years, the increasing number of indigenous peoples' fora provides an ever-growing coherent set of principles surrounding the indigenous concepts of the term territory.

This chapter will look at the concept of territory from several different angles. Initially, it will trace the emerging concept of territory from 19th-century juridical anthropology until the present day, comparing the term with the overlapping concepts of land, earth and landscape and relating these to current discussions of indigenous rights. The article then looks at indigenous peoples' views of their relationship to their surrounding world. Although the word "territory" is of European origin, we have to understand how and why it means so much to indigenous peoples. By comparing the non-indigenous and indigenous approaches to the concept of territory, we can place the discussions which are taking place internationally in a broader context.

For over a century the term territory has been discussed by anthropologists, ethologists and lawyers in markedly different contexts. The theoretical position from the 19th century divided political organisations into two types. Lewis Henry Morgan (1877: 6) provides the clearest example of connecting the concept of territory with the state:

> It may be here premised that all forms of government are reducible to two general plans [. . .] The first, in the order of time, is founded upon persons, and upon relations purely personal, and may be distinguished as a society *(societas)* [. . .] The second is founded upon territory and upon property, and may be distinguished as a state *(civitas)*.

Morgan contrasts society based on kinship with the state defined by property and territory. During the 19th century the evolutionary ideas which prevailed placed peoples on a graded hierarchy of progress. Those who were not organised into a state with a territory and private property were seen as pertaining to a lower stage in the evolutionary ladder. This theory of "primitive society" was constructed on the basis of theoretical speculation and had no basis in reality. It is about something "which does not and never has existed" (Kuper 1988: 8). Yet at the same time this perspective fitted neatly into the colonial framework where states with territories were able to colonise and incorporate other peoples.

The contemporary position of governments which denies indigenous peoples the rights to their territories is similar to Morgan's view in that it preserves a priority of state over society, where the former has a collective right to territory, but where the latter consists of "relations purely personal" and consequently has no territory. For Morgan, the priority was expressed through an evolutionary framework; nowadays it is based on state hegemony. Both positions share, however, the fact that states appropriate the concept of territories to justify the colonisation of indigenous peoples and gain access to their resources.

Among social anthropologists this conjectural hierarchy between societies based on kinship and states based on property and territory encountered opposition as the evolutionary paradigm underwent a marked shift in the 1920s and 1930s. In the United States, Robert Lowie, a pupil of Boas, published various critiques of evolutionary theory. In his book *Primitive Society* (1920: 378–379), Lowie uses Aboriginal peoples in Australia to show that territory plays an important part in the formation of non-state social systems, using the Kariera as an example. However, at the same time he says that there are other examples of people without notions of territory.

The idea that indigenous peoples had no notion of territory was contradicted by Radcliffe-Brown in 1930:

> It should be noted that the most important determining factor in relation to this wider structure is the strong social bond between the horde or local clan and its territory. The strong local solidarity which is the most important thing in the social life of the Australians, is correlated with a

very strong bond between the local group and its territory. (Radcliffe-Brown 1977: 161)

Ten years later, Radcliffe-Brown made one of his characteristic sweeping statements which turned around what Morgan and Maine had said:

> Every human society has some sort of territorial structure. We can find clearly defined local communities the smallest of which are linked together in a larger society, of which they are segments. This territorial structure provides the framework, not only for the political organization, whatever it may be, but for other forms of social organization also, such as the economic, for example [. . .] To try to distinguish, as Maine and Morgan did, between societies based on kinship [. . .] and societies based on occupation of a common territory or locality, and to regard the former as more 'primitive' than the latter, leads only to confusion. (Radcliffe-Brown 1940: xiv)

By 1940 anthropologists had dismissed the idea that indigenous peoples had no territory. Their view was increasingly reinforced by anthropologists over the next twenty-five years during the period of decolonization, when indigenous territories were converted into independent states. This process was carried out unilaterally by the colonising powers and through ignoring many ethnic boundaries, which led to disastrous consequences and the formation of new indigenous peoples within nation-states.

The discussion of the notion of territory continued in several directions from Radcliffe-Brown. His broad statement that all human societies have a territorial structure operating as a framework for organisation is vague. Subsequent anthropological work over the next few decades illustrated a variety of ways in which territory related to the social and cultural systems of indigenous peoples and produced a much more flexible perspective of the concept. Indeed, the emphasis on indigenous political systems occasionally gave the impression that territory was the only element of indigenous political life (Balandier 1970: 26).

The first aspect of the diversity within the notion of territory appears in the collection of essays on African political systems (Fortes & Evans-Pritchard 1940). The authors contrast political organisations that constitute indigenous states where the administrative unit is territorial and there is centralised authority with acephalous systems. An acephalous system would not have been considered as existing on a territory by the 19th-century evolutionists, but according to the authors:

> In the other group of societies there are no territorial units defined by an administrative system, but the territorial units are local communities the extent of which corresponds to the range of a particular

set of lineage ties and the bonds of direct co-operation. (Fortes & Evans-Pritchard, ibid.: 10)

The writers from 1940 gradually established a more flexible sense of territory than Radcliffe-Brown. When Evans-Pritchard writes about the Nuer, who are pastoralists of the southern Sudan, he describes them as a nation (ibid.: 279) consisting of "tribes" each with their territory. This territory "is divided into territorial segments which regard themselves as separate communities" (ibid.: 281). The social relationships between people according to these territorial segments constitute Nuer political structure. This approach could be taken straight from a contemporary indigenous representative's approach to international legal standards.

Fortes gives an example of territorial units in an acephalous political system which has no clearly defined territorial boundaries. He says, "indeterminate frontiers roughly demarcate the Tallensi of Ghana as an aggregate of communities" (Fortes 1940: 240). The word for community (*teng*) is also used to refer to the Earth "in its mystical aspect," sacred spots and clusters of these places. In this sense the territoriality of the Tallensi is clearly marked on a local level although the people as a whole do not have a marked frontier. This notion of "earth" also has a contemporary flavour of indigenous peoples' view of the world (Burgess 1987).

The increased flexibility of the concept of territory in Africa was reinforced by Schapera (1956), who looked at, among other things, territory from the perspective of four peoples in South Africa, ranging from the Bushmen and Bergdama who live in bands which recognise clearly their territories, to large scale organisations of peoples such as the Swazi. He concludes, "It may be said, therefore, that in South Africa each political community not only has its own territory, but occupies that territory to the exclusion of all others" (Schapera, ibid.: 15).

In 1962 Lucy Mair summarised the main findings of anthropologists to date with material from Africa. She took the argument to its logical conclusion and explained the concept of "government without the state." She argues that just because states have legislative, executive and judicial functions and an authority extended over a fixed territory does not mean that they have a monopoly over government (ibid.: 11). In the first place she reiterates clearly that "the political community, then, has its own territory whether or not it is organised in the form of a state" (ibid.: 16). Furthermore, she explains the relevance of the concept of "nation," and the sense in which it can be understood that indigenous peoples have their own law and government.

The 19th-century sense of territory as bounded state systems within a colonial context was "decolonised" during the first half of the 20th century. All peoples were capable of having territories based on political and religious criteria. This reflects the current indigenous position in the international legal arena, where it is consistently argued that the defining features

22 *Andrew Gray*

of territory are political control over an area and a spiritual relationship with the land. This is expressed in Article 25 of the draft Declaration on Indigenous Rights as follows:

> Indigenous peoples have the right to maintain and strengthen their distinctive spiritual and material relationship with the lands, territories, waters and coastal seas and other resources which they have traditionally owned or otherwise occupied or used, and to uphold their responsibilities to future generations in this regard.

EXPANDING CONCEPTS: TERRITORIES AND SOFTENING BOUNDARIES

In the late 1960s the concept of territory was broadened so to be not only a feature of human societies, but of all animals. Robert Ardrey in his book *The Territorial Imperative* states:

> A territory is an area of space, whether of water or earth or air, which an animal or group of animals defends as an exclusive preserve. The word is also used to describe the inward compulsion in animate beings to possess and defend such a space. A territorial species of animals, therefore, is one in which all males, and sometimes females too, bear an inherent drive to gain and defend an exclusive property. (Ardrey 1967: 3)

This extension of the notion of territory into a different domain from political anthropology, where it had been hitherto, satisfied the theoretical enterprise of the late 1960s to unpeel the cultural surface of human beings to reveal the animal aggression beneath.

This extreme position has received strong critiques from anthropologists from several sides. On the one hand the theory of the human as an aggressive animal confirms unreflectingly Western prejudices (Howell & Willis 1989: 8–9). Furthermore, Ardrey (1967: 313) uses his theory of territoriality to support linear social evolution, which as he himself admits has been "scorned by many a social anthropologist as an affront to human dignity."[1]

The key evidence against this view of human territoriality as the focus for the "aggressive instinct" comes from countless examples from all over the world where indigenous peoples do not fight over territorial boundaries but have a clearly flexible approach to them. After the 1960s, more studies demonstrated that territoriality was not about defending boundaries, but internal organisation within a spatial context. An example of this comes in Henriksen's (1986) account of Naskapi (Innu) hunting methods in the 1960s: "[T]he Naskapi are a small group of people who hunt in a vast tract of land with almost no competition from outside groups. The boundaries of their hunting territory are determined by the distance they wish and are able to travel" (Henriksen, ibid: 5).

Work from Australia around the same period demonstrated flexibility in a different way. According to Hiatt (1968), although different Aboriginal bands have their own territories, these are defined through kin relationships and access to sacred sites. As Godelier (1975: 16) puts it, "Members of other bands living near by are linked to it through overlapping section membership and therefore have the right to use each other's territory."

Since then, this observation has been analysed in detail by several writers on the subject (Morphy 1993: 230; 1995: 204; Layton 1995: 210ff). These Australian examples demonstrate the sophistication of territorial rights where economic access, participation at ceremonies on sacred sites, and section membership all inter-relate to produce a flexible, but not vague, multi-levelled definition of territory (Maddock 1982: 35). These different levels—economic, political and religious—have increasingly become the focus of studies over the past twenty years, with different emphases waxing and waning with anthropological theoretical positions.

By the late 1960s, the concept of territory was accepted as a fundamental part of the political organisation of indigenous peoples. Its earlier association with the term "tribe" had been replaced by works on ethnicity where the need for rigid boundaries was demonstrated to be unnecessary and discussions of other features such as flexible boundaries made sociocultural and environmental factors more prominent (Barth 1969: 24–27). However, the main focus of this period was a shift in emphasis from the concept of territory to that of "land" and its position in production activities.

Part of the change came through the theoretical origins of the influential Marxist approach to social investigation. Marx and Engels both relied heavily on Morgan, who as we noted earlier saw territory as an aspect of state societies.[2] Engels says: "In contrast to the old gentile organization, the state is distinguished firstly by the grouping of its members *on a territorial basis*" (Engels 1973: 229, my italics).

However, more significant for the Marxist approach was the increasing stress on economic factors in social formation. In this context the term "land" was used predominantly. For Marx, land was "inorganic nature," which is "an agent of production in creating a use-value, a material product" (Marx 1977: 494). The important element in this discussion is the fact that economic relations involving land are relations between people. The rise of capitalism constitutes a transformation of land from an object of labour to which all have access, to a commodity held by a landlord.

The theoretical overshadowing of the term territory by land in social anthropology reflected the new emphasis of subject matter dominating social scientific thought in the 1960s and 1970s. Territory was seen as the "juridical sphere" (Godelier 1974: 54), and during this period scholars became more interested in the structural relationship between "man and nature" and the economic role of land as providing the resources for production. Political anthropology thus became overshadowed by economic anthropology and the influence of Marx.

While "land" became a focus of study, Marx's analysis of the exploitation that arises when land is transferred from collective to private ownership was also under review by social scientists. With the rise in indigenous organisations during the 1960s and 1970s many of the demands centred on the invasions of indigenous peoples' lands. The Marxian analysis of land expropriation and exploitation of labour through land became highly relevant. This focus accounts for the emphasis on the term "land rights," which covers both access to resources and territorial control. This context shows the concept of territory approached from an economic perspective.

A further parallel concept has appeared occasionally with the notions of territory and lands. Anthropological interest in cosmology, religion and spirituality when applied to notions of territoriality has led to other terms. Here the words refer either to the specific areas under discussion (forest, river, sky or earth) or in a broader sense to the term "earth." The all-encompassing nature of the term "earth" has reflected indigenous perspectives of spirituality and territory.

Fortes (1940: 254) referred to the Tallensi's "cult of the Earth" in the sense of ground. Later, Evans-Pritchard (1956: 63) used the term "spirits of the earth" more broadly in contrast to "spirits of the above or of the sky." In this sense the term "earth" has been used frequently as relating religious or spiritual aspect of lands and territories. The Americas have provided many examples of the concept of the earth in a spiritual context. Ortiz (1969: 21) explains how Tewa villages in the American southwest have villages whose centres are known as "Earth mother earth navel middle place." Throughout the Highland areas of Peru and Bolivia, Pachamama is the female "ancient space/time concept immanent in the earth" (Nash 1979: 120–121).

When discussing earth we have entered into another dimension of the relationship between indigenous peoples and their environment. When we were discussing the concept of territory and land the orientation of the language was in the form of possession, access, ownership and control. These terms thus look at indigenous peoples in terms of their prior rights to their territories and lands over those of invaders or encroaching colonists. When we look at the notion of earth, on the other hand, possession is not the question, but, rather, a respect for spiritual and religious values. The earth or the spirituality connected with their territories and lands are a sign of the specific bond and understanding between indigenous peoples, which ties them to the place where they live.

The concept of "Mother Earth" has become a common phrase throughout the indigenous world, although the term is by no means universal. Furthermore, some indigenous peoples do not specify their ties with the earth solely in a spiritual way. They also demonstrate these ties by seeing in the world around the imprint of history. Indigenous peoples can see the remains of settlements, natural features and creatures as demonstrating their long residence of the place since "time immemorial."

The term which is coming into prominence in this context is "landscape." Whereas the concept of landscape has a set of connotations bound up with the aesthetics of painting and gardening between the 16th and 19th centuries in Europe, among indigenous peoples, landscape studies look at a broad range of factors such as the relationship between personal identity and the environment, the meaning embedded in particular places and the inscription of history over the surface of an area.

Like "earth," landscape denotes a special understanding or relationship with a territory. For many indigenous peoples, time and space are intimately related, and through analysing historical activity it is possible to see the past in the present layout of the world.[3] Landscape has become significant in anthropology as a way of looking at the process whereby human beings create their environment (Bender 1993: 1). This can be expressed in the form of how people perceive and act on their surroundings (Hirsch & O'Hanlon 1995).

This aspect of landscape creation is being understood as an important aspect of indigenous peoples' rights. In a recent report, Darrell Posey says:

> Despite international recognition, Indigenous Peoples' roles in biodiversity conservation have been underestimated. One reason is a failure to perceive the *anthropogenic* (i.e., human-created) or *humanised* (i.e., human-modified) nature of apparently pristine landscapes ... recognition of anthropogenic landscapes has important implications for ownership and, consequently, IPRs [Intellectual Property Rights]. [...] Species or landscapes that have been moulded or modified by human presence, however, are not automatically in the public domain and, consequently, local communities may claim special rights over them." (Posey 1995: 3)

Landscape, like the concept of land before it, has therefore drawn attention to another aspect of territoriality, which has not been emphasised much in anthropological writings hitherto. It is also a timely parallel with the rise in importance of concepts such as intellectual, scientific and cultural property and the rights which adhere to these aspects of indigenous resource control.

The initial attempt by the evolutionary anthropologists to deny the concept of territory for indigenous peoples gradually disappeared with the shift in paradigm during the first decades of the 20th century. By the 1960s the use of the term territory was accepted by anthropologists as a general notion covering all peoples. Subsequent work looked at more detailed variations in the way in which people control their territory, emphasising flexibility in the definition of borders and contexts in which they could be crossed. Some ethologists broadened the term territory and took it far beyond the specific anthropological use relating to political control of an area.

Anthropological use has also approached economic, religious, cultural and historical aspects of relating people to their environment. The different uses of the terms land, earth and landscape show how shifts in the language accompany theoretical changes of expression and how these also reflect different elements of indigenous peoples' territorial rights. The theoretical positions placed here delve further into the question as to whether indigenous peoples have rights to their territories or not. There are three points that should be addressed.

First of all, any attempt to deny indigenous peoples their claims to territory on the basis that they "have no territory" is anthropologically unsound. This position is an unadulterated restating of the 19th-century evolutionary position of Maine and Morgan (1877) that only states have territory. The opposite of this position is the ethological idea that everything has territory. Ardrey (1967) and Malmberg (1980) extend the notion of territory to such an extent that it refers to any behavioural demarcation of space. In order to overcome the confusion, Malmberg then distinguishes primitive, rural and urban territories. This smacks of a similar evolutionary principle but within the concept of territory.

Territory is not an evolutionary concept. Territorial rights exist in any indigenous social formation. However the way in which those rights are articulated depend on the way in which the territory is used and how it is conceptualised. These differences are not evolutionary; they vary according to time, place and historical context.

The four words which have arisen in the previous discussion, territory, land, earth and landscape can be approached in two ways. One is through a type of mutually exclusive series of monothetic definitions, and the other is as flexible aspects of one polythetic definition. The different elements in any discussion of territory will look at the relationship between peoples and their environment through the following terms:

1. *Territory* is the area which people need to live, comprising economic and social activities—including all aspects of the environment—forests, rivers, air, sea ice, etc.
2. *Land* is the soil or ground on which a settlement is built and where people grow their crops and forage.
3. *Earth* is the general term that according to its context can mean planet, ground as opposed to sky or soil and refers to the locus of spirituality.
4. *Landscape* comprises the surface features of an environment and its relationship with a people.

According to these mutually exclusive concepts, territory, earth, landscape and lands are substantially different. Unfortunately, this carving up of concepts relating to the environment ignores how they overlap considerably.

We have seen, for example, that the word "lands" frequently appears as an alternative for territory. An interesting illustration of this comes from the ILO:

> The ILO's Convention n°169 now has seven separate articles on land or territorial issues and related aspects of resource management. The first (Article 13) deals with the concept of land in its application. In particular, the collective aspects of the relationship between indigenous peoples and their lands or territories is to be respected; and the use of the term 'lands' is to include the concept of territories, covering the total environment of the areas which the peoples use or occupy. (Plant 1991: 60)

This illustrates the blurred boundary line between "lands" and "territories." When Australian Aboriginal peoples claim "Land Rights Now!" they do not mean "We want rights to land but forget our territories!" On the contrary, territoriality is fundamental to the existence of Aboriginal peoples and includes their control over their resources. In practice, landscape and religion are intimately bound up as is shown throughout the highland areas of Latin America among the Maya (Wilson 1993) and the Quechua (Skar 1994) connecting land, landscape, and the mountain spirits. The only conclusion which arises from this is that the four concepts which we have used here, and which at different times have been used to trace the relationship between indigenous peoples and their surroundings, are not discrete. They are, on the contrary, aspects of one element. We cannot really call this "environment" in that the concept is not particularly a human focused phenomenon, whereas territory, lands, earth and landscape involve political, economic, spiritual and cultural factors. My approach to this is that the four concepts are aspects of a "polythetic" definition (Needham 1975) of the relationship between human beings and their environment. We can place these as follows:

1. *Territory*—a word which refers to the political control of a people over the area they consider as their own.
2. *Lands*—the territory looked at from the point of view of the resources contained in the environment.
3. *Earth*—the religious or spiritual relationship they have with their territories.
4. *Landscape*—the historical and semantic relationship they have with their territory.

These are not discrete entities but ways of looking at the same relationship. For indigenous peoples these elements are not necessarily separate but are aspects of life. Separating the spiritual from the territorial is a compartmentalisation, which distorts analysis and does not reflect indigenous perspectives.

At different times in their intellectual history or according to their needs, anthropologists have used each of these elements as a starting point. In some cases they have argued a causal priority in explanation. For example, land as a resource is the fundamental element in the relationship with the environment or that cultural understanding of the landscape shapes other aspects of life. To use these elements in a reductionist fashion as a form of explanation is to lose the polythetic flavour of the relationship. In certain contexts one or other of these terms could be a useful heuristic starting point for analysing the relationship between indigenous peoples and their environment. Some may wish to start with the notion of lands if they are looking at access to resources, on the other hand others may wish to look at the concept of Earth if they are concerned with spirituality. The conclusion which arises from these concepts is that territoriality is the most appropriate starting point for looking at the rights of indigenous peoples in relation to their environment because the other elements are all incorporated into its broad framework. The parallel development of anthropological theory from territory through land to landscape has paralleled the interest of international legal standards in certain fundamental rights: rights to political control (territory), rights to resources (land) and rights to intellectual, scientific and cultural property (landscape). At all times the concept of "earth" and spirituality has existed in the background of these discussions. This fits in with the conclusions of Hirsch, which argue that potentiality remains forever in the background of a landscape and has spiritual dimension (Hirsch 1995: 4).

The parallels between anthropological theory and the interests in legal questions for indigenous peoples have not necessarily been directly connected. Anthropological interest in territory occurred during a period of decolonisation; the interest in land rights and resources occurred at the period in the indigenous movement when Marxism was influential. The concern with landscape and intellectual property is also paralleled at a period of predominant semantic—oriented post-modern paradigm. Although there are anthropologists throughout the world who make connections between their discipline and the indigenous movement in practice, this is not sufficient to say that anthropology has had a direct influence on legal questions. On the contrary, the parallels are, if anything, the results of more general paradigmatic interests that have been activated by changes that have taken place in indigenous communities.

A recent exploration in critical anthropology advocates the importance of moving away from the idea that the world is a series of "discrete territorialized cultures" (Gupta & Ferguson 1997: 3). In a world where there are an estimated fifty million refugees (Korten 1995: 255–256), flexible approaches to territoriality and ethnic identity are critical. However, this should not detract from the importance with which concepts such as territories are currently held by millions of indigenous peoples throughout the world. Indigenous peoples have clear notions of territoriality, but they are not fixed. Rather than dissolve the idea of territory, we should be looking to see how it operates as an object of study, something shifting and reformulating, and also as something so powerful as a marker of identity that some people are prepared to defend it to the death.

Over time, territoriality can change markedly according to historical circumstances. Nowhere is this more apparent than through the process of colonisation. The second half of this chapter investigates one example of an indigenous community in lowland Peru, which has changed its view of territoriality as a result of colonisation, and how this relates to trends in national and international law.

CONTRACTING CONCEPTS: TERRITORIES AND HARDENING BOUNDARIES

This section consists of an analysis of indigenous territorial rights in the Amazon. Indigenous territory is the key concept in the Amazon. A recent book (Chirif, Garcia & Chase Smith 1991) provides a detailed definition of territory in an Amazonian context that brings together all the aspects we have discussed hitherto:

> Mountains, valleys, river and lakes which are identified with the existence of an indigenous people and which have provided their means of life; the wealth inherited from their ancestors and the legacy which they are obliged to pass on to their descendants; a space in which each little part, each manifestation of life, each expression of nature is sacred in the memory and in the collective experience of that people and who share an intimate inter-relation with the rest of living beings respecting their natural evolution as a unique guarantee of mutual development; the range of freedom over which the people exercises its dominion, allowing it to develop its essential national elements and for whose defence or claims it will be disposed to spill the blood of each member of its people before enduring the shame of having to be seen despoiled in the eyes of its people. (Chirif, Garcia & Chase Smith, ibid.: 27–28)

The context of this definition, which is one of the most comprehensive to date, is to demonstrate and explain how indigenous peoples can demarcate their territories and defend them against encroachment. Territorial rights can be used as a starting point for including all the other aspects noted above in the "polythetic" definition of the relationship of indigenous peoples to their environment reviewed above.

Territorial rights are a "bundle" of different rights (Leach 1961: 104) relating to control over an area. The consequences of the recognition of this right are political control, access to resources, and freedom of religious and cultural expression. The example here looks closely at how in one Amazonian people, the Arakmbut of southeastern Peru, the notion of territorial rights proves an appropriate beginning for recognition of indigenous rights.

The Arakmbut (also known as Amarakaeri) are a Harakmbut-speaking people from the Madre de Dios region of Peru who first encountered the national society in the 1950s. Numbering just under 1,000 people, during the last forty years they have suffered elements of colonisation which have affected indigenous peoples all over the world—missionisation, land invasions, and attempted ethnocide.[4]

Prior to contact with missionaries, the Arakmbut lived in communal houses (*malocas*) along the banks of rivers flowing into the main Eori (Madre de Dios). There were twelve Arakmbut *malocas* constituting self-sufficient communities that mixed horticulture with hunting, gathering and fishing. Relations with the other *malocas* were frequent and consisted of alliances through marriage and mutual invitations to feasts and ceremonies. Each community had a flexible territorial area that blended into the territories of its neighbour.

When relations were good between *malocas* the territorial interaction was flexible and open. The influence of one community would weaken as a hunter or visitor approached the next one. Large areas of hunting grounds were shared by several *malocas*. When relationships deteriorated with other peoples (usually with neighbouring non-Arakmbut people) raiding occasionally took place, consisting of ambushes and attacks on *malocas* and gardens. These would occasionally result in deaths or the stealing of women or crops. The stories of fighting with the Taka (outsiders) are still enjoyed at dusk-time story-telling sessions.

This flexible territorial pattern did not necessarily consist of marked physical boundaries but social boundaries reflected on the ground. Friends came close to the community and enemies were repulsed. At the same time, land was sufficiently open that communities could move their communal houses (*hak*), after an attack, after a death or simply because they wanted to. Occasionally communities would break up and reform according to the political conditions and relationships with the other groups.

This flexible notion of territoriality, noted above among the Innu, is reported in other parts of lowland South America, particularly by Overing Kaplan (1975: 57), although some writers (e.g., Gallois 1998: 174) consider that the flexibility is so great that the concept of territory only becomes relevant with the process of demarcation. Whereas this is a reasonable approach, for the Arakmbut, the concept of *wandari* is present throughout their recent history. It is their word for a general extension of land and is their generic word for "territory." However, the Harakmbut language has several words that relate to their conceptualisation of territory. There are four distinctions that cover the word:

1. *Wandari* is a broad expanse of area which includes the forest, the river and the sky where there are resources ranging from fish under the water, gold under the ground to the birds in the air. In the past *wandari* was open-ended until an Arakmbut person encountered an enemy. Boundaries between groups reflected the political relations between groups. This term fits in our word for territory, lands and earth.
2. *Wandari* is divided into four domains. The *hak* (house, settlement) is surrounded by three others: *kurudn* (sky), *dumba* (forest) and *wawe* (river). All human and animal species and spirits are divided into these domains.
3. The domains are characterised by different elements. *Wae* is water while air has the same word as sky (*kurudn*). Sorok means soil. *Sorok* does not refer to anything beneath the soil. Whereas *sorok* has nothing growing above it, *barak*, on the other hand, consists of ground which has trees or scrub on the surface. Other substances are *kuwadn* (sand) and *widn* (stone).
4. The domains are further characterised by aspects of the landscape. These are specific features which people will know and which are too numerous to mention here. Examples are: *wakumbogn* (bank), *wakupa* (undulating ground), *mbayo* (a place where there is anything observable, e.g., *kotsimbayo*—where the *kotsi aguaje* grow). Salt licks where animals congregate are also known as *sorok* and are usually named.

This classification is extremely general, but it shows that indigenous peoples need not necessarily share the same way of ordering the environment. We can say however that *wandari* refers to political territory, access to resources and the earth as a whole. The domains refer to a classification of beings both visible and invisible within the *wandari* and are consequently the way of relating the invisible spiritual world to the visible. The third series of categories refer to the elements constituting the domains—water, air, soil etc., while the final one relates to features of the landscape. The classification which I use here is ever more specific, working from the large category of *wandari* to particular features found there.

All the elements mentioned in the discussion of anthropology and the law (territory, earth, land and landscape) appear in the Harakmbut classification, but they are embedded within the notion of territory that is the most all-embracing category. However, these concepts are not static in their application, and it is possible to see how the concept of *wandari* developed with colonisation through Arakmbut history.

After contact with missionaries in the early 1950s, the Arakmbut were plagued with sickness and disease. Fearing the decimation of their people, they followed the encouragement of the priests and eventually moved to the mission of Shintuya in the Upper Madre de Dios in 1957. They spent ten years in the artificially concentrated mission where 350 Harakmbut were living in close proximity to each other. During this period increasing conflicts with each other and the priests led to various crises. The Arakmbut responded by fleeing in several waves between 1969 and 1973 and settling once more in communities in their traditional homelands. They founded communities, but in the intervening years, colonists had already moved on to what had been their territories.

The small number of colonists at first was not a problem. The Arakmbut were prepared to share their resources. However, during the 1970s, gold in the rivers Karene, Pukiri and Inambari where the Arakmbut had their communities became the focus for an unprecedented invasion of colonists. The old *patrónes* who were already living in the area attracted peon labour from the highlands of Peru. Many of these workers were fleeing economic devastation and, later, warfare between the armed forces and the guerrilla organisation Sendero Luminoso.

The increase in colonisation became serious after 1979, when there were about 60 people on the lands of the community of San José de Karene where I stayed. By my first return in 1985 there were 300 people. By 1991 this figure had reached 550. For a community of 150 men, women and children, this was an enormous threat. After the murder of a young Arakmbut from the community in 1986, the old flexible manner of territorial protection was no longer possible.

Whereas in the pre-contact period territoriality had been agreed through alliance or fought out, after colonisation outsiders treated the lands as "empty," moved in and took over beaches to work gold. They prevented the Arakmbut from making their livelihood. Threats became common after the murder and the community was terrorised. Throughout this period of increasing conflict the Arakmbut struggled to gain their land titles.

In 1978 the Peruvian government enacted its Law of Native Communities (Law 22175) under the Ministry of Agriculture. This law had been originally instigated as the legal equivalent of the Agrarian Reform in the highlands which had been in operation since the time of President Velasco in 1974. The law sets out procedures for the titling of indigenous territories on a community basis where lands are recognised as inalienable and the area is demarcated on the basis of local needs. The process is complicated and usually not supported by the authorities, which prefer to encourage colonisation into the area. In addition to demarcation, the law also recognises indigenous community institutions provided that they are based on a standardised format, and grants tax exemption for indigenous peoples of the Amazon.

This law was not initiated by indigenous people but was part of a left-wing government's attempt to integrate peoples into the state by strengthening corporatist institutions. The main proponents of the law were indigenists who, as non-indigenous professionals working with indigenous peoples, produced an enlightened, but top-down, solution for land titling.

Indigenous peoples resented having conditions for demarcation imposed on them, and many would have preferred titling to be done according to a people as a whole rather than for each community. Nevertheless, by utilising the strengths of the law, the indigenous peoples of Peru have secured a patchwork of titles covering several millions of hectares throughout the Amazon.

Thus although the law was not indigenous, the indigenous peoples of Amazonian Peru have come to defend it, and many anthropologists have worked with the communities to fight for the demarcation process against a recalcitrant Ministry of Agriculture. The Arakmbut produced evidence for titling in 1979 to the state titling organisation SINAMOS, but with the return to democracy, the titling process was frozen.

An important aspect in the titling of the community was the rise of an indigenous community representative organisation, FENAMAD (the Native Federation of the Madre de Dios), which was founded in 1982 and contained representatives of every indigenous community in the Madre de Dios. FENAMAD worked consistently to obtain territorial recognition through titles with technical assistance from a support institution, the Centro Eori, based in Puerto Maldonado. The communities received their titles eventually in 1986.

The titles provided areas ranging from 3,000 to 50,000 hectares for five Arakmbut communities, recognising their inalienable territorial rights. The main problem was that the territorial rights had already been violated and expelling colonists from these lands, even though their presence is illegal, has proved impossible.

At least now each community has a fixed area delimited as its own territory where it can exploit its resources in relation to the needs of the community. Within the area the Arakmbut organise themselves politically and try as best as they can to defend their land from invaders. Without legal protection of their territories, however, the Arakmbut would have been destroyed by an open field raid on their lands. In spite of the enormous number of colonists now living on their community territory, about half that number again left the area soon after they first arrived when they realised that the indigenous community held titles.

The Arakmbut, as most of the indigenous peoples of the world, have a collective holding of and ownership at the territorial level. This means that no member of the community has the right to dispose of the land to anyone else. The territory is held in trust from the past generations for the future generations. The justification of this is connected with the spirit world which, being outside of time and space, is in a position to oversee the continuity of territorial holdings. Individual families can utilise lands within the territory for their production activities on a usufruct basis. However, this takes place within the broader context of the collective territorial holdings as a whole. The main change over the notion of territory has therefore been that the concept of *wandari* now refers to bounded units which the Arakmbut try to defend, rather than the more flexible social boundaries which they had prior to colonisation.

A further development that is taking place in the Madre de Dios is the formation of an Amarakaeri Communal Reserve through the work of FENAMAD and Centro Eori. The idea here is to link together the community lands into a wider protected area that can be controlled by representatives of the community to prevent illegal logging and the uncontrolled killing of animals. These areas will be shared by the communities, rather in the way that territorial overlap took place before contact. In this sense, community territory is surrounded by a broader homeland belonging to the native peoples as a whole. However, colonists already have plans to log this delicate ecological habitat and vigorously oppose the approval of the communal reserve.

To make matters worse, the oil company Mobil has carried out an environmental impact study in the area, and, in the face of great concern by the local Arakmbut communities, is considering exploration in the area of the reserve. The government should, by rights, have approved the reserve three years ago, but on the possibility it might gain from the oil reserves, the Minister refuses to sign recognition of the communal reserve. In this way, a great opportunity for the Arakmbut to control at least half of their traditional territory is slipping into the hands of the oil companies and the bureaucrats in Lima.

The colonists invading the *wandari* affect the capacity of the Arakmbut to control their own territory and also plunder their gardens, steal their gold deposits and frighten away the animals. This has consequences for their spirit world. The Arakmbut hunt and fish by means of contact with spirit world—the most important for production purposes are the forest (*dumberi*) and river (*waweri*) spirits. Every hunter and fisher through dreaming can communicate with the spirits, who tell him where he can find prey and how many can be killed. The capacity to provide meat comes therefore from spirits associated with the domains where the species live. The *wandari* is imbued with spiritual significance. As the gold rush brings more colonists, so the animals and fish are killed or frightened away. Consequently, the dream contact between the Arakmbut and the forest and river becomes less effective.

For hundreds, if not thousands of years, Harakmbut peoples have lived in this area. Throughout the *wandari* where the communities are settled, and in the communal reserve, are the old settlements of the ancestors. It is not uncommon for Arakmbut people to find fish poison, peach palm, pineapples or plantains in gardens that had been planted before contact with the national society. These old settlements are sacred to the history of the Arakmbut, who define their sense of time through the settlement patterns over the last hundred years.

By remembering the locations and names of old *malocas*, people can refer to events, myths, and stories which make up their oral culture. As these lands become invaded they are desecrated. The landscape of the Arakmbut is thus a text on which their history is written. As this is destroyed, so is the heritage of the people.

This example illustrates the intimate connections between political control, access to resources, spirituality and cultural continuity, which cluster together through the relationship of the Arakmbut to their environment. It also shows that unless territorial control is recognised and supported through defence programmes, access to resources will be eroded and spiritual and cultural life desecrated. For this reason the front line of decolonisation is territorial protection. The effect of colonisation for the Arakmbut has led to the need to define territorial rights more markedly. The reason for this is not that the Arakmbut lacked a territory before they encountered the national society, but that a change has taken place over the last forty years over the application of their notion of territory. Whereas the fixed boundaries of the communal house defined the community in the past, now this has been replaced by the fixed boundaries of community *wandari* recognised by Peruvian law.[5]

The need for territorial rights only emerged historically with the rise in colonisation of indigenous peoples. Before that time indigenous peoples used their own laws to regulate inter-community relations over territory. Now, to repel the colonising frontier, the Arakmbut use other methods. Fighting and arbitration do not work with colonists and international companies, so campaigns and protest are their main weapons. Particularly important defence mechanisms have been Western legal concepts. Fortunately, these, as we have seen, are highly appropriate for indigenous conceptualisations of territory.

As the territory of an indigenous people becomes threatened, so the need for territorial rights arises. In order to defend themselves the indigenous peoples can press to ensure that their territories are recognised and guaranteed as theirs by right and recognised by the state. This will provide them with a basis for defending their territory in the future. This is where indigenous peoples connect with national and international law. Until 1995, the Arakmbut defended their rights using Law 22175 and argued that their community titles enabled them to decide who should live on their lands. Recent cases in 1992 and 1994, for example, took place when San José, with the help from FENAMAD and a lawyer in Centro Eori, expelled a German adventurer from their lands and later a *patrón* who was beginning to impose himself on the community.

However, territorial defence is a constant struggle. Not only do the Arakmbut strive to defend themselves from colonists, but also from arbitrary changes in national legislation. On 18 July 1995, this means of redress was curtailed by the passing by President Fujimori of Law 26505, "The Law of Private Investment in the Development of Economic Activities in Lands of National Territories and of Native and Peasant Communities." This law brings into line unilateral changes that the government made in 1992 to weaken the provisions for indigenous peoples in the national constitution with the land law. The revised constitution removed the inalienable right of indigenous peoples to their lands, the prohibition on mortgaging indigenous land was lifted and any land that was not in use (as defined by the government) could be confiscated. The "Land Law," as it is known, transferred these constitutional amendments into practice without any discussion with indigenous peoples or with the representative organisations, although the International Monetary Fund was consulted (Garcia 1995: 21).

The indigenous peoples of Peru were extremely concerned about this, as the new law allows the decision of two-thirds of any Amazonian community to sell off its lands, and should a community get into debt, its lands can be confiscated in lieu of the amount owed. The communities are quickly trying to become acquainted with the law so that they can defend their communities from its overall aim, which is to turn indigenous political institutions into private companies. This makes land alienation even more of a threat because every time a community company goes bankrupt, it could lose its lands.

One way of defending themselves has been by recourse to international law. Peru is one of the few countries to ratify ILO Convention 169; this took place at the same time as the constitutional amendments in 1992. Convention 169 is considerably weaker than the Law of Native Communities, but it is very much stronger than the Land Law of July 1995. The indigenous peoples of Peru and their legal advisors know that ILO Convention 169 is now part of national and international law. One of its provisions is the recognition of the right of participation of indigenous peoples in any measures that affect them. The new Land Law involved no participation or consultation and therefore contradicts Article 4, Clause 2 (Garcia, ibid.: 71).

Even though the indigenous peoples of Peru have an excellent case to present to the ILO (it would have to be presented via an international trade union), so far there has been little enthusiasm among Latin American ILO officials to take up the case because it might dissuade other countries from ratification. In a trip through the Arakmbut communities in August 1995, it was clear that they are aware that the law is like a two-edged sword. Whereas the Law of Native Communities protects them, the Land Law threatens them. Whereas the ILO Convention provides the means to challenge the Land Law, in practice it is difficult to use.

This case study has demonstrated several points. The Arakmbut concept of *wandari* has shifted in meaning through the process of colonisation and increasingly means the same as the Spanish concept of territory. The sense of a right to territory arose from the injustice that the Arakmbut felt as colonists moved illegally onto their lands. Their recourse to rectify this has been to become aware of both national and international law. However, as was noted with anthropology and anthropologists earlier, the law and its practitioners can be either supportive or threatening. The indigenous struggle can really not rely on disciplines, but on friendly institutions and persons.

THE IMPORTANCE OF TERRITORIES

The experience of the Arakmbut is not unique but demonstrates a process of colonisation that can be seen globally. Examples from all over the world could illustrate the problems that can arise when indigenous peoples' territorial rights are not recognised. Should indigenous peoples lose control over their territories land invasion, despoliation and unilateral appropriation quickly follow. The main threats come from uncontrolled colonial frontiers, military force and the extension of state administrative control into indigenous territories (Bodley 1982: 23).

There are four main ways in which a breakdown of indigenous territorial control can lead to devastation for indigenous peoples.

1. *Establishing reservations.* In Australia, as in the United States, a policy of forcing indigenous peoples onto reservations was undertaken. This took place through the three dangers mentioned by Bodley above:

> The process of the destruction of Aboriginal peoples consisted of first being swamped and forced into submission by the colonial frontier and after that more specific government control took over. The government was pressed by the settlers to get them off all the land they wanted and by philanthropic groups who wanted them 'protected.' This is how the reserves were established. Where Aborigines did not wish to be resettled, they were forcibly relocated. As settlers demands increased the reserved areas decreased. (IWGIA 1985: 8)

The recognition of ethnic and community rights is only distinct from reservation practices when local people have sufficient territory to live according to their desires and aspirations. Wherever governments are land-titling indigenous territories, they frequently show a marked desire to reduce recognition to a minimum, something which can be observed in Brazil where a commitment to title indigenous areas was counteracted by Presidential Decree 1775 in 1996, which opened up fifty-four per cent of indigenous territories to claims by companies, local authorities or individuals.

2. *Allotment—Privatisation.* When outsiders want reservation land, a frequent policy of governments has been to "privatise the land" by means of allotment. This way of breaking down the inalienable element of land into disposable units has been used in the Chile, Bolivia and Japan to dispossess indigenous peoples. The most notorious example of this comes from the United States, where:

> During the period of most active allotment between 1887 and 1932 more than 60 per cent of the 56.7 million hectares then in Indian hands

was lost and the tribes were left with only 20 million hectares of often marginal land. (IWGIA, ibid.: 89)

3. *Dispossession and forced relocation.* In South Asia, land alienation of the indigenous tribal peoples was a problem from the British period onwards. The consequences for indigenous peoples in the plains have been total alienation from the land and dispossession. The presence of the British began a process of alienation of tribal peoples' territories, which still continues:

> Unable to resist the gradual alienation of their ancestral land, the aboriginals of many regions either gave way by withdrawing further into hills and tracts of marginal land or, if no such refuge areas were left, had no other choice than to accept the economic status of tenants, share croppers or agricultural labourers on the very land their forefathers had owned. (Fürer-Haimendorf 1982: 34–35)

The British tried to stem the tide of colonists onto indigenous territory in the hill areas by means of regulations preventing colonisation. The Inner Line Regulation in Nagaland is one example (IWGIA 1986: 14). The net result was an effective demarcation of Naga territory. The Chittagong Hill Tracts Regulation of 1900 initially had a similar effect (Chittagong Hill Tracts Commission 1991: 9–10). In both cases the laws related to local people's control over their territories and provided restrictions on those non-hill people wanting to settle there.

4. *Transmigration.* While there was some measure of territorial control, these areas were largely protected, but when, particularly after independence of India and Pakistan, the laws no longer had any territorial political element, outsiders rushed in to the areas as colonists. They were encouraged by the transmigration policies of the Indian and Bangladesh governments. The resulting unrest from the hill peoples led to militarisation and the tragic and violent consequences that occurred subsequently.[6] Similar devastating results of transmigration policies can be seen in Indonesia and Kanaky (New Caledonia).

These four examples of control of indigenous territories reflect clearly on the Arakmbut experience. Although the Arakmbut were not forced onto reservations, their titled lands comprise about one tenth of their original pre-mission territory. The alienation of Arakmbut lands through allotment is taking place by means of the current Land Law, which encouraged the formation of private businesses and allowed land alienation. Complete dispossession of Arakmbut has taken place in certain areas, such as the river Pukiri on San José del Karene's territory, which is now almost entirely a "no-go" area for the community who are threatened with death if they try to work gold on their own lands. Transmigration of outsiders onto indigenous protected territories occurs more as a spontaneous wave of colonists moving from the highlands down onto Arakmbut territory. This demonstrates that the case study in the previous section relates clearly to a process of colonisation that is international.

The gradual trend within the world until twenty years ago was a degeneration from territory and reservation to allotment and complete dispossession. However, since the 1960s, there has been an upsurge in the struggle of indigenous peoples for guaranteed recognition of their territorial rights. This is currently taking place on two fronts. One of these is through programmes of land titling and the other is through the establishing of indigenous rights to their territories.

Recognition of indigenous peoples' territories is a prerequisite for the exercise of the right to self-determination (Henriksen 1989: 15). Land-titling projects have been taking place in the Amazon. Pertinent examples include the recognition of eighteen million hectares of indigenous territories in Colombia (Bunyard 1989: 5) and a two million hectare community titling project in Peru (Gray & Hvalkof 1990: 230). In Brazil the recognition of the Yanomami Park has also been a step forward, although reports coming from the area indicate that the invading miners have still not all been removed from indigenous territory.

The recognition of titles is fundamental for the practical guarantee of indigenous territorial rights. This is particularly problematic in areas where there are protected areas and parks. For example, over eighty per cent of the protected areas in Latin America have indigenous peoples living inside them, while in India over 600,000 tribal people and forest-dwellers have been displaced from protected areas (Colchester 1994: 12, 19). The initiatives which have taken place in South America are just the beginning of a concerted effort on the part of indigenous peoples to make governments and other institutions all over the world understand the importance of territory for their survival.

The evolution of international standards complements the work on a national level for the recognition of indigenous rights. The most comprehensive process has been the UN Working Group on Indigenous Populations, which has met since 1982 to produce the draft Declaration on Indigenous Rights mentioned at the beginning of this chapter. On average about 500 indigenous representatives have attended this meeting annually and contributed to a text which, although not indigenous in itself, is supported by most indigenous peoples of the world. This meeting provides the focus for linking together all of the themes described hitherto.

Whereas it is impossible to show that anthropology and human rights connect directly at the inter-disciplinary level, they are subject to similar influences and work within the same historical paradigms. Nevertheless, there are moments when clear practical relationships emerge. The Arakmbut illustrate this. Between 1991 and 1993 the indigenous organisation of the Madre de Dios, FENAMAD participated at the UN Working group on Indigenous Populations. In each case, they were prepared by anthropologists and lawyers from the Centro Eori and support was found for them by anthropologists at the International Work Group for Indigenous Affairs (IWGIA) in Copenhagen.

During these three occasions FENAMAD, leaders and indigenous students were invited to the meeting to participate in the setting of international standards and to present publicly their concerns. At the meeting in 1992, the representatives made a presentation of the situation of the Arakmbut and the gold colonisation. A detailed report by a national commission analysed the situation from the perspective of national law and on this basis suggested that it is important that the new Declaration on the Rights of Indigenous Peoples protects subsurface rights to minerals and other resources. This was subsequently included in the draft Declaration. At this moment indigenous law, national law and international law were addressed by indigenous representatives. However, demonstrating interconnections is not necessarily a solution to the enormity of the daily problems facing indigenous peoples. As Elias Kentehuari, an Arakmbut student who defended his community in 1992 at the UN Working group, said in an interview afterwards:

> I thought with much illusion, that I would be able to find a solution here in the United Nations. I thought it was something else, that it was a meeting for the defense of the native communities. But I see now this is not the case. I am not as content as I hoped to be, I see that analyzing the situation, there are always obstacles to keep us marginalized. Regrettably the state and the laws put obstacles in our way. They don't pay us any attention and they don't acknowledge our rights. (Moksnes 1992: 28–29)

This chapter has brought us to the same point from two different directions. By analysing the shifting themes in anthropological writing on territory and related concepts, we have been able to throw light on the context of the current refusal by some governments to recognise indigenous rights to their territories. This myopia parallels the 19th century evolutionary approach to anthropology, which was immersed in discrimination, colonialism and racism, while the more progressive decolonisation approaches to territories from the 1940s–1960s reflect the concepts used by indigenous peoples today. This has been further elaborated by the concepts of land and intellectual property rights in the context of resources and landscape. However, there is no necessary relationship between anthropology and human rights theory, except through the connection of similar intellectual paradigms. This is not to say that a relationship cannot be created, but it will be through specific personal and institutional connections and interests.

A major factor of all the problems facing indigenous peoples today is the lack of recognition of their rights to their territories. Without recognition of territorial rights, indigenous peoples face alienation, dispossession and landlessness. The need for this guarantee has arisen as a result of colonisation from where the awareness of asserting the right arises. The Arakmbut show, as do indigenous peoples from all over the world, that rights emerge as a result of the injustice of colonisation. Only with the recognition of territorial rights can the decolonisation of indigenous peoples really begin. The struggle for rights operates at the levels of indigenous, national and international law—usually all three simultaneously. As this struggle necessitates a pro-indigenous perspective, it is unlikely that one will ever see a general link between anthropology and indigenous rights except one forged personally and institutionally through the practical mediation of indigenous peoples.

The conclusion is that the ambivalence felt by indigenous peoples for anthropologists is well founded. The discipline is a set of theories and techniques, which can on the one hand analyse human rights from a local perspective and which can, on the other hand, use human rights as a basis for pro-indigenous or anti-indigenous activities. In the end, the relationship is one of potentialities, which is only made actual through the activity of each person or institution.

NOTES TO CHAPTER 1

1. This approach was taken further by Torsten Malmberg in his book *Human Territoriality* (1980), where in a chapter called "Primitive Territories" he compares children, mental deficiency, stone-age spatial behaviour and "primitive societies." The cluster of such diverse and unrelated subjects within a chapter called "Primitive Territories" can only be seen as extremely unhelpful in this context. The notion of territory is stretched in these ethological works far beyond the notion of sovereignty and political control to be of any use whatsoever.
2. To be fair to Morgan we should note that in 1871 he wrote in "Systems of Consanguinity and Affinity of the Human Family": "Each tribe is individualised by a name, by a separate dialect, by a supreme government and by the possession of some territory which it occupies and defends as its very own." (cited in Godelier 1974). However, Morgan's later position in *Ancient Society* (1877) appears to have been the approach for which he is more famous.
3. A recent seminar series in Oxford looking at the relationship of identity with the environment included several papers on the importance of landscape among Arctic peoples. In particular, Mark Nutall's account of the Inuit of Greenland demonstrated clearly their cultural and historical knowledge inscribed upon the landscape.
4. Most of the information presented here is based on three years living with the Arakmbut in the Peruvian Amazon. Written material also comes from Gray (1983, 1986, 1987a, 1987b) and the Arakmbut Trilogy (Gray, 1996–1997).
5. The Amazon is not the only example where territorial rights have become more fixed as a result of colonisation. Schapera (1956: 14) noted in Africa:

"In general it is only within the past century and a half, and largely owing to the spread of European domination, that tribal territories have become fairly stable and precisely defined. But much of what was formerly tribal land has been appropriated for European settlement."

6. Johnson (1982) relates events that took place in Nagaland, Burma, India and Bangladesh.

REFERENCES

Ardrey, R. 1967. *The Territorial Imperative: A Personal Inquiry into the Animal Origins of Property and Nations.* London: Collins.
Balandier, G. 1970. *Political Anthropology.* London: Allen Lane, the Penguin Press.
Barth, F. (ed.). 1969. *Ethnic groups and Boundaries: The Social Organization of Cultural Difference.* London: Allen & Unwin.
Bender, B. (ed.). 1993. *Landscape: Politics and Perspectives.* Oxford: Berg.
Bodley, J. 1982. *Victims of Progress.* London: Benjamin Cummings.
Bunyard, P. 1989. *The Colombian Amazon: Polices for the Protection of Its Indigenous Peoples and Their Environment.* Bodmin, Cornwall, UK: The Ecological Press.
Burgess, H. 1987. Traditional Territories of the Earth. In *IWGIA Yearbook 1986,* pp. 133–140. Copenhagen: IWGA.
Chirif, A., P. Garcia, and R. Chase Smith. 1991. *El Indigena y Su Territorio son Uno Solo: Estrategias para la Defensa de los Pueblos y Territorios Indigenas en la Cuenca Amazonica.* Lima: Oxfam America/COICA.
Chittagong Hill Tracts Commission. 1991. *Life is Not Ours: Land and Human Rights in the Chittagong Hill Tracts, Bangladesh.* London: Calvert's Press.
Colchester, M. 1994. *Salvaging Nature: Indigenous Peoples, Protected Areas and Biodiversity Conservation.* Geneva: World Rainforest Movement, World Wide Fund for Nature, and United Nations Research Institute for Social Development. DP 55.
Deloria, V. 1970. *Custer Died for Your Sins: An Indian Manifesto.* New York: Avon.
Engels, F. 1973. *The Origin of the Family, Private Property and the State.* London: Lawrence and Wishart.
Evans-Pritchard, E.E. 1940. The Nuer of the Southern Sudan. In M. Fortes and E.E. Evans-Pritchard (eds.), *African Political Systems.* Oxford: Oxford University Press.
Evans-Pritchard, E.E. 1956. *Nuer Religion.* Oxford: Oxford University Press.
Fortes, M. 1940. The Political System of the Tallensi of the Northern Territories of the Gold Coast. In M. Fortes and E.E. Evans-Pritchard (eds.), *African Political Systems.* Oxford: Oxford University Press.
Fortes, M., and E.E. Evans-Pritchard. 1940. *African Political Systems.* Oxford: Oxford University Press.
Fürer-Haimendorf, C. von. 1982. *Tribes of India: Their Struggle for Survival.* Delhi and Oxford: Oxford University Press.
Gallois, D. 1998. Brazil: The Case of the Waiapi. In A. Gray, A. Parellada and H. Newing (eds.), *From Principle to Practice: Indigenous Peoples and Biodiversity Conservation in Latin America,* pp. 167–185. Copenhagen: IWGIA Forest Peoples Programme/AIDESEP.
Garcia, P. 1995. *Territorios Indígenas y La Nueva Legislación Agraria en el Perú.* In IWGIA Documento 17/ Racimos de Ungurahui. Lima: IWGIA.

Godelier, M. 1974. *Perspectives in Marxist Anthropology*. Cambridge: Cambridge University Press.
Godelier, M. 1975. Modes of Production, Kinship and Demographic Structures. In M. Bloch (ed.), *Marxist Analysis and Social Anthropology*. ASA Studies 2. London: Malaby Press.
Gray, A. 1983. *The Amarakaeri: An Ethnographic Description of an Harakmbut People in Southeastern Peru*. Ph.D. Thesis. University of Oxford.
Gray, A. 1986. *And After the Gold Rush . . . ? Human Rights and Self-Development among the Amarakaeri of Southeastern Peru*. IWGIA Document No. 55. Copenhagen.
Gray, A. 1987a. Perspectives on Amarakaeri History. In H. Skar and F. Salamon (eds.), *Natives and Neighbours in South America*. Gothenburg: Göteborgs Etnografiska Museum.
Gray, A. 1987b. Indigenous Affairs and Anthropology. In H. Skar and F. Salamon (eds.), *Natives and neighbours in South America*. Gothenburg: Göteborgs Etnografiska Museum.
Gray, A. 1990. Report on the International Labour Organisation Revision of Convention 107. *IWGIA Yearbook 1989*, pp. 173–191. Copenhagen: IWGIA.
Gray, A. 1996–1997. *The Arakmbut Trilogy (Vol. 1: Mythology, Spirituality and history; Volume 2: The Last Shaman; Volume 3: Indigenous Rights and Development)*. Oxford: Berghahn Books.
Gray, A., and J. Dahl. 1991. Report on the Eighth Session of the UN Working Group on Indigenous Populations. *IWGIA Yearbook 1990*, pp. 167–173. Copenhagen: IWGIA.
Gray, A., and S. Hvalkof. 1990. Indigenous Land Titling in the Peruvian Amazon. *IWGIA Yearbook 1989*, pp. 230–243. Copenhagen: IWGIA.
Gupta A., and J. Ferguson (eds.). 1997. *Culture, Power, Place: Explorations in Critical Anthropology*. Durham, NC: Duke University Press.
Henriksen, G. 1986. *Hunters in the Barrens: The Naskapi on the Edge of the White Man's World*. Newfoundland Social and Economic Studies 12.
Henriksen, G. 1989. Introduction to Indigenous Self-Development in the Americas. *IWGIA Document 63*. Copenhagen: IWGIA.
Hiatt, L. 1968. Ownership and Use of Land among the Australian Aborigines. In R. Lee and I. Devore (eds.), *Man the Hunter*. Chicago: Aldine.
Hirsch, E. 1995. Introduction. In R. Hirsch and M. O'Hanlon (eds.), *The Anthropology of Landscape: Perspectives on Place and Space*, pp. 1–30. Oxford: Clarendon Press.
Hirsch, E. & M. O'Hanlon 1995. The Anthropology of Landscape: Perspectives on Place and Space. Oxford: Claredone Press.
Howell, S., and R. Willis (eds.). 1989. *Societies at Peace*. London: Routledge.
Johnson, C. 1982. Eastern India: The Plight of Ethnic Minorities: 'He who lays down his gun lays down his freedom.' *IWGIA Newsletter No. 31–2* pp. 90–99. Copenhagen: IWGIA.
IWGIA (ed.). 1985. Land Rights Now: *The Aboriginal Fight for Land in Australia*. IWGIA Document 54, Copenhagen.
IWGIA (ed.). 1986. *The Naga Nation and its Struggle against Genocide*. IWGIA Document 56. Copenhagen.
Korten, D. 1995. *When Corporations Rule the World*. San Francisco: Kumarian Press/Berrett-Koehler.
Kuper, A. 1988. *The Invention of Primitive Society*. London:Routledge.
La Rusic, I. 1985. Expert Witness? In R. Paine (ed.), *Advocacy and Anthropology*. Institute of Social and Economic Research, Memorial University of Newfoundland, St John's.

Layton, R. 1995. Relating to the Country in the Western Desert. In E. Hirsch and M. O'Hanlon (eds.), *The Anthropology of Landscape: Perspectives on Place and Space*, pp. 210–231. Oxford: Clarendon Press.

Leach, E.R. 1961. *Rethinking Anthropology*. London: Athlone Press.

Maddock, K. 1982. *The Australian Aborigines: A Portrait of their Society*. London: Pelican Books.

Mair, L. 1962. *Primitive Government*. London: Pelican Books.

Malmberg, T. 1980. *Human Territoriality: Survey of Behavioral Territories in Man With Preliminary Analysis and Discussion of Meaning*. The Hague: Mouton.

Marx, K. 1977. *Selected Writings*. Edited by D. McLennan. Oxford: Oxford University Press.

Moksnes, H. 1992. Culture is how we survive: Interviews with five indigenous representatives from the Americas about the 500 years and the UN. *IWGIA Newsletter*. No. 3, pp. 24–29. Copenhagen: IWGIA.

Morgan, L.H. 1877. *Ancient Society*. New York: Holt.

Morphy, H. 1993. Colonialism, History and the Construction of Place: The Politics of Landscape in northern Australia. In B. Bender (ed.), *Landscape: Politics and Perspectives*, pp. 205–244. Oxford: Berg.

Morphy, H. 1995. Landscape and the Reproduction of the Ancestral Past. In E. Hirsch and M. O'Hanlon (eds.), *The Anthropology of Landscape: Perspectives on Place and Space*, pp. 184–209. Oxford: Clarendon Press.

Nash, J. 1979. *We Eat the Mines and the Mines Eat Us: Dependency and Exploitation in Bolivian Tin Mines*. New York: Columbia University Press.

Needham, R. 1975. Polythetic Classification. *Man*, n.s. 10: 349–369.

Ortiz, A. 1969. *The Tewa World: Space, Time, Being and becoming in a Pueblo Society*. Chicago: Chicago University Press.

Overing Kaplan, J. 1975. *The Piaroa, A People of the Orinoco Basin*. Oxford: Clarendon Press.

Plant, R. 1991. Land Rights for Indigenous and tribal Peoples in Developing Countries: A Survey of Law and Policy Issues, Current Activities, and Proposals for an Inter-Agency Programme of Action World Employment Programme. *Research Working Paper*, WEP 10–6/WP108.

Posey, D. 1995. *Indigenous Peoples and Traditional Resource Rights: A Basis for Equitable Relationships?* Oxford. Green College Centre for Environmental Policy and Understanding.

Radcliffe-Brown, A.R. 1940. Preface. In M. Fortes and E.E. Evans-Pritchard (eds.), *African Political Systems*. Oxford: Oxford. University Press.

Radcliffe-Brown, A.R. 1977. The Social Organization of Australian Tribes. In A. Kuper (ed.), *The Social Anthropology of Radcliffe Brown*. London: Routledge.

Schapera, I. 1956. *Government and Politics in Tribal Societies*. London. Watts.

Skar, S. 1994. *Lives Together, Worlds Apart: Quechua Colonization in Jungle and City*. Oslo: Scandinavian University Press.

Wilson, R. 1993. Anchored Communities: Identity and History of the Maya-Q'eqchi. *Man* (n.s.) 28: 121–138.

2 The Reconstruction of Waimiri-Atroari Territory

Stephen G. Baines

The recent history of interethnic contact between the Waimiri-Atroari indigenous people and segments of the national society which have invaded their territory clearly shows how Western economic exploitation of land and natural resources leads to redefinitions of indigenous concepts of space and the imposition of new definitions by the dominant invading populations on the dominated Indian people. These redefinitions of indigenous concepts of space occur within the context of, and as part of, violent changes in the Indian way of life brought about by interethnic contact. Although the indigenous ways of apprehending the new imposed definitions pass through a cultural filter, and are often interpreted very differently from what the mentors had imagined, the social relations of domination/subjection which characterise interethnic contact in Brazil (Cardoso de Oliveira 1976: 9, 56–57; 1978: 83–98; 1996 [1964]) subordinate and devalue indigenous concepts.

Native Americans are by no means passive recipients of imposed Western ideologies, as the long struggle they have kept up since colonisation began shows. However, under the threat of brute force and powerful corporations, their perspectives are frequently ignored and trampled on, so that they, in an effort to survive, and faced with immensely more powerful forces, often take up versions of the colonising discourse, in an attempt to accommodate to a colonial situation. As Varese (1996: 15–30) emphasises, with the "New World Order" and weakening of the sovereignties of the nation-states, native peoples increasingly have to deal directly with transnational corporations.

This chapter looks at the reconstruction of space in the case of the Waimiri-Atroari and the ways in which their concepts have been moulded by a colonial situation. I conclude the chapter by looking at the question of the reconstruction of space in the light of globalisation rhetoric, and how this rhetoric can verbally neutralise the violence of situations of interethnic contact.

WAIMIRI-ATROARI CONCEPTS OF SPACE

The Waimiri-Atroari, an Indian population of the Carib language family, inhabit part of the north of Amazonas State and the south of Roraima, in the basins of the rivers Alalaú, Camanaú, Curiuaú and the Igarapé Santo Antônio do Abonari. Up to the beginning of this century the territory occupied by these Indians was very much more extensive than today, including the basins of the rivers Jauaperí and Uatumã. After a long history of violent invasions,[1] closely related to fluctuations in the prices of forest products on the international market such as Brazil nuts, latex, otter and alligator skins, and tropical hard woods, the Waimiri-Atroari were driven into a territory where they remained until the 1970s.

Estimates of the Waimiri-Atroari population in the past are very contradictory. Hübner and Koch-Grünberg (1907: 232) mention that there were "6.000 Indians on the River Jauaperí, according to the Brazilians." However, the regional population to whom they refer, being at war with the Indians at the time and having just incited the local government to undertake a punitive expedition against them (ibid.: 229), had an interest in presenting a high estimate of the Indian population. According to the Indian Census of August 1959, undertaken by the government Indian agency Serviço de Proteção ao Índio (SPI), there were 957 Waimiri-Atroari in contact with the Camanaú and Alalaú Indian Posts. There are, however, no estimates of the Indian population that was not in contact with the Indian Agency Posts. In 1973, the administrator of this area, Gilberto Pinto Figueiredo Costa, of the Fundação Nacional do Índio (FUNAI—the new name given to the government Indian agency in 1967), admitted that "The Attraction Front does not have real data about the number of Indians... However, estimates of the signatory of this Report are of around 600 to 1000 Indians."[2] In 1983, after more than a decade of lethal epidemics, which increased at an unprecedented rate during the construction of the BR-174 Highway, only about 332 Waimiri-Atroari survived (Baines 1991a: 78), although the population has been recovering rapidly since then, especially during the period 1983–1987.[3]

To understand the impact of interethnic contact on Waimiri-Atroari concepts of space, it is necessary to examine their cosmovision prior to the massive occupation of their territory. The spatialised construction of social alterity, explicit in their system of sorcery, was centred on the village. When I began fieldwork with the Waimiri-Atroari, there were no longer any villages independent of the Waimiri-Atroari Attraction Front (Frente de Atração Waimiri-Atroari)—FAWA—set up by the FUNAI in 1970 with the intention of promoting an accelerated integration of the Indian population into the national society (Baines 1994a). According to what the Waimiri-Atroari told me, and judging by the number and distribution of old village clearings and recently abandoned villages, during the years immediately prior to the establishment of the FAWA, there were three principal agglomerations of villages, connected by several large pathways. Each village consisted of a large round or elliptic communal habitation and its gardens. Each agglomeration of villages was spread over the hydrographic basin of one of the rivers of the region: Camanaú, Alalaú and Santo Antônio de Abonari.[4]

Like other Indian groups of the Guiana massif region (Rivière 1984), the Waimiri-Atroari conceptualised their villages as if they were, politically and economically, almost autonomous units, expressed in a basic dichotomy between "inside" and "outside"—on the one hand, *a'yaska* ("Our real kinspeople"), and on the other hand, *aba_i'ra 'amba mïdï'tanï* ("Our people, from another village"). The expression *a'yaska* includes both co-residence and cognatic kin ties, which are often, but not always, overlapping.[5] The expression *aba_i'ra, 'amba mïdï'tanï*, which includes all people considered *a'yaska ka'bï* ("S/he who that other person calls, 'Our real kinsperson'" i.e., "We do not" = "S/he is not our real kinsperson"), is used in reference to individuals from other local groups of Waimiri-Atroari, with the exception of those considered to be close cognatic kin of the speaker. Co-residents who go away to live in other villages are no longer referred to as *a'yaska* unless they are considered to be close cognatic kin. The Waimiri-Atroari kinship terminology has some similarities with the Dravidian type,[6] with a strong preference for marriages between people who are included in the category of bilateral cross-cousins.

The dichotomy *'aska/ba_i'ra* reflects the strong preference that the Waimiri-Atroari express for endogamy at the village level, and, when this is not possible for demographic reasons, for endogamy at the level of neighbouring villages. People from other villages were treated with extreme distrust, especially those from distant villages, being the most common object of accusations of sorcery. The Waimiri-Atroari stressed the difficulties that an individual faced to be accepted by members of distant villages and to marry people from distant villages. Animosities within a Waimiri-Atroari village were solved by fission, which continued to occur in the settlements of the FAWA, despite the mediation of FUNAI workers who tried to prevent it. In this aspect, the Waimiri-Atroari village was similar to the Trio village described by Rivière (1970: 253), which "cannot support divisions within itself, and the appearance of tensions can be resolved only by fission." The village was conceived by the Trio "as an isolated, independent, and self-sufficient unit" (Rivière 1984: 72). According to Rivière, "The basic dichotomy in Trio thought is inside versus outside. Sorcery acts to confirm the distinction" (1970: 254), and "accusations of sorcery are directed against other villages, particularly unknown shamans and strange visitors" (ibid.: 248). Rivière (1969: 30) points out that "The Trio have known for a long time that sickness and death is related to visits of strangers."

The Waimiri-Atroari relaxed this tension between members of different villages during intervillage ritual activities (*'marïba*), during which children were initiated. For periods of about three days, during the ceremonies members of different villages socialised intensively. However, these inter-village rituals often ended in conflict and the rapid withdrawal of visitors following insinuations or accusations of sorcery.

The Waimiri-Atroari present a vision in which they place people according to degrees of increasing and decreasing social distance and proximity, which corresponds, approximately, to geographical distance, although not necessarily so. The more socially distant a person is from ego, the more potentially dangerous. Waimiri-Atroari referred to any village by citing its political leader and the group of men who lived in it, since inter-village political relations were mediated by men. Other than an individual's placing him/herself within the network of known people and configuration of neighbouring villages, there was no concept of territory in terms of a continuous geographical area belonging to an ethnic group.

On several occasions I walked with Waimiri-Atroari to the few villages where groups of Waimiri-Atroari still returned after misunderstandings in the FUNAI Indian Post settlements, or when there was a lack of food in the plantations near the Posts. We followed old paths where they associated every trace of a camp and every site of an abandoned village with events of the past: places on the paths where there had occurred specific meetings of people from different villages; places where people had died; the place where a man had been attacked by a jaguar; the place where the elderly man, known as Janu'ma, ill and too weak to accompany the group with whom he was walking, requested the others to go on and wandered off to his death in the forest[7]; the sandy place in the clearing of an abandoned village where the FUNAI manager Gilberto Costa had landed in a helicopter when the inhabitants of several villages were participating in an intervillage ritual; the pathway where the FUNAI manager had passed when he visited villages; the place where a Waimiri-Atroari man had angrily perforated some aluminium pots supplied by FUNAI, when his wife died during an epidemic; places where people had spent the night during journeys. . . .

Waimiri-Atroari historical references were mapped on the forest landscape. They represented their lives as a sequence of periods in which they lived in certain villages. To say where one was living when a certain incident occurred was a way of letting those Waimiri-Atroari who were listening situate that incident in a wider sequence of past events. In this way, each spatial reference was imbued with a historical dimension.[8]

SPACE AND INTERETHNIC CONTACT

Waimiri-Atroari themselves related the impact of contact on the spatial organisation of the network of villages. How the intrusion of people of the national society was reflected in the displacement and redistribution of villages? There was an initial withdrawal due to the construction workers building the BR-174 Highway (in the early 1970s), followed by sporadic visits to the Indian Posts of the Attraction Front and the gangs of road workers. The time of attacks against Indian Posts in an attempt to expel the invaders who brought sickness (1973–1974) was marked by a prolonged withdrawal, followed by new visits. Later, some young men who had lost their parents in the epidemics came to live at the Indian Posts (from 1978). In the following years the inhabitants of the villages were redistributed among three large settlements near Indian Posts, on the orders of FUNAI workers and young Waimiri-Atroari "captains"[9] (1978–1982), with a subsequent fragmentation brought about by further directed displacements of Waimiri-Atroari to new settlements set up by the FAWA administration. Later (from 1984), there began a process of withdrawal of some Waimiri-Atroari factions to places situated at a greater distance from the Indian Posts but of easy access. These places were incorporated into the productive system of the Attraction Front by setting up new Indian Posts beside the Indians residences.

These spatial displacements directly contributed to the imposition of a new way of conceptualising space, which reproduced the social relations of domination between the FUNAI staff and the Waimiri-Atroari. The new version censured Waimiri-Atroari ways and was imposed especially through the new Waimiri-Atroari leaders, or "captains," appointed by the indigenist[10] administration. Incorporated as subdominators who presented an "official version" as the only legitimate version, the young "captains" emulated the FUNAI workers, talking about requesting transference from the co-ordinator between Indian Post settlements.

The dominant versions did not totally obliterate Waimiri-Atroari spatial concepts, despite the extremely repressive practical and ideological control exercised by the Attraction Front workers. An attempt was made to resocialise the Waimiri-Atroari through agricultural labour projects imposed by relations of subjection–domination, with the intention of preventing any indigenous social reorganisation and forcing the Waimiri-Atroari to adopt the rules of the game of the Attraction Front and aspire to be "civilised Indians" and "Indian FUNAI workers."

Oliveira (1994: vii) affirms that it was the situation of attraction and pacification which moulded the paradigms of government indigenist policy. In his concept of "territorialization" as a social process, Oliveira discusses the ways in which indigenous populations enter into a colonial situation in which the guarantee of their land passes through the government indigenist organ.

THE OCCUPATION OF WAIMIRI-ATROARI TERRITORY

From the late 1960s, the federal government started a massive occupation of the Waimiri-Atroari territory through large-scale development projects based on transnational capital. This large-scale occupation of the region was put into action through an articulation made between a large export-directed group of mining companies, the electric sector directed to the production of cheap energy, especially for companies installed in the industrial zone of Manaus, the Brazilian army, and FUNAI.

The BR-174 Highway that links Manaus to Boa Vista was cut through the middle of the Waimiri-Atroari territory, with a tremendous loss of Waimiri-Atroari lives, and without ever consulting the Indian people. The extension that passes through their area was constructed between 1972 and 1977. In the beginning of 1979, mining companies of the Paranapanema Group invaded the Indian Reserve, which had been delimited some years before by Decree n°68.907, 13-07-71. In 1979 work was also begun on the construction of the Balbina Hydroelectric Scheme by the government company, Electronorte. The Presidential Decree n°85.898, 13-04-81, declared an area of approximately 10,344.90 km^2 to be of public utility for expropriation, superimposed over the area delimited as an Indian Reserve. The expropriated area includes the lake and the region of influence of the Hydroelectric Scheme, which resulted in the flooding of approximately 2928,5 km^2 (Ibama 1992) of territory occupied by the Waimiri-Atroari up to the 1970s. The limits of the Indian area, especially along the BR-174 Highway, were taken over by cattle-raising and colonisation projects.

After having invaded and occupied part of the Waimiri-Atroari Reserve, mining companies of the Paranapanema Group resorted to cartographic manipulations to "legalise" the dismemberment of approximately 526,800 hectares (see Baines 1991b). The dismemberment of the area of immediate interest to Paranapanema was brought about by Presidential Decree n°86.630, 23.11.81, and has since become one of the largest tin mines in the world.

From 1970 the Waimiri-Atroari were submitted to a FUNAI "Attraction Front," which accompanied the construction work of the BR-174 Highway within the Indian territory. In this, a large contingent of FUNAI workers imposed an "accelerated integration" plan, congregating the Waimiri-Atroari survivors in settlements close to the Indian Posts, where they were incorporated into a disciplinary regime of agricultural labour directed by FUNAI employees. From 1987, the Programa Waimiri-Atroari[11] took over the direction of the indigenist policy in the area.

To show the extent to which their own cosmovision, including concepts of space, was being questioned by the Waimiri-Atroari, I shall cite an incident that occurred in 1982. During the initial phase of my fieldwork, while at the Camanaú Indian Post, when I was trying to increase my vocabulary, I pointed, one day, to the sky, and then to the ground, to elicit words and sentences. A young man asked me: "Under the ground? Are there not our people under the ground?" I replied that I had no knowledge about this, and he was astonished by my reply. After I had spent several months in the area, I was told of a Waimiri-Atroari belief that there are "other people, the same as us" under the ground and below the riverbed. What surprised me most on this occasion was that the man had asked me about the Waimiri-Atroari concept of the cosmos, which had already been put in question by the disdain and ridicule of many FUNAI workers. In addition, he was astonished by the fact that I had not "taught" him, as the workers usually did. In declaring that I "did not know," I had put my own word in doubt, since the Waimiri-Atroari already believed in the system of ideas which the workers had imposed on them, that is, that they "didn't know" and that the workers "did know." I revealed to them that I did not share the implicit attitudes of the workers, who constantly affirmed to the Waimiri-Atroari that they "knew" about everything, as part of their concept of being *civilizados* or "civilised Indians," in opposition to the Waimiri-Atroari, who, as "Indians," "did not know" and had to be "taught."

On another occasion, I was asking some Waimiri-Atroari about the moon and the stars. They asked me if there is water in the sky. This time, remembering their previous consternation and the sequence of doubts that it had provoked, I returned the question to them. They told me that a lot of water falls from the sky. They were so accustomed to receive orders and teachings from the workers that they expected the same from me, and were astonished that I did not give them. They put in question their own concepts about the cosmos, subordinating these to the concepts imposed by the staff and reinterpreting them in the light of the latter.

However, Waimiri-Atroari continued to express their own concepts when talking together, even when the imposed explanations negated, or attempted to remodel, the indigenous explanations. The discourse of negation, even when appropriated by many Waimiri-Atroari in interethnic contexts to satisfy the demands of FUNAI workers who believed that they were "civilising" the Waimiri-Atroari, did not make the indigenous concepts disappear, as the "civilisers" liked to imagine. On the contrary, the discourse of negation coexisted with the discourse of the negated, in often apparently contradictory discourses. New imposed interpretations coexisted with traditional explanations and interpretations which reinterpreted the latter. The reinterpretations passed through a cultural filter to make them intelligible within Waimiri-Atroari terms. Nevertheless, the fact that many native concepts persist, in spite of the violence of interethnic contact, in no way diminishes the impact of this violence, which has led to the suppression of many aspects of Waimiri-Atroari society, such as shamanism (Baines 1993).

The remodelling of villages to conform to regional "civilised" standards imposed by the FUNAI workers (Baines 1991a: 216–232) clearly shows how traditional communal houses were rejected by the Waimiri-Atroari in their efforts to conform to imposed standards and gain favours (access to manufactured goods and privileged positions in the administration) from the FUNAI staff. However, the new villages, made up of smaller residential units composed of domestic groups, followed Waimiri-Atroari patterns of residence in periods when they camped away from the large communal houses. Later, the Waimiri-Atroari followed the orders of indigenists, building *malocas* to reinforce an appearance of revitalisation of traditions.

In the late 1980s, the pressures exerted by large companies over the area increased dramatically. A new mega-project was started—Calha Norte Project (Projeto Calha Norte)—which is different from previous projects in that it "does not have the rigid and systematic structure of a programme or plan . . . It consists of the formulation of a group of directions and aims with which all government initiatives directed towards this region should become compatible" (Oliveira 1990: 18). Most of the Waimiri-Atroari territory was incorporated within the space called "Regional or 'Interior' Nucleus" by this Project (p. 2), situated between the spaces called "Frontier Strip" and "Riverine Zones." The Calha Norte Project, elaborated in secrecy by the National Security Council in 1985, is a military project having as its ostensible objective the occupation of the northern frontier of Brazil by implanting military outposts. It is presented in a rhetoric of national security, the so-called foreign threat of socialist regimes in the Caribbean region, Colombian guerrillas, and narcotraffic. However, the military and strategic interests are only one part of the intentions of the Calha Norte Project, and among the "fundamental and immediate necessities, judged as a top priority" for the region by the General-Secretary of the National Security Council, are the "amplification of the highway infrastructure; acceleration in the production of hydroelectric energy; inland penetration of poles of economic development; and amplification of the offer of basic social resources."[12] Taking this into consideration, the Waimiri-Atroari territory served as a precursor of the new military–big business model for occupying the north of Amazonia. In this process of occupation, indigenist policy has been constantly subordinated to economic interests that involve large private and government companies. Ramos (1990) stresses that among the problems created by the Calha Norte Project for the Indians was the drastic reduction of their traditional territories (see also Albert 1991; Buchillet 1990; Oliveira 1990).

From the early 1980s, the indigenist policy for this region has been shaped by and subordinated to the interests of two large companies—Paranapanema and Eletronorte—which have far greater economic powers than FUNAI, creating a unique situation of large company action over the Indian population that fits in well with the objectives of the Calha Norte Project. This can be seen by the amplification of the infrastructure in the Reserve, the increase in control over the Indians, the promotion of Indian leaders who act as spokesmen for the indigenist administration and the companies which are advancing over their territories, incorporated in roles created by the indigenist administration as obedient executors of orders and middlemen who transmit orders with the duty to obey their superiors and keep silent about matters considered inconvenient to the administration.

The new indigenist policy is also characterised by the prohibition over the access of ethnologists and missionaries to Indian territory (see Oliveira 1990: 30). As Oliveira (ibid.: 20) stresses, "[P]eople who work with Indian groups in this region [Amazonia] who are not part of the FUNAI staff, are characterized as enemies of the country, since they practise actions which are contrary to the so-called national interests."

"THE WAIMIRI-ATROARI ATTRACTION FRONT": THE CENSORSHIP

During the periods that I was in the area, the FUNAI team was made up principally of workers who identified themselves as Indians,[13] from other ethnic groups than the Waimiri-Atroari. Following a policy of putting a minority of non-Indian workers in jobs as heads of Indian Posts to which a large contingent of acculturated Indian workers were subordinated as labourers, FUNAI created, in this area, a situation which aggravated the Indian/White opposition. There was a constant tension between White heads of Indian Posts and Indian auxiliary workers, many of the latter scheming together to try to get White workers banned from the area, with the aim of gaining the much higher paid jobs as heads of Indian Posts. They frequently appealed to the generic identity of "Indian," valued in an indianised counter-culture discourse of "Indian" to "Indian" against "Whites," establishing intimacy with the Waimiri-Atroari with the principal object of instigating them to reject the White heads of Indian Posts and to demand that the administrative director of the FAWA appointed Indian workers in their place.

The power struggle in the FAWA came to be expressed in an indigenist rhetoric which masked the fact that the FUNAI workers who identified themselves as "Indians" or "civilised Indians" were treating the Waimiri-Atroari with the same stereotyped prejudices of the national society, as "Indians" and *caboclos*,[14] as were the non-Indian workers. They identified themselves, in the first place, as FUNAI workers, presenting themselves to non-Indians as being more adequate to work with the Waimiri-Atroari on the grounds of being "Indians too," while their behaviour, as FUNAI workers, was little different from that of the non-Indians. Many of the Indian workers, placed as subdominators between the non-Indian FUNAI workers and the Waimiri-Atroari, also resorted to a discourse of "Indian" to "Indian" against "Whites" when addressing the Waimiri-Atroari, as a strategy to exercise control over the information that the Waimiri-Atroari gave to me, who was labelled by these same FUNAI workers as a "White."

The indigenist rhetoric used by many of the FUNAI workers of the FAWA, demanding that the Waimiri-Atroari adopt a posture of being "self-conscious politicised `Indians,'" in the generic sense, who position themselves and act in opposition to "Whites," presented a contradiction in the context of the Attraction Front. It proposed a redefinition of "Indian" as united against "Whites," when the asymmetrical social relations, imposed on the Waimiri-Atroari by the team of FUNAI workers (Indians and Whites), were contradictory ones of subordination–domination (Cardoso de Oliveira 1976: 55). In this context, in addition to plotting intrigues against White workers and involving the Waimiri-Atroari, some of these Indian workers tried to monopolise the local commerce of Waimiri-Atroari handicrafts (officially controlled by the administrative direction of FUNAI), entering into private agreements with the "captains" to sell the Waimiri-Atroari products in Manaus and bring industrialised goods. They also told the Waimiri-Atroari that, as Indian workers, they had been authorised by FUNAI to have sexual access to the Waimiri-Atroari women[15] and, in exchange, took some Waimiri-Atroari men to centres of prostitution when these were staying at the FUNAI's "Indian House" in Manaus. They also entered into agreements with the "captains" to conceal from some White heads of Indian Posts and administrative directors the fact that they frequently consumed alcoholic beverages while working at Indian Posts.

In these plots, the Indian identity was extended to include all the FUNAI workers who participated in them, independent of ethnic criteria: it was equally manipulated to exclude Indian workers who did not participate. In order to reconcile these contradictions in the use of ethnic identities, the workers involved often redefined the Indian/White opposition as "FUNAI"/"real Whites." They also used the opposition *peão* (manual labourer)/"White" (to refer to functionaries in jobs as heads of Indian Posts or administrative directors). Thus, the Indian Post situation reproduced at the local level the power structure of FUNAI and the national society: the establishing of social relations of subordination/domination between generic Indians and Whites, and also between Waimiri-Atroari Indians on the one hand, and White and Indian workers from other ethnic groups on the other hand.

The indigenist administration acted as a total institution (Goffman 1971 [1961]) and many workers (Indians and Whites) transmitted to the Waimiri-Atroari a developmentalist model which defended the interests of mining companies of the Paranapanema Group to advance further into the Indian territory, presented in a rhetoric of Indian self-determination. The very concept of "self-determination" was subordinated to a context of domination, imposed by functionaries in the form of a "directed self-determination" transmitted as an order from the indigenist administration to the Waimiri-Atroari "captains" who were incorporated in subaltern positions in its bureaucratic hierarchy. This became clear to me in the control exercised by the indigenist administration over my access to information through the Waimiri-Atroari "captains." I cite, as an example, a visit which General Euclydes Figueiredo, ex-Military Commander of Amazonia, made to this Indian area in 1984, together with a retinue of seventeen representatives of FUNAI, Mineração Taboca S.A. (Paranapanema) and the Army, to inaugurate a school constructed by Paranapanema at one of the FUNAI Indian Posts. The FUNAI workers and the Waimiri-Atroari maintained total secrecy about the matter. During the days before the inauguration of the school, I heard commentaries about a future visit to the area. However, when I asked the Waimiri-Atroari and workers about the matter, they withheld information. The principal "captain" delegated two Waimiri-Atroari to take me to visit some abandoned Indian villages and, when I returned to the Terraplenagem Indian Post some days later, I was informed that the retinue had visited the area and that the principal "captain" had made a speech thanking the General and representatives of Paranapanema.[16] Any attempts I made to directly or indirectly approach the question of the presence of the mining company in the area dismembered from the Indian Reserve were met with censorial attitudes from the "captains" and younger Waimiri-Atroari who worked together with the FUNAI team, and from the majority of FUNAI workers.

As a consequence of this recent development of rhetoric about Indian identity imposed on the Waimiri-Atroari at all the Indian Posts and settlements, the "Indian" identity was extended by the workers, in their indianised rhetoric addressed to the Waimiri-Atroari, to include all the FUNAI workers who participated in the imposition of a censorship over information to people labelled "Whites," regardless of their ethnic identity. The censorship was reinforced in my case, as a researcher, by the fact that some White FUNAI functionaries in the administrative direction often reminded the workers and the Waimiri-Atroari that I "was not a FUNAI employee."

If the conditions for the Waimiri-Atroari and for the field-worker were difficult at that time, they became even more so in the period which followed. Since the creation of the Programa Waimiri-Atroari (FUNAI/ELETRONORTE) in 1987 there has been a consistent policy of hostility towards the presence of ethnologists, as a result of which my own research was banned from June 1989.

PROGRAMA WAIMIRI-ATROARI

The Programa Waimiri-Atroari had, in 1990, fifty-seven employees[17] and, in the part of the Indian Reserve that was dismembered by Presidential Decree in 1981, there were several thousands of workers of Mineração Taboca. At that time, this mining company had armed workers of a security company controlling the access to a private road inside the Indian area.

Several months after the banning of my research in the Waimiri-Atroari area, I found out that on 24 June 1989, the same day on which I had been taken to the Waimiri-Atroari in a vehicle of the Programa to consult the Indians, and a few hours before my arrival at the FUNAI base, a new agreement ("Termo de Compromisso n°001/89") had been signed directly between Mineração Taboca S.A. (Paranapanema) and ten Waimiri-Atroari "captains" appointed by FUNAI, to undertake development projects for the Indian community, allocating "advanced monthly payments of future royalties that will be owed by the *company* to the *community* for the mining activities" that Paranapanema intends to carry out within the remaining Indian area. This "Agreement" was also signed by representatives of

Paranapanema together with the same manager of the Programa Waimiri-Atroari (a FUNAI employee) and the then Regional Superintendent of FUNAI,[18] who signed as witnesses.

This "Termo de Compromisso" includes a "Declaration" signed by five Waimiri-Atroari "captains" on 15 May 1987, as well as correspondence between FUNAI and the mining company which followed, dated June 1989. The "Declaration," signed also by the manager of the Programa and an ex-Regional Superintendent of FUNAI, as witnesses, together with representatives of the mining company, states that the Waimiri-Atroari community, represented by five leaders, decided to exploit mineral wealth within the Indian area in exchange for royalties, choosing, exclusively, the Paranapanema Group to carry out the prospecting and mineral extraction. The "Declaration" is written in a rhetoric of Indian self-determination, giving the impression that the decision to exploit minerals and the exclusive choice of Paranapanema came from the Waimiri-Atroari. However, the wording of the document and the asymmetry of the proposal reveal that the Waimiri-Atroari "captains" who signed it had not been adequately informed of the tragic consequences for their survival as an ethnic group of any advance of mining companies over their territory, which was already threatened by invasions of the same company, which is seriously polluting the River Alalaú, the major river in the Indian area. It reveals, on the contrary, that these "captains" were enticed to sign the document under company pressures articulated by local FUNAI functionaries, including the then manager of the Programa.

All these documents, signed by a few Waimiri-Atroari and representatives of Paranapanema and the FUNAI, go against the Brazilian indigenist legislation, as does also a "Contract of Utilisation of the ground for Mining Purposes" between six companies of the Paranapanema Group and FUNAI, signed by its then president, Romero Jucá Filho, that authorises the exploitation of minerals in all the Waimiri-Atroari Indian area. The FUNAI functionaries who articulated this "contract" with Paranapanema in 1987 also enticed the principal "captain" of the Waimiri-Atroari and his brother to sign it. It is worth mentioning that the signing of this "contract" occurred when the principal "captain" and his brother were brought to Brasília by FUNAI in 1987, accompanied by the Regional Superintendent and the same manager of the Programa. It is part of a series of irregularities used against this Indian population to favour private mining companies by means of illegal agreements of ethnocidal consequences.

The mining companies of the Paranapanema Group have not been able to use these documents to advance further over the Waimiri-Atroari lands, since the complementary legislation governing mining in Indian territories according to the 1988 Brazilian Constitution has not yet been drawn up, making the documents invalid. The Programa has also demarcated an area for the Waimiri-Atroari.[19] However, the demarcation of their lands is, in itself, no guarantee that their territory will be respected. The mining companies are adopting a new strategy in collaboration with the government—to favour the demarcation of Indian areas and to exercise economic pressures to entice new Indian leaders to enter into direct agreements with the companies in exchange for royalties, in the name of "self-determination." The Programa Waimiri-Atroari thereby reveals itself to be a closed "total institution" that has captured the Waimiri-Atroari.

In the past few years, the indigenist administration has adopted a rhetoric of Indian "resistance" to cover up a situation of extreme domination, and spread an image of a model assistential programme. The indigenous strategy to learn the rules of the game of the official indigenist policy for this area can be seen not as a passive reaction, but an active reaction of accommodation to this situation of extreme domination, which reflects the immense power of huge companies. The indigenist administration constructs and publicises images of Waimiri-Atroari both nationally and internationally, incorporating them in its intensive marketing policy (Silva 1993: 70; Baines 1994b, 1995).

Presenting the action of the Programa Waimiri-Atroari as "alternative indigenism" that has "saved the Waimiri-Atroari from extinction" (see Baines 1994b), and as respectful of the Indian culture, together with the fact that its implantation, in 1987, coincided with the period of rapid demographic recuperation four years after the Waimiri-Atroari population had reached its lowest point, the administration vehicles images of this Indian people that conceal the domination to which they have been subjected in recent years. On the contrary, the propaganda makes it appear that the action of the Programa Waimiri-Atroari is contributing to a renovation of Indian resistance, especially through declarations made by the new Indian leaders, recruited as spokespersons of the administration.

In documentary films and TV reports[20] local leaders appear, dialoguing with technicians and administrators, creating images for the public, with all the power of the media, as if they operated in symmetrical and more democratic relations. In addition, TV reports show the Waimiri-Atroari practising rituals, which is presented to the public as a "full return to their rituals" and a cultural revitalisation, as a demonstration of the success of the Programa Waimiri-Atroari. They themselves appear, saying that they are practising their own "culture" and expressing their own claims. Without putting in doubt the words of the Waimiri-Atroari, the images and editing of films are controlled by others, and are presented in contexts over which the Waimiri-Atroari have no control. Yet again, the control exercised by the indigenist administration is concealed behind images of a cultural resistance prepared by others. The role of the leaders is similar to that of the Indian functionaries in Mexico who, according to Bartolomé (1995: 363), are "used ritually to 'represent the Indians' in official political campaigns." In the Waimiri-Atroari case, in addition to a seminar organised in Manaus in 1990, and an exhibition in a Manaus shopping mall in 1993, the ritual use is recorded and set up in films and propaganda leaflets.

The Waimiri-Atroari leaders have been subjected to intensive publicity campaigns, and incorporated in them, thus being prevented from having access to information which would give them the opportunity to question the entrepreneurial interests behind this indigenist policy. The Waimiri-Atroari case is a clear example of the way in which pressure exerted by large companies can produce a rhetoric of Indian resistance that covers up the immense inequalities of a situation of interethnic contact between large companies and Indian communities. Through its publicity campaigns, the Programa Waimiri-Atroari moulds the "official version" of the Waimiri-Atroari reality, incorporating the Indians themselves in this "reality" created by publicity. In this way, the administration constructs images of Indians as part of its publicity policies, with the Indians participating in the reconstruction of their own image directed to attend company interests. They appear in propaganda films wearing T-shirts of the Programa Waimiri-Atroari with a printed image of a Waimiri-Atroari and the name "Waimiri-Atroari," serving as a uniform of the Programa.[21]

CONCLUSIONS

I conclude by pointing out the danger of representing the Waimiri-Atroari within a rhetoric of globalisation. The indigenist action of the Programa Waimri-Atroari, through its intensive marketing campaigns, has won the support of the public at large, both nationally and internationally, including some anthropologists (Hart 1991; Baines 1997: 74). The recent history of spatial concepts in Waimiri-Atroari society reveals the passage from a spatialised traditional history to more recent concepts expressed in an impoverished language of the administration employees, in which the Waimiri-Atroari reality has been moulded and coerced to conform with the ideology and perspectives of the administrative staff. The new leaders, recruited since the time of the FUNAI's Attraction Front, present themselves as spokespersons for, and representatives of, the new model of an Indian society imposed by the totalitarian indigenist policy. With a new cultural legitimacy based on a politicised Indian rights rhetoric borrowed from the Indian movement, and captives of a memory reconstructed by the indigenist administrators (Baines 1993), they censured Waimiri-Atroari history before the "pacification," imposing an official model to construct a new Waimiri-Atroari as a "civilised Indian," productive and docile, who displays, folklorically, "traditional indigenous culture" in propaganda films in order to legitimise the Programa Waimiri-Atroari as being respectful of Indian culture.

Within the Programa seven sub-programmes have been created, including a "sub-programme of vigilance of the limits." According to reports and a propaganda leaflet,[22] "expeditions are constantly made,

The Reconstruction of Waimiri-Atroari Territory   59

in all the limits of the area, aiming to prevent possible invasions, always with the participation of the Waimiri-Atroari." Thus the Waimiri-Atroari are incorporated into activities programmed by the administration and within the latter's spatial concepts. The indigenist action introduced a reading of space founded on a protectionist policy and taught to the Waimiri-Atroari. Another more recent and bilingual (Portuguese/English) government propaganda leaflet,[23] in the section on "Environment," states that

> Among these activities, the work done with the Waimiri-Atroari Indians stands out. Their reserve was marked and enlarged from 1,850,000 to 2,585,911 hectares. In a project with FUNAI an Action Program was set up and, even today, it has represented an effective instrument for bettering the living conditions and the preservation and valorisation of the Indian community culture. (ibid.)

The propaganda, written in a developmentalist rhetoric to promote company interests (Eletronorte plans to build many more hydroelectric schemes, which, if constructed, will flood other Indian lands in Amazonia), presents Indians as subjects of the environment, of the hydroelectric scheme (Viveiros de Castro & Andrade 1988), and of policies of social engineering which aim to preserve and value their culture. This developmentalist rhetoric coincides with the position held by many sympathisers of globalisation. In the words of Segato,

> [S]ome voices which celebrate the process of 'globalization' and do not interpret it as an exacerbation of imperialism, cling to the idea that it is only as a consequence of the internationalization of modern ideas of citizenship and human rights that the emergence of peoples who were previously invisible, and today claim rights in the name of their identity, has been made possible. (Segato 1998: 3)

Segato proposes that this is only partly true and that it is an "ambiguous and unstable process, capable, on the one hand, of affirming the rights of minorities but, also, on the other hand, of homogenising cultures, flattening their lexicons and values so that they can enter the generalized dispute for resources, yet leaving outside the political horizon a deeper reflection about the very nature of these resources, and the plurality of their forms of production and utilization" (ibid).

In the case of the Waimiri-Atroari, the implantation of the Programa Waimiri-Atroari, planned and financed as a model of indigenist action, has improved health assistance, compared with the inefficient and poorly funded health programme of the previous FAWA. On the other hand, the Programa is being used by Eletronorte as propaganda to promote its interests in the construction of newly planned hydroelectric schemes that will flood other Indian territories if constructed. Despite the fact that many aspects of Waimiri-Atroari society have survived interethnic contact, the violence against the Indian society has been immense. This can be seen in the way indigenous concepts of space have been subordinated to hegemonic concepts that redefine their way of life.

NOTES TO CHAPTER 2

1. The history of invasions and massacres has been documented since the middle of the 19th century (Barbosa Rodrigues 1885; Payer 1906; Hübner & Koch-Grünberg 1907; Bandeira 1926; in the Reports of the Province of Amazonas (Amazonas, 1906–1908, and in the Indian Protection Service [SPI] and National Indian Foundation [FUNAI] reports). In 1856, Major Manoel Pereira de Vasconcellos and fifty soldiers undertook a massacre in Indian villages in the River Jauaperí basin, marking the beginning of thirty years of war and military expeditions against the Indians. Barbosa Rodrigues established peaceful contacts with the Indians and founded a settlement on the banks of the River Jauaperí in 1885. Later interethnic conflicts include the sending of fifty soldiers from the police in 1905, who killed 283 Indians, taking eighteen prisoners. Documented massacres of Waimiri-Atroari by members of the regional population continued into the 20th century.
2. Report of the Waimiri-Atroari Attraction Front, 27-10-73, FUNAI, pp. v–vi.
3. In the following four-year period the rate of population increase shows a slight decline, from 26.5% to 20.2% (Silva 1990).
4. See Rivière's (1969, 1970) description of Trio villages and Butt Colson's (1966) of Akawaio villages, other Indian groups of the Carib linguistic family which are rather similar to the distribution of Waimiri-Atroari villages. See also Albert's (1985) description of the Yanomami, also in the Guiana massif region.
5. The Waimiri-Atroari do not make a rigid distinction between cognatic kin ties and those of co-residence to include someone in the category *a'yaska*. As Rivière (1969: 65) observes in the Trio case, "Co-residence can be as closely binding as the ties of genealogical connection, and in Trio thought they are not truly distinguished."
6. For a stimulating discussion, see Silva (1993).
7. The death of Janu'ma occurred after January 1974. In that month the FUNAI manager Gilberto Costa made contact with him at the place where the Alalaú II Indian Post was reinstalled.
8. For other cases of the spatialisation of time in indigenous societies, see e.g. Albert (1985: 126, 1988: 94), Rappaport (1990: 11, 147–153, 180), Rosaldo (1980: 55–56), and Seeger (1981: 75–77), for the Yanomami, Páez, Ilongot and Suyá, respectively.
9. The role of "captain" was institutionalised by FUNAI during the "pacification" period. The "captains" were, principally, young men, recruited from among the Waimiri-Atroari as intercultural agents rendering services to the indigenist administration, who transmit orders from the team of functionaries to the other Waimiri-Atroari in exchange for privileges such as an unequal access to manufactured goods. Since 1978, a young man and his brother, among the first Waimiri-Atroari who came to live in an Indian Post, were chosen by the administration as the principal captain and his substitute.

10. I use the word "indigenist" to apply to policies formulated by non-Indian directed administrations for Indians, to distinguish from "Indian" policies formulated by the Indians themselves.
11. The "Programa Waimiri-Atroari" (Agreement FUNAI/ELETRONORTE), financed by ELETRONORTE with funds from the World Bank, substituted the Frente de Atração Waimiri-Atroari in 1987, and was planned for 25 years duration. It was intended as a means of compensating the Indians for the flooding of part of their territory, in consequence of the decision to construct the Balbina Hydroelectric Scheme, without previously consulting the Indian population. The programme of assistance was created in the final phase of construction of the Balbina dam and just a few months before the floodgates were closed in October 1987, flooding an area of about 2360 km^2. All the area flooded was part of the traditional territory of the Waimiri-Atroari up to the early 1970s, and about 311 km^2 of flooding was inside the reduced area that has been reserved for the Waimiri-Atroari. The flooding transformed all the headwaters of the rivers Uatumã, Santo Antônio do Abonari and Taquari into an uninhabitable area with putrefaction of the submerged tropical forest, forcing the removal of about one third of the total Waimiri-Atroari population to other parts of the Reserve. Viveiros de Castro and Andrade (1988: 16) affirm that these "palliative and tardy measures, of cosmetic character, taken when all decisions about the construction work had already been carried into effect" have been used to create "a false idea of 'participation.'" The present Programa Waimiri-Atroari offers an assistential infrastructure subordinated to the *fait accompli* of the flooding of part of the Indian territory and the irreversible modification of the environment.
12. Exposition of Motives n°018/85, 19th June 1985, Gen. Bda. Rubens Bayma Denys, Minister of State, General-Secretary of the National Security Council (Brasil, 1985).
13. The report "Analysis of Workers Posted in the NAWA (Waimiri-Atroari Assistance Nucleus) in 08-07-79," written by the FUNAI administrative director of the area, Giuseppe Cravero, reveals that 68% of the workers were from "several 'acculturated' Indian areas." According to this Co-ordinator, of the "Indian" workers, there were twenty-nine from the Rio Negro, twenty-nine from the Lower Amazonas, three from the River Purus and seven from other areas. The majority of these employees had worked in cities of the region for several years and some in large development projects such as the construction of the "Perimetral Norte" Highway in the region of São Gabriel da Cachoeira in the early 1970s, the construction of the BR-174 within the Waimiri-Atroari territory (1972–1977) and the construction of the Balbina Hydroelectric Scheme, begun in 1979.
14. Pejorative term often used with several meanings such as "half-caste," "civilised Indian," and frequently with the connotation of "yokel," "country bumpkin."
15. The Regional FUNAI Delegate discovered later that this was happening: radio message No.840, 09-04-85, and removed about thirty workers involved.
16. The inauguration of the school took place on 06.01.84 (A Notícia, e Jornal do Comércio, Manaus, 07.01.84). This school was constructed in 1983, beside Terraplenagem Indian Post on the edge of the BR-174 Highway, following a request made by General Euclydes Figueiredo, who had promised a school to the Waimiri-Atroari's principal captain during a previous visit to this Indian area on 24 June 1983, together with a retinue of army personnel, representatives of Paranapanema and the Regional Delegate of FUNAI. On 28 June 1983 and the following days, a series of meetings were held in Manaus between representatives of Mineração Taboca and the Army to

discuss a proposal for a government edict aiming to revise government indigenist policy to facilitate the entry of private mining companies in Indian areas.
17. Of the fifty-seven functionaries, forty-six were posted in the Waimiri-Atroari area, according to the Technical-Administrative Report of the Programa Waimiri-Atroari (FUNAI/ELETRONORTE), 1990.
18. The name of the Regional Superintendent of FUNAI who signed this "Agreement" appears as Co-ordinator of Special Projects in FUNAI's "Calha Norte Special Project: Yearly Operative Plan 1988."
19. Decree n°94.606, 14-07-87. According to information provided by the Programa, an area of 2,585,911 hectares has been demarcated, with homologation Decree n°97.837, 16-06-89. The area does not, however, reincorporate the tributary streams of the River Alalaú, occupied and polluted by the mining company, and polluting one of the principal rivers which passes through the Waimiri-Atroari territory.
20. Such as the documentary broadcast on the TV programme "Fantástico" of the Rede Globo, on 22 October 1995.
21. They also serve as a symbol of alternative values, following the model of T-shirts sold by non-governmental organisations which defend human rights, such as Survival International/CCPY (Root 1996: 74), and the Indigenous Missionary Council of the Catholic Church (CIMI).
22. Report: Programa Waimiri-Atroari, agreement, FUNAI/ELETRONORTE, 21 September 1990; propaganda leaflet: "Ambiente, desenvolvimento, comunidades indígenas (Environment, development, indigenous communities)," Eletronorte/ Ministério de Minas e Energia, 1993: 14-15.
23. "Ambiente de Envolvimento: Hidroelétricas na Amazônia (Environment of Involvement: Hydroelectric schemes in Amazonia)," Eletronorte, n.d., p. 13.

REFERENCES

Albert, B. 1985. Temps du Sang, Temps des Cendres: Représentation de la maladie, système rituel et espace politique chez les Yanomami du sud-est (Amazonie brésilienne). Doctoral dissertation. Université de Paris X, Nanterre.
Amazonas (Província). Presidência da Província. 1906–1908. *Relatório da Presidência da Província do Amazonas desde a sua creação até a Proclamação da República*, mandados colleccionar pelo Governador Coronel Silvério José Nery e novamente publicados por ordem do Coronel Antônio Constantino Nery 1852–1877. Rio de Janeiro, Typ. do "Jornal do Commercio" de Rodrigues & Cia. V volumes.
Baines, S.G. 1991a. *'É a FUNAI que sabe': A Frente de Atração Waimiri-Atroari*. Belém: MPEG/CNPq/SCT/PR.
Baines, S.G. 1991b. Dispatch: The Waimiri-Atroari and the Paranapanema Company. *Critique of Anthropology* 11 (2): 143–153.
Baines, S.G. 1993. Censuras e memórias da pacificação Waimiri-Atroari. *Série Antropologia* 148. Brasília: UnB.
Baines, S.G. 1994a. A política indigenista governamental e os Waimiri-Atroari: administrações indigenistas, mineração de estanho e a construção da 'autodeterminação indígena' dirigida. *Revista de Antropologia*, vol. 36. São Paulo: USP.
Baines, S.G. 1994b. Epidemics, the Waimiri-Atroari Indians and the politics of demography. *Série Antropologia* 162. Brasília: UnB.

Baines, S.G. 1995. Os Waimiri-Atroari e a invenção social da etnicidade pelo indigenismo empresarial. *Anuário Antropológico/94*, pp. 127–159.
Baines, S.G. 1997. Uma tradição indígena no contexto de grandes projetos: os Waimiri-Atroari. *Anuário Antropológico/96*, pp. 67–81.
Bandeira, A. 1926. *Jauapery*. Manaus.
Barbosa Rodrigues, J. 1885. *Pacificação dos Crichanás, Rio Jauapery*. Rio de Janeiro: Imprensa Nacional.
Bartolomé, M. 1995. Movimientos etnopolíticos y autonomías indígenas en México. *América Indígena* 1–2: 361–382.
BRASIL. Poder Executivo. 1985. Desenvolvimento e Segurança na Região ao norte dos Rios Solimões e Amazonas—Projeto Calha Norte. Relatório do Grupo de Trabalho Interministerial criado pela Exposição de Motivos 018/85. Brasília. Mimeo.
Buchillet, D. 1990. Pari Cachoeira: le laboratoire tukano du projet Calha Norte. *Ethnies (Brésil: Indiens et Developpement en Amazonie)* 11–12: 128–135. Paris: Survival International.
Butt Colson, A. 1966. The Shaman's Legal Role. *Revista do Museu Paulista 5* (XVI, 1965–1966): 151–186.
Cardoso de Oliveira, R. 1976. *Identidade, Etnia e Estrutura Social*. São Paulo: Livraria Pioneira Editora.
Cardoso de Oliveira, R. 1978. *A Sociologia do Brasil Indígena*. Rio de Janeiro: Tempo Brasileiro.
Cardoso de Oliveira, R. 1996 [1964]. *O Índio e o Mundo dos Brancos*. Campinas: UNICAMP.
Goffman, E. 1971 [1961]. *Asylums: Essays on the Social Situation of Mental Patients and Other Inmates*. New York: Doubleday & Co., Anchor Books.
Hart, C. 1991. A Brazilian Tribe Escapes Extinction: Waimiri Indians Are on a Journey Towards Survival. World Development, New York. PNUD, Vol. 4 (2): 15–18.
Hübner, G., and Th. Koch-Grünberg 1907. Die Yauapery, Georg Hübner, Manaus. Critical revision and introduction by Koch-Grünberg. *Zeitschrift für Ethnologie* 39 (1–2): 225–248 (Berlin).
Oliveira, J. Pacheco de. 1990. Segurança das Fronteiras e o Novo Indigenismo: Formas e Linhagem do Projeto Calha Norte. In J. Pacheco de Oliveira (ed.) *Projeto Calha Norte: Militares, Índios e Fronteiras*. Rio de Janeiro: UFRJ/PETI/Museu Nacional, (Antropologia e Indigenismo n° 1).
Oliveira, J. Pacheco de. 1994. Os instrumentos de bordo: expectativas e possibilidades do trabalho do antropólogo em laudos periciais. In O. Sampaio Silva, L. Luz, & C.M. Helm (eds.), *A Perícia Antropológica em Processos Judiciais*. Florianópolis: UFSC.
Payer, R. 1906. Reisen im Jauapiry. *Gebiet. Petermanns Geogr. Mitteilungen* 10: 217–222 (Gotna).
Ramos, A.R. 1990. An Economy of Waste: Amazonian Frontier Development and the Livelihood of Brazilian Indians. In Working Paper *Economic Catalysts to Ecological Change*. Center for Latin American Studies. Gainesville: University of Florida.
Rappaport, J. 1990. *The Politics of Memory: Native Historical Interpretation in the Colombian Andes*. Cambridge: Cambridge University Press.
Rivière, P. 1969. *Marriage Among the Trio: a Principal of Social Organization*. Oxford: Clarendon Press.
Rivière, P. 1970. Faction and Exclusion in Two South American Village Systems. In M. Douglas (ed.), *Witchcraft Confessions and Accusation*. ASA Monographs 9. London: Tavistock.

Rivière, P. 1984. *Individual and Society in Guiana: a Comparative Study of Amerindian Social Organization.* Cambridge: Cambridge University Press.

Root, D. 1996. *Cannibal Culture: Art, Appropriation, and the Commodification of Difference.* Boulder, CO, and Oxford: Westview Press.

Rosaldo, R. 1980. *Ilongot Headhunting 1883–1974: A Study in Society and History.* Stanford, CA: Stanford University Press.

Seeger, A. 1981. *Nature and Society in Central Brazil: The Suya Indians of Mato Grosso.* Cambridge, MA, and London: Harvard University Press.

Segato, R.L. 1998. Alteridades históricas/identidades políticas: una crítica a las certezas del pluralismo global. *Série Antropologia* 234. Brasília: UnB.

Silva, M. 1991. Taxa de crescimento da População Waimiri-Atroari cai nos últimos quatro anos. Universidade Estadual de Campinas (UNICAMP), São Paulo. Ms.

Silva, M. 1990. Romance de primas e primos: uma etnografia do parentesco Waimiri-Atroari. Doctoral Thesis. Programa de Pós-Graduação em Antropologia Social, Museu Nacional, UFRJ.

Varese, S. 1996. Parroquialismo y globalizacion: Las etnicidades indígenas ante el tercer milenio. In S. Varese (coord.), *Pueblos indios, soberanís y globalismo.* Quito: Abya-Yala.

Viveiros de Castro, E., and L.M.M. de Andrade. 1988 Hidrelétricas do Xingu: O Estado contra as Sociedades Indígenas. In L.A. Ayer de O. Santos & L.M.M. de Andrade (eds.), *As Hidrelétricas do Xingu e os Povos Indígenas.* Comissão Pró-Índio de São Paulo.

3 Legal Process of Abolition of Collective Property
The Mapuche Case
Jorge Calbucura[1]

Between 1884 and 1927 the Mapuche of Chile were confined to about three thousand reservations. Forty years later this number had been reduced to two thousand. During the 1980s the number of reservations did not exceed 600. Two reasons explain the decline in Mapuche reservations: usurpation of land by landowners and the privatisation of collective property. The latter is the result of a series of legislative actions promoted by the Republic of Chile beginning in 1927. From a historical perspective the legal premises advanced by the Republic of Chile have had as an objective to deny the legitimacy of the juridical basis of collective property. At the same time, the privatisation of collective property implies the abolition of the *de facto* minority status which the Mapuche have held. This chapter describes the legislative process used by the Republic of Chile, which has resulted in the disappearance of most indigenous reservations.

In the South American continent there are about 410 indigenous groups, which differ widely. The Mapuche[2] inhabit the southern Andean region of Chile and Argentina. With approximately 1,400,000 people, they constitute one of the largest groups, along with the Aymarás, Quechuas, Mayas, Cackchiqueles, Mixtecas, Nahuatles, Otomies, Piles, Quichés, Yacatecos and Zapatecos (Hernández 1985: 11). About one million are located in Chile and the rest in Argentina.

The majority of the Mapuche in Chile inhabit the region known as La Frontera (The Frontier). This region encompasses the former provinces of Bío-Bío, Arauco, Malleco, Cautín, Valdivia, Osorno, Llanquihue and Chiloé. The largest number of Mapuche is found in Malleco and Cautín, where they constitute approximately 40% of the population. It is estimated that about one hundred thousand Mapuche reside in the urban centres of Santiago, Concepción, Valparaíso, Temuco and Valdivia. Until the 1970s the majority of the Mapuche could be found in 2,060 reservations. In the 1980s, after the military dictatorship decreed the division of collective property and issued titles of ownership to individual Mapuche, the number of reservations decreased to 665.

In Argentina the Mapuche live in the provinces of Neuquén, Rio Negro, Chubut, and Santa Cruz, where they constitute roughly 30% of the population. Until the 1980s they were concentrated in 32 Reservations.[3]

MAPUCHE TERRITORIAL AUTONOMY: HISTORICAL SURVEY

In contrast to what happened to other indigenous peoples in North and South America, the Spanish Empire was never able to subjugate the Mapuche. On January 9, 1641, after decades of bloody fighting between the Spanish and the Mapuche, hostilities ceased with the signing of the Treaty of Quilín. This Treaty recognised the River Bío-Bío as the southern border of the General Captaincy of Chile. It established that the Araucania started at the Bío-Bío. In 1811, one hundred and seventy years later,[4] under less advantageous conditions for the Mapuche, representatives of the new Republic of Chile ratified the principles of the Treaty of Quilín. Thus the Mapuche preserved their territorial autonomy for two hundred and forty-two years.

On the Argentinean side, the Mapuche, allied with other tribes, established their territorial autonomy in 1835 with the establishment of the Confederation of Salinas Grandes. Under the leadership of the Cacique Juan Calbucura,[5] the Ranqueles, Salineros, Pampas, Manzaneros, Tehuelches and Arribanos peoples were brought together. This Confederation controlled the largest indigenous territory to date. Thanks to the peace treaty signed between General Urquiza and the Cacique Juan Calbucura this Confederation preserved its territorial autonomy for over forty years.

The war against the Mapuche is one of the longest in history. Military aggression covers more than three centuries, beginning with the Spanish invasion on Mapuche territory by Pedro de Valdivia in 1541, and lasting through the "Conquest in the Desert" (1833–1881) in Argentina[6] and the "Pacification of the Araucanía" (1862–1883) in Chile.[7] Historically, the focus of the fighting between the Mapuche against the Spanish Empire and its successor republics has been land: the Mapuche have struggled to defend their territory, while the Spanish, Chile and Argentina have tried to expand their territory by conquering Mapuche lands.

Much like other indigenous groups in the Americas, the Mapuche suffered a drastic reduction in numbers in latter centuries.[8] According to Hernández (1985: 14), at the start of the Spanish invasion the Mapuche population in what is now Chile reached about one million.[9] Three decades later they had been reduced to 600,000. Two hundred years later, during a war of extermination launched by the governments of Argentina and Chile, the genocide reached its peak. It is estimated that in Chile no more than

150,000 Mapuche survived. Hernández's figures are confirmed by official data. In 1907, the first indigenous census reported only 107,000 Mapuche[10] in Chilean territory.

Before the Republics of Chile and Argentina exercised sovereignty over Mapuche territory, the "indigenous question" was a political–military problem. After the military conquest and the relocation of the native population to reservations, the "indigenous question" became a political and social problem. The Republics of Chile and Argentina have treated the Mapuche in different ways in their condition as conquered people. In the case of Chile, one hundred and nine years after relegating the Mapuche to reservations, we can establish that the state has not guaranteed the legal existence of its indigenous communities.[11] It has, instead, uninterruptedly taken legislative action promoting the abolition of the collective property system. Within this framework, we see an arbitrary legal process that progressively denied the rights of those recognised by law as Mapuche. A similar process is absent in Argentina.[12]

THE MILITARY OCCUPATION OF ARAUCANÍA: RELEGATION OF THE MAPUCHE TO RESERVATIONS

In January 1883 the Chilean Army occupied the Araucanía and Chile took possession of approximately 55,800 square miles. The Government of Chile, by decree, declared this territory property of the Republic. Based on legal principles formulated in 1813 the "Commission for the Relocation of Indigenous Peoples"[13] was created. The task of this commission was to place the surviving Mapuche in reservations.[14] In the course of thirty-five years (1884–1919) approximately 80,000 Mapuche were confined to some three thousand reservations. During the same period, approximately twenty-two million acres of Mapuche land were given to Chilean and foreign settlers.

In the reservations, we find small concentrations of families under a hierarchical structure. The Cacique was given a *Titulo de Merced*[15] with the task of distributing the property among its members. The Mapuche became isolated in a territory slightly above 1,235,000 acres, in a mountainous zone and devoid of government assistance. The reservations became enclaves of an agrarian subsistence economy.

THE DISAPPEARANCE OF MAPUCHE RESERVATIONS: THE USURPATION

From different sources we are able to determine that a few years after the process of confinement to reservations was completed, the number of Mapuche Reservations began to decrease. Between 1884 and 1919, according to Labbe (1950, cited in Bengoa 1985: 356) and Morales (1982: 145), 3,078 *Titulos de Merced* were granted, equivalent to an equal number of Mapuche Reservations. The area covered by these titles was approximately 1,173,250 acres, favouring about 78,000 persons. These authors estimate that about 40,000 Mapuche were left without a community to live in.[16] According to Lipschuts (1972a: 115), in 1959 there were in Chile about three thousand Indigenous Reservations with a total of about 1,370,000 acres. The population of these Reservations exceeded 323,000 individuals. According to the Interamerican Committee on Agricultural Development (CIDA 1966: 79), in 1963, in the provinces of Arauco and Llanquihue, there remained 3,048 Reservations with 322,916 individuals and a total of 1,397,850 acres.

In 1970 Chile officially recognised the existence of 2,060 Mapuche Reservations with a population of 700,000. According to Tordera (1982: 152), in 1979, in the provinces of Arauco, Cautín and Malleco, there were about two thousand Reservations covering an area of 864,500 acres.

From the above we can establish that between the 1950s and 1970s about one thousand Mapuche Reservations disappeared. The majority of studies concerning this period emphasise the usurpation of land, carried out mostly by settlers, as a contributing factor to the decrease of land originally assigned to the Mapuche. In this respect, figures from other investigators strengthen the extent of the usurpation.

Bengoa (op. cit.: 372) estimates that in the first half of the 20th century approximately one third of the land originally granted to the Mapuche through *Titulos de Merced* was usurped by private individuals. According to Fernández (1985: 29), between 1927 and the 1970s the settlers, not big landowners, had usurped 25% (about 323,570 acres) of the original 1,299,926 acres assigned through *Titulos de Merced*.[17]

The above figures do not allow us to determine to what extent the usurpation contributed to the disappearance of complete reservations or whether it affected them only partially. Besides corroborating the extent of the usurpation, available data allow us to determine that this process is as old as the Mapuche reservations themselves. Another factor contributing to the disappearance of Mapuche reservations has been the privatisation of collective property. Beginning in the 1980s, this phenomenon acquires alarming proportions. It should be mentioned at this point that both the process of usurpation and privatisation of Mapuche collective property have neither been documented nor studied by investigators.

THE PRIVATISATION OF COLLECTIVE PROPERTY

The privatisation of Mapuche collective property has been the primary cause of the disappearance of Mapuche reservations. Of the approximately 2,000 reservations at the beginning of the 1970s, 665 remained by the 1980s. At the beginning of the 1980s, 1,335 reservations dissolved themselves, becoming small private holdings.[18] The force behind this drastic reduction was the enactment of Law n°2,568 (22nd March 1979), decreeing that in order for collective property to be divided into private holdings it was sufficient that only one member of the community request such a division.

The existence of expedited legal means of dissolving collective property is not new in Chilean legislation. The privatisation of collective property has been promoted by the Chilean Government through a series of legislative acts spanning more than fifty years. This period begins when the process of issuing *Títulos de Merced* ended (1927), that is to say, when the Mapuche were relegated to reservations.[19] Since then, two legal premises have been used to promote the abolition of the collective property system: (1) the progressive denial to the Mapuche of their legal right of expression and self-determination, and (2) the gradual weakening of the position of those whom the law recognises as Mapuche.

The chronology of the laws enacted to regulate the existence of Mapuche reservations that follows[20] indicates the formulation of the legal processes created to facilitate the abolition of the collective property system.

- 1927 August. Law n°4,169 "Division of Indigenous Communities." The division of Mapuche collective property can be at the request by any one of its members.
- 1930 January. Law n°4,802. Eliminated the Comisión Radicadora de Indígenas of 1866 and 1883. This law created the Indian Courts,[21] whose objective was to proceed with the division of collective property.
- 1931 June. Law n°4,111. This law authorises the division of Mapuche collective property. For a division to take place, it must be requested by a third of its members.
- 1931 June. Decree-Law n°4,111, Article 54. An individual is considered "indigenous" (i.e., Mapuche) when s/he belongs to a family whose chief is a member-owner of collective property granted by a *Título de Merced*. Excepted from this law are those indigenous individuals who have complied with the law of Obligatory Primary Education.[22]

- 1959 December. Law n°14,511 replacing Law 4,111. This law decrees that the President of the Republic has the right to expropriate Mapuche collective property.
- 1960 January. Law 14,511 modifying the functions of the Indian Courts created in 1930 by Law n°4.802.
- 1960 January. Law 14,511, Article 29. A person is considered Mapuche when s/he belongs to a family whose chief is a member co-owner of collective land in a community possessing a *Título de Merced*. Excepted from this law are: (1) individuals who have successfully completed high school or its equivalent, as determined by the Director General of Secondary Education, and (2) Indigenous individuals who have been granted a professional degree by the University of Chile or by other accredited University.
- 1967 July. Agrarian Reform, Law n°16.640. This law includes the Mapuche as beneficiaries of the agrarian reform, considering them as another type of "peasant" (farmer).
- 1972 September. Law 17,729 decrees that Mapuche collective property is "indivisible." Division of collective property can now be achieved only when 100% of the community members agree to it.
- 1979 March. Law n°2,568 modifying Law n°17,729. This law decrees the "indivisibility" of collective property, but now a single member of the community may request the division of property. The law declares that "upon the division of collective property both the land and the individual cease to be classified as indigenous."

In the above chronology we can observe a legal process which has progressively restricted and reduced the existence of Mapuche reservations. The legislative sequence also indicates how Chile promoted legal expedients designed to abolish Mapuche collective property, starting when the Mapuche were first relegated to reservations. Since then, two legal premises have sufficed to promote the abolition of the collective property system.

With respect to the first, the enacted legislation systematically and arbitrarily made it easier to proceed with the abolition of the collective property system. We can also see how over time the number of members required to formalise the division of land varied. In the majority of legal enactments the demands of a minority of community members were legitimised. Only once was legislation enacted with the intent to protect the collective property system, namely, in 1972, during the administration of Salvador Allende. Allende reversed the trend by establishing that the division of collective property can take place only when 100% of the members of the community agree to it.

Legal Process of Abolition of Collective Property 71

In more specific terms, the second legal process complements the restrictions of the first through progressive legislation based on exclusion; the law now recognises only as "indigenous" those who belong to a family whose chief is a member and co-owner of a community holding collective property, and who do not possess higher education. The law establishes that education is the excluding factor formally institutionalising the discrimination of those individuals with the potential to exercise their constitutional rights in their status as "indigenous."

It is necessary to call to the attention of the reader an important aspect of the legislative sequence above. Law n°4,169 of 1927 and Law n°2,568 of 1979 are similar in context. Both laws were enacted by military administrations. They illustrate the case that in Chile, the existence of the Mapuche as an ethnic minority has been seriously threatened whenever the military have assumed control of the government. Throughout Chile's short existence, on three occasions, 1813, 1927 and 1979, legislation was enacted with the purpose of definitely ending the "Indigenous Issue." On the first occasion,[23] the new Republic had the Army to counter the Royalists; on the second[24] and third, Chile was under a military administration.[25]

In the course of this century the Mapuche have gone through a significant deterioration of their standard of living and of their rights as an ethnic minority group. There is nothing in the American continent resembling the legal restrictions that Chile has imposed on the Mapuche. It is important to note that in Canada[26] there was, in 1968, an attempt to legally establish the collective property rights of Indian reservations. This attempt was unanimously rejected. On the other hand, it needs to be mentioned that in later years some nations have initiated constitutional reforms to legitimise collective property rights to the benefit of their indigenous population. Such is the case of Colombia, Brazil, Peru, Nicaragua, Argentina and Australia.

We must therefore ask ourselves: Why has the Chilean Government maintained a policy designed to restrict, deny and nullify the constitutional rights of the Mapuche? Without interruption, Chile has legislated towards the abolition of the right of collective property in by indigenous reservations. There is a relationship between this fact and what all the studies related to the situation of ethnic minorities have shown: the worst social and legal conditions are found in countries where ethnic minorities have been militarily subjugated. From a historical perspective, the arbitrary treatment of the Mapuche by Chile is such a case.

Secondly, the problem is found within a global juridical–political reality.[27] The development of republics in the Americas presupposes the problem of incorporation of the indigenous population within the state of law.[28] Their eventual incorporation implies a confrontation with the legal system of the state—an extraordinarily complicated process.

The legal basis of a republic is the Constitution. This, in turn, is based in the right of private property.[29] The concept of private property recognises the constitutional legitimacy of individual rights. However, as indicated by Stavenhagen (1988: 313), the continued legal existence of indigenous groups requires legal recognition of their right to own property collectively. In turn, the incorporation of the right to own collective property as a constitutional right is the only legal guarantee this system has.

Historically, the problem of constitutional incorporation brings with it the need to draw a line of demarcation between the constitutional right of collective property and that of individual rights. How the relation between these rights is viewed in terms of importance constitutes a political-doctrinaire reasoning.

From the perspective of the political-doctrinaire reasoning fundamental in the founding of the Republic, the "indigenous issue" has been considered from two points of view: first, as a political–military problem, and second, as a political–social problem. A logical consequence of the first has been the use, and abuse, of violence. From the second viewpoint, the "Mapuche question" is judged as the problem of an impoverished social group (the "peasants"). Both viewpoints bring about as a political way out the dilemma of proceeding with the objective of integration and assimilation. This reasoning assumes that a policy oriented towards integration and/or assimilation is the required precondition which will allow for the improvement of living conditions and for a way out of poverty.

Within this framework, it must be noted that in the instances when legislation respecting collective rights has been passed in Chile, it has followed a political purpose: for example, Law 17.729, 1972, decreeing that "indigenous community property is indivisible." On the other hand, examples of laws obeying political dictates are Law 4.169 (1927) and Law 2.568 (1979), decreeing the "division of indigenous communities."

As has been mentioned above, the existence of the Mapuche as an ethnic minority has been seriously threatened whenever the military have taken control of the government. This fact denotes the political ill will of military administrations towards the Mapuche, since the concern over the problem of their incorporation or exclusion of the Mapuche from the framework of a state of law is again revived.

In Chile, whenever the military have taken over the government, they have done so with clear political purposes, as illustrated by the military coup of 1973. The military intervention of 1973 was inspired by ultra-liberal political and economic principles. A logical consequence of the implementation of these principles is the exclusion of the constitutional right to collective property. In practical terms, the only possibility is the execution of a policy oriented towards the assimilation of the Mapuche.

Within the historical process of the founding and consolidation of the Republic, the treatment of the "Mapuche question" has gone through the recognition (or lack thereof) of the constitutional right to collective property. The treatment of this problem in Chile has been dictated by political-juridical realities inherent to the nature of the Republic. It is evident that Chilean has legislated continuously for the abolition of collective property. The historical quest remains in its original state, as Simon Bolivar said in his Angostura speech of 1819: "[W]e find ourselves in the conflict of disputing with the Natives the rights to possession."

SUMMARY AND CONCLUSION

The successful application of the 1979 Law of "Division of Mapuche Communities" has allowed the Republic of Chile to accomplish a double historical purpose: (1) to legitimise the illegal usurpation of Mapuche land by settlers, and (2) to legally deny the system of collective property.

The transformation of the majority of Mapuche reservations into small private holdings is another step towards the abolition of the legal exception guaranteeing the existence of collective property. The governmental purpose over the last fifty years to convert privatise collective property proves that Chile has, historically, denied the incorporation of the Mapuche into the State of Law.

This statement is based on the legal importance, hopefully established here, of the existence of collective property. The Mapuche find, in the right to collective property, the only condition that legitimises and guarantees them as a minority group with constitutional rights. The state has systematically denied the Mapuche the legal guarantees to their existence, which rests on the principle of owning land collectively. It has also been established that the State has denied the legal guarantees on which to base the existence of the system of collective property.

The majority of investigators in this field claims that the incorporation of indigenous groups into a state of law must go through the formalisation of legal recognition of language, culture, and religion.[30] This reasoning defines the problem from an "integrationist" point of view, which has merits. On the other hand, it is a fact that the collective property system lacks the solid legal guarantees that could warrant their institutionalisation. This situation is neither new nor unknown. Paradoxically, it is not discussed.

The Chiapas insurrection in Mexico has once again brought to light the "political–juridical" realities that harm the legal existence of indigenous groups in America. The North American Free Trade Agreement (NAFTA) erodes the legal guarantees legitimising collective property as a constitutional right in Mexico.

74   *Jorge Calbucura*

From a historical perspective, the question is: until what point is the system of collective property compatible with a constitutional Republic?

In the case of the Mapuche, the collective property system is the only condition required for establishing them as an ethnic minority group. Until this condition can be guaranteed by legal means, the Mapuche will not be able to exercise their rights within the State of Law.

NOTES TO CHAPTER 3

1. A previous version of this chapter was presented at the 48th International Americanist Congress (ICA), in the symposium Borders and Indigenous Groups in South America 16–19th Centuries. Stockholm–Uppsala, July 1994. The author wishes to acknowledge the comments and suggestions of Peter Ekegren, Katarina Marklund and Ingvar Enghart. He also thanks Fernando de Pierris for his generous help in translating the original Spanish text into English. The author is also especially grateful for the comments and suggestions of the participants of the Development Sociology Seminar of the Sociology Department, University of Uppsala.
2. *Mapu*: land, *Che*: man. Mapuche: Man of the Land.
3. Officially, eighteen are recognised.
4. Congress of Concepción (1811).
5. In the Mapuche alphabet the letters C and B do not exist, which explains why different authors have written this name with different spellings. In all events, they refer to the same person. Thus: Kalfukura: Jules Verne (1975); Calvukura: Guevara (1913); Calfucura: Yunque (1956); Calvucura: Zeballos (1961); Calbucura: Bengoa (1985). *Calfu*: blue, *Cura*: stone. *Calfucura*: Blue Stone.
6. The "Conquest of the Desert" military campaign began on 22 March 1833, with three armies invading the Pampas. The first, from Chile, was commanded by General Bulnes; the second, from Mendoza and Cordoba, by Generals Aldao and José Ruiz Huidobro; and the third from Buenos Aires by General de Rosas. The expedition failed; Yanquetruz, Cacique of the Ranqueles, defeated the Army under the command of José Ruiz Huidobro. In 1881, the troops of the Federation of Salinas Grandes were defeated. The Argentine army occupied Patagonia. On 28 July 1881, the President of Chile, Anibal Pinto, signed the treaty whereby Chile renounced its historical rights over Patagonia and which established the Andes as the border between Chile and Argentina. Patagonia became the property of the Argentine Republic, which took possession of 102,642,577 acres. On 5 May 1885, Namuncura, successor to Juan Calbucura, formally surrendered to General Winter, "Governor of Patagonia."
7. In 1862 the cities of Mulchén and Lebu (south of the Bío-Bío) are founded and the Chilean army begins its advance south of the Bío-Bío. On 1 January 1883, Toqui Epulef is defeated. The Chilean army occupies the Araucanía. Chile takes possession of territory amounting to 24,500,000 acres.
8. The reasons for the decrease of the indigenous populations have been and continue to be the subject of much discussion among investigators. The majority consider a combination of disease, wars, and natural catastrophes as factors for the decrease in population (see Bengoa 1985). On the other

hand, the studies of León (1987, 1989) illustrate and give an idea of the intensity of the war against the Spanish.
9. This number is corroborated by Hidalgo (1973, quoted by Solis 1996), who based his estimates on a detailed study of the chronicles pertaining to the first stage of the Spanish conquest. According to some researchers, the estimate of a population of one million is considered "optimistic" (see Solís 1981).
10. 117,000, according to Guevara (1911).
11. Chile recognises the existence of different types of collective property of land. An example would be the legislation concerning indigenous communities and Agricultural Communities. For further details, see e.g. Baraona, Aranda and Santana (1961) and Solís de Ovando (1989). There is an absence of detailed studies on the subject.
12. My statement is based on the studies of Cloux (1991) and Hernández (1991) concerning the conditions of the indigenous peoples of Argentina and the policies towards them carried out by Argentina in latter years. The results of these studies allow us to see both the differences and similarities in policies. The reasons for the different treatment of the Mapuche by Chile and Argentina do not fall within the scope of this paper. To my knowledge, there are no comparative studies on the subject.
13. On the 1 July 1813, a decree designating a "Commission for the Reduction and Sale of Indigenous of Land of Indigenous Lands" is published. Its objective is to auction indigenous lands and with the proceeds to build formal towns with some adjacent land for the Mapuche.
14. According to Berglund (1977: 69), "The reservation of Chile are those pieces of land which, from 1866, were allocated to the Mapuche, and are remainders of those lands which the Mapuche once possessed independently. The legal document of ownership was called *título de merced*, and was granted to the *cacique*, while members of his group had right of usufruct. The family elders were, admittedly, named in the document of title, but it was the *cacique* who administered the communally owned land." For detailed information concerning the legal process involved in the assignment of titles to property to the Mapuche, see Errázuriz (1914).
15. According to Berglund (1977: 44), "When the reservations were created, it was [. . .] the chief of the family or the person claiming to be leader of a certain agricultural community, who was recorded as owner of this large area. The document of title was called *Título de Merced* and contained, besides the name of the accredited leader, the names of the members of the group, known as *radicados*. The topographical limits of the larger area were also given. The individual members of the family then had right of usufruct to those plots of land to which their claim was generally accepted by the others in the group. These plots could not be sold."
16. Morales (1982: 145). Other studies refer to time limitations. According to Fernandez (1985: 27), between 1883 and 1930 the "Commission to Relocate the Mapuche" issued 2,919 Titles, covering 1,300,000 acres, to 83,170 Mapuche.
17. According to Fernandez (1985: 29), between 1961 and 1971 different Mapuche reservations filed 1,434 law suits demanding the return of community property before the Indian Courts. In the course of ten years, the Mapuche prevailed in 352 actions, awarding them 8,350 acres. Only 3,365 acres were actually returned to the Mapuche. According to Bengoa (1985: 356), in 1929, there were 2,173 Mapuche Reservations in Cautín, and 1,709 legal actions for restitution against private landholders in the courts.
18. According to an estimate by Velázquez, a national leader of Ad-Mapu, in an interview by Calbucura (1986). Others sources complementing

Velázquez's are mentioned by Délano (1991), who learned that the division of Mapuche reservations resulted in the issuance of 70,000 titles to private property.
19. According to the Inter-American Committee for Agricultural Development (CIDA 1966: 79), "Between 1884 and 1929 Titles to private property were given to individual Mapuche." That is, until 1929 the policy of relocating the Mapuche into reservations continued.
20. The selection and reference to laws is partial and based on the following authorities: Errázuriz (1914), Lipschutz (1972b), Jara (1956), Ormeño and Osses (1972), Hernández (1985), Bengoa (1985).
21. To cite Berglund (1977: 94), "[An] Indian Court [is] a court with considerable powers in questions concerning the division of Indian-owned land, the settling of disputes, and the buying and selling of private or collectively-owned land." The purpose of the Indigenous Courts was to proceed with the division of collective property.
22. That is, those who have completed the 6th grade.
23. See footnote 9.
24. Colonel Carlos Ibañez del Campo became President of Chile on 21 July 1927. He was the only candidate in the presidential election. His administration was a military dictatorship.
25. Augusto Pinochet's dictatorship lasted from 1973 to 1989.
26. On becoming Prime Minister of Canada, Pierre Trudeau proposed the abolition of the Indian Act. A similar situation developed in Brazil in 1987.
27. This concept was originally used by Stavenhagen (1988). In the present case, the use of the concept differs from its original application.
28. The problem has receded somewhat with the passage of time. The founders of the American Republics understood the limitations of the problem. This is illustrated by Simon Bolivar when he stated that: "We are not Europeans, we are not natives, but rather a middle specie between the aborigines and the Spanish. We are Americans by birth and Europeans by right. We find ourselves in the conflict of disputing the property of the natives and to remain in the country that gave us birth, against the opposition of the invaders; our case is extraordinary and complicated" (Angostura speech, 1819).
29. For a discussion on the conflict between private and collective property, see Fernández (1953), Stavenhagen (1970, 1988), and Urban and Sherzer (1991).
30. It has been formulated, for example, that "Indigenous peoples fit the concept of an ethnic minority; with rights guaranteed by international law, because as a group they share a common language, culture, race and religion which distinguishes them, and they deserve to be treated as such for their differences" (García 1985).

REFERENCES

Baraona, R., X. Aranda and R. Santana. 1961. *Valle de Putaendo. Estudio de Estructura Agraria*. Santiago: Instituto de Geografia de Universidad de Chile.

Bengoa, J. 1985. *Historia del Pueblo Mapuche Siglo XIX y XX*. Santiago: Editorial Interamericana Ltda.

Berglund, S. 1977. *The National Integration of the Mapuche.* Stockholm: Almqvist & Wiksell.
Calbucura, J. 1986. Entrevista a J. Velázquez Dirigente Nacional de AD-MAPU. *Pueblo Indoamericano* 4(23):14–15.
Cloux, H. 1991. Perfil de la Política Indigenista Llevada a Cabo el la República Argentina en los Últimos Años. *América Indígena* Vol LI(1):55–62.
Comité Interamericano de Desarrollo Agrícola, CIDA. 1966. Chile Tenencia de la Tierra y Desarrolllo Económico del Sector Agrícola. Santiago: Talleres Gráficos Hispano. Suiza Ltda.
Délano, M. 1991. El Retorno de los Mapuches. *El País* (2 Novenber).
Errázuriz Ovalle, I. 1914. *Títulos de Propiedad en el Territorio Indíjena.* Santiago: Imprenta Universitaria.
Fernández, R. 1953. *Propiedad Privada Versus Ejido.* Mexico: Universidad Autónoma de Mexico.
García, S. 1985. La Cuestión Aborigen y la ley. *El Despertador* (3)47.
Guevara, T. 1911. Los Araucanos en la Guerra de Independencia. *Anales de la Universidad de Chile,* número especial. Santiago: Imprenta Cervantes.
Guevara, T. 1913. *Las Ultimas Familias y Costumbres Araucanas.* Santiago: Imprenta Litografía y Encuadernación Barcelona.
Hernández, I. 1985. *Derechos Humanos y Aborígenes. El Pueblo Mapuche.* Buenos Aires: Ediciones Búsqueda.
Hernández, I. 1991. Etnicidad y Marginación: la Situación Indígena en Argentina. *América Indígena* Vol LI(1):9–53.
Jara, A. 1956. *Legislación Indigenista de Chile.* Mexico: Instituto Indigenista Interamericano.
Lenz, R. 1895–1897. *Estudios Araucanos.* Santiago: Imprenta Cervantes.
León, L. 1987. La Resistencia Anti-Española y el Rol de las Fortalezas Indígenas en Chile Central 1536–1545. *CUHSO* No. 4.
León, L. 1989. *Comercio, Trabajo y Contacto Inter-Étnico en las Fronteras de Chile, Cuyo y Buenos Aires, 1750–1800.* RUNA.
Lipschuts, A. 1972a [1948]. La Propiedad Indígena en la Reciente Legislación de Chile. Pp. 104–110 in A. Lipschuts, *Perfil de Indoamérica de Nuestro Tiempo.* Habana: Editorial de Ciencias Sociales.
Lipschuts, A. 1972b [1959]. La Comunidad, y el Problema Indígena en Chile. Pp. 111–126 in A. Lipschuts, *Perfil de Indoamérica de Nuestro Tiempo.* Habana: Editorial de Ciencias Sociales. Mariqueo, V. 1986. División de la Comunidad Mapuche, leyes etnocidas del huinca contemporaneo. *Aukiñ* (12):4–9.
Morales, A. 1982. Chilenos y Mapuches. *Araucaria* (20):147–157.
Ormeño, H., and J. Osses. 1972 Nueva Legislación Sobre Indígenas en Chile. *Cuadernos de la Realidad Nacional,* No. 14.
Solís, L. 1981. Alianzas Militares entre los Indios Araucanos y los Grupos de Indios de las Pampas: la Rebelión Araucana de 1867–1872 en Argentina y Chile. *Revista Nueva Historia,* (1):3–49.
Solís de Ovando, J. 1989. *Normativa Legal de las Comunidades Agrícolas, Estudio Crítico del D.F.L. No. 5 de 1967 de Ministerio de Agricultura con sus Modificaciones Posteriores.* Santiago: Editorial Antártica S.A.
Stavenhagen, R., ed. 1970. *Agrarian Problems & Peasant Movements in Latin America.* Garden City, NY: Doubleday & Company.
Stavenhagen, R. 1988. *Derecho Indígena y Derechos Humanos en America Latina.* México D.F.: El Colegio de Mexico, Instituto Interamericano de Derechos Humanos.
Tordera, P. 1982. El Pueblo Mapuche y la Sociedad Chilena. *Araucaria* (20):135–146.

Urban, G., and J. Sherzer (eds.). 1991. *Nation-States and Indians in Latin America*. Austin: University of Texas Press.
Verne, J. 1975. *Los Hijos del Capitan Grant*. Barcelona: Editorial Bruguera.
Yunque, A. 1956. *La Conquista de las Pampas*. Buenos Aires: Ed. Zamora.
Zeballos, E. 1961 [1884] [1890]. *Calvucura y la Dinastía de los Piedras*. Buenos Aires: Hachette.

4 Religion, Belief and Action
The Case of Ngarrindjeri "Women's Business" on Hindmarsh Island, South Australia, 1994–1996

James F. Weiner[1]

> Moses said to Israel: 'How can you let your doing precede your listening? Does not the deed usually arise from learning what to do?' They answered him: 'We will do whatever we will hear from God.'
>
> From this also derives the saying: 'He whose works exceed his wisdom, his wisdom will endure.' (Midrash [21], in Plut, M., *The Torah: A Modern Commentary*)

The anthropological investigation of the "beliefs" of non-Western people has been one of the century's crucial foci for assessing anthropology's methodology and the nature of cultural difference this methodology implicates. Evans-Pritchard (1937), Needham (1972), Gellner (1985) and more recently Sperber (1996) have all contributed significantly to the perennial question concerning the function of apparently "irrational" or unverifiable beliefs, especially those we usually term religious, cosmological or supernatural, and the role of cultural relativism in assessing the social and cultural functionality of these and other beliefs. They have been aided by the abiding concern with the nature of knowledge, language and translation on the part of many notable analytic philosophers of this century, including Quine (1968), as well as philosophers of science such as Barnes and Bloor (1982) and Bhaskar (1979).

However, more recently the whole question of the legitimacy of beliefs has been made to bear a significantly heavier political, ethical and epistemological burden, given a number of contemporary developments in the world(s) of indigenous people. First, there is the controversy concerning the so-called "invention of tradition," revealed in its sharpest terms in the debate between Allan Hanson and his critics over the recency of Maori tradition.[2] Second, and related to the first point, there is the increasing literary documentation that has been accumulating about indigenous peoples and their history and culture, and, more to the point, the growth of literacy and academic interest in such documents on the part of indigenous scholars and activists themselves. Because our indigenous interlocutors are thus bringing Western textual, exegetical and literary tools of analysis to bear upon their own cultures, these cultures are appearing more and more as things "cultivated" or produced, as indeed our own Western culture is largely an artifice of law and custom set up as a humanly constructed bulwark against nature. Along with this—and this is a critical point for the case I will discuss below—I suggest we also see evidence for the attributing of specifically Western forms of subjectivity, individuality and autonomy not just to indigenous persons but to the entire domain of contemporary indigenous action, intention, deliberation and production, forms which may very well be in marked contrast to the pre-Western manner in which indigenous people revealed aspects of the world to themselves. Even as anthropological involvement with indigenous people is becoming more and more linked to global political movements for indigenous rights—that is, as the notion of the Western legal *persona* increasingly underwrites the global discourse of indigenous autonomy and survival—politicians and legalists seem to assess the task of describing non-Western forms of personhood, intention and subjectivity as less important than contriving arguments in support of such global legislation.[3]

This pressure derives directly from the third recent development in contemporary indigeneity: the challenging of indigenous culture and its status as traditional and authentic by a number of States against whose interests recent indigenous aspirations, especially concerning the reclaiming of control and proprietorship over ancestral land, appear to be poised, in such countries as Canada, New Zealand, the United States and Australia. In the face of these challenges, which more and more are taking place in the highest courts of law in these countries, anthropologists are called upon to analyze, interpret and evaluate indigenous peoples' attempts to confront the state and other non-indigenous interests to which indigenous peoples see themselves in conflict.

All three of these developments in the articulation of contemporary indigeneity came together dramatically in Australia in 1995, when a group of Ngarrindjeri women were accused by the State of South Australia of deliberately fabricating a claim for a sacred site in order to halt the construction of a bridge between the South Australian mainland and an island in the mouth of the Murray River. In this chapter, I re-visit the question of how "beliefs" can be tested anthropologically, as indeed the question was raised in the context of the Ngarrindjeri sacred site claim, and the role of the anthropologist as both adjudicator of and witness to the events surrounding clashes between indigenous peoples and states.

THE HINDMARSH ISLAND BRIDGE SACRED SITE CLAIM

In 1995, a group of Ngarrindjeri women from South Australia whose spokesperson was Doreen Kartinyeri, a well-known local Aboriginal historian and activist, lodged a claim under the Commonwealth Aboriginal and Torres Strait Islander Heritage Protection Act (1984) to prevent a bridge that was to be built between the mainland town of Goolwa and Hindmarsh Island, which lies just opposite Goolwa in the mouth of the Murray River. The women (who would come to be known as the "proponent women") claimed that building the bridge would fatally impair the reproductive capacity of women's bodies and the reproductivity of their cosmos more generally. They also claimed that this knowledge was of great antiquity but that awareness of the existence of this cosmological nexus was very restricted, and its transmission from generation to generation was through a line of select women who had purportedly demonstrated skill, sensitivity and receptivity to the knowledge and whatever ritual practices were associated with it in the past. The selectivity of transmission accounted for the observation that no mention or hint of its existence had been reported since numerous anthropologists and other researchers had been studying the Ngarrindjeri since the 1940s, including such renowned Australian anthropologists as Norman Tindale and Ronald and Catherine Berndt. An anthropologist hired by the developers of the marina complex on Hindmarsh Island a few years previously likewise did not mention the existence of this women's business. As it was subsequently explained by another anthropologist who facilitated the transmitting of the claim (Fergie 1994), only when the knowledge complex was under threat by the imminent start of bridge construction did the women feel it necessary to reveal its existence for the purposes of utilizing the Federal Act as a means of halting the bridge.

The then Federal Minister for Aboriginal Affairs took the advice of the female Professor of Law, Cheryl Saunders, whom he had appointed as official reporter. She herself took advice from the above-mentioned female anthropologist, who had been hired initially for a two-day period to act as "facilitator" between the Aboriginal women claimants and the Professor of Law, even though this anthropologist had no background knowledge, either first hand or with the literature, of the Ngarrindjeri. Acting on this report, the then Minister ultimately used the power of the 1984 Act under Section 10(4) to place a 25-year ban on the bridge's construction.

Shortly after this, reports began to appear in the news media that the claim of "secret women's business" as it came to be known had been deliberately fabricated for the purpose of stopping the bridge. In April 1995, remarks from other senior Ngarrindjeri women (who would become known as the "dissident women") appeared maintaining that they knew nothing of the existence of such secret women's knowledge. By June 1995 these media reports had received enough national attention that the Liberal State government of South Australia was spurred to hold a Royal Commission to determine whether the claim had been fabricated for the purposes of stopping the bridge.

On the second day of the Royal Commission hearings, the Queen's Councilor representing the Aboriginal Legal Rights Movement of South Australia (the body which lodged the claim on behalf of the proponent women) announced that the Royal Commission was inappropriately questioning the religious beliefs of Aboriginal people and that her clients were withdrawing from the Inquiry.[4] With one exception, none of the proponent women appeared before the Royal Commission (though three Ngarrindjeri men gave evidence in support of the applicants). After over five months of taking testimony from a host of witnesses, both Aboriginal and Euro-Australian, the Commissioner opined that the so-called secret women's knowledge had originated no earlier than 1993, and intimated that the claimant women had probably been encouraged to act by others such as environmental activists who were also opposed to the bridge, and who continue to publicly defend the proponent women's case at the present time.[5]

Very shortly after the Commissioner issued her report, the Federal government instituted its own Inquiry into the original claim. It employed several senior anthropologists, both male and female, from within and outside Australia, all with long experience and extensive publications in the areas of Aboriginal culture, religion and gender. In April 1996, a Federal election in Australia resulted in the defeat of the incumbent Labour Party, traditionally sympathetic to Aboriginal empowerment, and the election of a Liberal/National Party coalition representing politically the conservative middle and rural right, though the Federal Inquiry proceeded despite the change in administration. In this inquiry, the "proponent" Ngarrindjeri, both men and women, cooperated fully with the anthropologists aiding Justice Jane Mathews, who led the Inquiry. However, at the last moment, a court decision in West Australia over another Aboriginal sacred site claim ruled that developers would be denied natural justice if they could not learn of the reasons why a site had been placed off-limits to them for Aboriginal religious purposes.[6] This decision caused the applicant women to withdraw their evidence, after Justice Mathews could no longer promise the material would remain confidential. Nevertheless, she concluded in her report that the material withdrawn represented the difference between "nothing and very little." Hence, from the point of view of the women claimants, the report of Justice Mathews did not provide the anthropological or legal confirmation of their claim that perhaps they anticipated.

Armed with this report, the new Federal Minister for Aboriginal Affairs tabled a special bill in Parliament in 1997[7] to allow the Hindmarsh Island Bridge to be built. The bill in effect asked that the Aboriginal Heritage Protection legislation be suspended in this one case. In response, the original claimants (now represented officially by the Ngarrindjeri Heritage Committee and supported by the major political figures in the Ngarrindjeri community) lodged an appeal in the Australian High Court, claiming that the special bill constituted a racist refusal to accept the validity of the asserted beliefs of Aboriginal persons. This was heard in the High Court (February 5–6, 1998). Subsequently, the High Court dismissed the appeal by a 5–1 majority.[8] As I will argue at the end of this chapter, the appeal

Religion, Belief and Action 83

and its dismissal represented a crucial turning in the progress of this case in terms of what it implied for our portrait of Aboriginal religion, belief and culture.

The most recent chapter of this saga occurred when on August 21, 2001, von Doussa J dismissed the appeal of the original Hindmarsh Island Marina developers and Binalong Pty. Ltd. against Luminis Pty Ltd., Dr. Deane Fergie, Professor Cheryl Saunders, Robert Tickner and the Commonwealth of Australia.[9] In general, the applicants charged that they had suffered financial damages as a result of misleading or deceptive information proffered (in the case of Fergie and Saunders) and misfeasance (in the case of Saunders and Tickner) on the part of the respondents. Although von Doussa J stated in his Reasons for Judgement (at 372) that he was not trying to anthropologically evaluate the cases made for and against the existence of the Ngarrindjeri women's business, in fact he heard evidence and received submissions from both the proponent and dissident women as well as Dr. Fergie, Dr. Clarke and other senior anthropologists acting on their behalf. In due course, he did make a judgement on the nature of Ngarrindjeri religion during the Hindmarsh Island Bridge Royal Commission, to which I will return in the conclusion.

I have commented on other aspects of the Hindmarsh Island case elsewhere.[10] Here I want to focus on the issue of belief as it emerged as a central plank in the original Ngarrindjeri applicant women's case, and discuss some of the problems, both legal and anthropological, with the testing and adjudicating of belief. The point I will make will be neither terribly complicated nor even new, as it merely reiterates a position put forward by Needham, Sperber, and Quine, among others: Anthropologically, the status of "belief," though enshrined in the Aboriginal Heritage Protection legislation throughout Australia, is plagued by definitional and methodological indeterminacies that have been identified by writers such as Needham and Sperber. I will maintain that anthropologists involved in such public interest cases have a responsibility to describe indigenous social life in such a way that the term "belief" becomes a reasonable gloss for a socially situated disposition to act and speak in particular ways. I will go on from there to suggest some problems with the convergence of Aboriginal and Western religiosity in the conjuncturally constituted "post-indigenous" world of settled, peri-urban Australia.

SOME ASPECTS OF TRADITIONAL NGARRINDJERI RELIGIOUS LIFE

The following account is summarized from the two main ethnographic records of the Ngarrindjeri, that of Ronald and Catherine Berndt (1993), and Norman Tindale's unpublished journals and notes, currently held at the South Australian Museum in Adelaide. Both records derive from fieldwork in the 1940s, primarily with elderly informants who still remembered pre-Colonial religious life. The Ngarrindjeri were one of a congeries of groups inhabiting the estuarine area of the Murray River in southeast South Australia. Due to the abundance of fish and game in their habitat, they were somewhat more sedentary than other, interior dwellers of more arid zones of Australia, and their political life was evidently more complex and on a larger scale than is reported to have been the case elsewhere on the continent. They had a well-developed interclan council which dealt with disputes and matters of public important and was called *yanarumi* (Berndt and Berndt 1993: chapter 5). It was a focus of public life and in the words of the Berndts, "generally enabled a flow of information between people" (ibid: 64). Important trade routes linked the Lower Murray populations such as the Ngarrindjeri to the interior. There was an institution by which newborn male babies could acquire an unseen trade partner in a distant land by the father sending the navel cord along such trade routes. The individual who laid claim to the cord would consider himself indebted to the child when it attained maturity and traveled through his territory to claim his protection and beneficence. This relationship was called *ngengampi* (ibid: 119). On the other side, neighboring groups raided each other, commonly for the purposes of capturing women.

There were several important religious concepts that apparently dominated traditional Ngarrindjeri life. Mythologically, they shared much in common with societies throughout Australia: they considered the most salient features of their landscape to have been formed by the actions of ancestral creator beings, the most important of which was the male Ngurunduri, who traveled along the coast of South Australia and made most of the significant features of coastal topography.

Similar to the totemic complex that dominated traditional Aboriginal life throughout the continent, the Ngarrindjeri accorded a central role in personal identity to the *ngaitje*, or personal totem, a species with which each individual associated, although the *ngaitje* had a territorial dimension as well. The personal aspect of totemic identification was accentuated by the emphatic assertion by the Berndts that the Ngarrindjeri lacked organized species-renewal rituals of the sort commonly reported for the desert populations of central Australia. Another was that of *miwi*, the seat of power, action, thought and cogitation. Third, there was the institution of initiation, apparently far more elaborated with respect to males than females, though females underwent their own rites of passage. In this regard, the Berndts claim that during initiation what boys "were told at this time, although sacred, was not secret; nor was it information that was kept from women" (ibid.: 163), though a few pages later they refer to "secret-sacred" interpretations of the boys' initiatory state known "only to the elders" (ibid.: 176).

The healer or *putari* was an important figure in Ngarrindjeri life. The consulting anthropologist's report linked the content of the secret women's business on Hindmarsh Island to the institution of female *putari* who were essentially midwives and experts in the matter of physical and presumably, in light of what was divulged of the applicant women's claim, also cosmological, reproduction. The Berndts also remark that "the possession of a strong *miwi* was a prerequisite for performing curative tasks" (ibid.: 251). Finally, sorcery was a well-developed institution and means of inter-personal aggression, and was a major source of social tension and conflict.

The portrait that emerges in the Berndts' account is that personal power, the individual perception of significance, was more highly developed among the Ngarrindjeri and Lower Murray populations than perhaps was the case elsewhere in Australia, although Berndt did make a case for a similar construct among the Wiradjuri (Berndt 1947). The Berndts remark on "the term *mulumi*, which was translated on the one hand as 'many dream songs' and on the other, as 'sacred'. In exploring this term, the closest meaning that can be implied is that of 'privacy', of 'belonging to a person', 'something that is not common', or 'quietness'" (ibid.: 213). We may be confronting a tradition in which there were not the highly institutionalized ways of publicly revealing restricted symbolic equations and interpretations well-known for Aboriginal populations of the Central Desert and northeast Arnhem Land. Reading the Berndts' and Tindale's accounts of the very personal totemic relationship of *ngaitje*, the concept of *miwi* as an internal source of power, discrimination and insight, the education and training of the healer/magicians the *putari*, one can at least countenance the possibility that the pre-Christianized Ngarrindjeri world included a pronounced contrast between inner, personal and external, public worlds. However, it must be remembered that the Berndts were dealing with reconstructions by a small number of Ngarrindjeri individuals of communal rites and practices that had not been carried out for many years. Hence, the contrast between the individual's interior state and the public world of ritual meaning was in all likelihood sharpened by the conditions under which Tindale and the Berndts elicited these accounts.

This set the stage for the anthropologically focused epistemic problem revealed by the Royal Commission's inquiry into the nature of Ngarrindjeri belief, a problem posed elsewhere in the ethnographic world (for example, among the Papua New Guinea Mountain Ok, and in the entire corpus of Carlos Castaneda's writings on the Yaqui sorcerer Don Juan): To which version of social life should we accord more legal and analytical legitimacy, the "public, sunlit world" of ceremonial, as Alfred Gell once termed it (Gell 1980), or the privileged insight of the adept, him(her)self an internal version of the anthropologist/synthesizer whose worldview is nevertheless as idiosyncratic and incommunicable as it is totalizing? In this chapter I will suggest that the dichotomy between the world of the ritual specialist and that of the non-specialist is largely a contrived one with respect to epistemic framework, that the articulation of a cosmology is an anthropological task and not necessarily an avowed goal of a ceremonial system, and that all beliefs, public and private are, as Needham suggested, essentially glosses or *post factum* theorizations of specific human actions, including verbal action, or utterances. Because beliefs cannot be divorced from the actions of individual agents, so-called collective and individual beliefs are empirically indistinguishable even though they may support different *post factum* interpretational assessments.

NGARRINDJERI "WOMEN'S BUSINESS" AND THE ROYAL COMMISSION

Let us now examine some of the components of the Ngarrindjeri women's claim that were challenged during the Hindmarsh Island Bridge Royal Commission.

There have been several accounts of what the secret women's business consists of, and in fact, such is the nature of talk under pressure that the Report of the Royal Commission was able to list at least twelve distinct aspects of the alleged secret women's business during the course of the Royal Commission Inquiry (see Stephens 1995). The main explanation provided by both the proponent women's spokesperson and the anthropologist was that the island had to remain separate from the mainland. When it was countered that the barrages, built in the 1930s and which control the flow of salt water into the Murray estuary, already provided this link, it was then suggested that the proposed bridge would provide a connection between sky and water and thus compromise the separateness of these domains upon which female reproductive efficacy depended. Thus, the barrages did not constitute a cosmological hazard because they rested on the surface of the water.

Another account was that Hindmarsh Island was sacred because it was a place where Aboriginal women went to abort fetuses conceived after liaisons with white whalers. This practice could by its very terms only have started after 1820.[11] We also learned from the archaeological evidence that Hindmarsh Island was probably an important site of Ngarrindjeri burial, which itself was cosmologically significant and a focus of ritual elaboration. Another claim put forth was that the shape of the island and the surrounding estuary were iconic of parts of the female reproductive anatomy, and there was also the suggestion that the name of the island, Kumarangk, was similar to the Ngarrindjeri word for pregnancy, or the word for woman.[12] Although it was not put forward as a component of the secret business, we also know that Ngurunderi, the Ngarrindjeri male creation hero, made many of the geographic features of the Murray mouth during his travels along the South Australian coast (though none of the Murray mouth islands are mentioned in the ancestral journey of Ngurunderi along the south Australian coast) and that cosmogonically, the Lower Murray people considered the Murray River and its estuary as literal parts of Ngurunduri's body.

These suggest a "deeper" cosmological gender significance that surely must have predated the white–Aborigine fetus abortion practice. But the assertion of the abortion practice is inconsistent with the claim of great antiquity for the women's business itself by Doreen Kartinyeri. If the island had to remain separate from the mainland to protect the reproductive capacity of women, why did women travel to the island to have abortions? I am not saying that there is necessarily a contradiction here (it may have had something to do with the foreign nature of the genitors); one could envision any number of frameworks in which such contradictory assertions could all nevertheless be valid. But here I am posing the anthropological questions: How did the question of the testing of beliefs as such arise? Why was the issue phrased as one primarily of "belief" in the first place? What would we have to know to make such assertions part of a behavioural/cosmological whole that had, as the consulting anthropologist asserted, a "cultural logic" (Fergie 1994)? What questions would the anthropologist have had to ask to do so? What alternatives, if any, existed for an alternative rendering of the proponent women's claim?

THE TESTING OF BELIEF

A foundation of the consulting anthropologist's defense was her insistence that such questions could not be posed, because she maintained that the empirical basis of a belief cannot be tested. [13]But even if we agree that religious beliefs are all, as the consulting anthropologist seemed to imply, irrational at their base, this is still not, nor has it been since Durkheim's time, a bar to the empirical study of belief. More to the point, it was not what the Royal Commission was attempting to determine. It is the case that demonstrating the factual existence of God or any other spiritual being is not a precondition of the "truth" of a religion. But all beliefs have an empirical dimension in that they make people *act and speak* in certain ways.[14] Hanson makes this point effectively, acknowledging Geertz' important debt to Ryle in this regard:

> There is no fundamental difference ... between someone saying 'I believe in a triune deity' out loud and silently entertaining the same belief in one's private thoughts. It is definitely not the case that the latter holds a privileged position and somehow causes or produces the former.... The only distinction between them is that the one is done overtly, in public view, and the other is done covertly ... [But] the consequences of these views are immense for anthropological understanding, for from them it follows that ... ideas, values and meanings are as empirical and can be studied as objectively as birth rates, election tallies, and calorie or body counts. (Hanson n.d.: 19–20)

88   *James F. Weiner*

This is how we as anthropologists are obliged to describe what we identify as a belief system in any social group we care to isolate. As Barnes and Bloor put it:

> It is not that all beliefs are equally true or equally false, but that regardless of truth and falsity the fact of their credibility is to be seen as equally problematic. The position we shall defend is that the incidence of all beliefs without exception calls for empirical investigation and must be accounted for by finding the specific, local causes of this credibility. (Barnes and Bloor 1982:31)

The question of belief, both of the "beliefs" of our informants, and our decisions "to believe" what they say, is of course a long-standing and central issue in anthropological investigation and was treated comprehensively by Rodney Needham in his classic work *Belief, Language and Experience* (1972). The point I want to make here is that the anthropologist who was asked to give an account of the women's claim did not, either in the original application or in her testimony before the Royal Commission, differentiate sufficiently between what Sperber terms *mental representations* and *public representations* (1996: 78). "Mental representations" he defines as internal to the agent. "Public representations" he defines as "material phenomena in the environment of people and which represent something for people who represent and interpret them" (ibid.).[15]

Sperber goes on to say that we speak about "cultural representations" to the extent that these are widely shared within a community. He adds that "what human communication achieves in general is . . . some degree of resemblance between the communicator's and the audience's thoughts" (ibid.: 83). What he calls an "epidemiology of representations" is an account of the mechanisms by which representations become distributed and shared. In the context of the current case, what we could say is that even an item of secret knowledge must be communicable, both in terms of its substantive content and as an item for which concealment from public consciousness is deemed appropriate.

The consulting anthropologist was, during the Royal Commission, subjected to the accusation that she did not attend sufficiently to such epidemiological considerations in assessing the cultural cogency of the Ngarrindjeri applicants' claim. She defended herself by maintaining, *contra* Sperber, that a belief could not be tested. An example of this can be found in the Royal Commission proceedings when the counsel for the developers, Mr. Meyer, in his cross-examination, asked her how she, the anthropologist, determines whether what she is being told, in fact, exists:

> A [Fergie]. It exists because you are being told it.
>
> Q [Meyer]. That is not necessarily so. I have been told lots of untruths in my life that don't exist.

A. No, you are asking a different question.

Q . . . . What I'm putting to you is in your doing this assessment, as you call it, do you assess what you're being told as to whether it's accurate, or do you just accept it.

A. The terms in which you are asking the question are terms that most anthropologists would take issue with; that, in a sense, belief is not something whose veracity you can determine. I will give you an example. My mother is a very, she is very religious. If I were to say to her 'Look mum, evolution discounts genesis', she would not in any way be swayed in her misbelief. I can't produce that empirical test as a confirmation of her belief. It's not my business to go around finding out what people have as a basis in empirical fact and in what they believe, my business is to explore what people believe.

Q. It is to find out whether that belief is truly held. (T: 5370)

I repeat—it is to find out whether the beliefs *are truly held*—that is, *whether they are in a definitive sense the extrusion in discourse of some embedded and conventionally held disposition to behave*. In contrast, what could the consulting anthropologist have meant by "misbelief" here except that some beliefs are erroneous, if not downright ridiculous, and that certain descriptions of the world are true (evolution) while others are not (Creation)? What is the difference between the distinction that the consulting anthropologist draws between evolution and Genesis and the following statement by one of the senior dissident women, Bertha Gollan, earlier in the Royal Commission?

Q [Counsel]. . . . When was it that you heard for the first time of any secret sacred women's business stories.

A [Gollan]. I read it in the paper, about, if the bridge went ahead, that is, down at Hindmarsh Island, it would stop the fertility of the women and I made a statement to that and I said it would never stop the fertility, because they still were breeding like rabbits. (T: 626)

The constructionist terms which dominate today's anthropological discourse of identity lead to a resurrection of the Frazerian notion of religion as error, because all acts of construction are seen as consciously and subjectively constituted (recall that Tertullian averred: "I believe because it is impossible," or that Hocart (1927: 28) had reason to remind us that *Credo quia non intelligo*). This is an important point to which I draw the reader's attention: Unless anthropology is to divorce the description of acts of constructioning, social or otherwise, from their observable behavioural manifestations, the consulting anthropologist's characterization of the strategy of the Royal Commission as "grossly empiricist" has to be rejected as inaccurate and misleading. Having insisted that there is not necessarily any empirical, historical or material basis to the belief in question, the consulting anthropologist and the Ngarrindjeri proponent women are forced to situate it entirely in the realm of the "spiritual" and leave the realm of the material to their "ethnocentric, empiricist" opponents, that is, the Royal Commission itself. But as the passage from the transcript quoted above indicates, the Commission was not charged with determining the "factual" basis of Ngarrindjeri belief, as the proponents' QC erroneously tried to insist on the second day of the Commission, but the historical and cultural "realities of social existence" out of which the allegations of restricted women's business arose.[16]

BELIEF, PRACTICE, CULTURE

"Belief," then, is a way of referring to a set of dispositions to act or speak that are amenable to sociological description and analysis of the sort that anthropologists characteristically engage in. In the case of Australian Aboriginal religion, ritual practice without exception forms the observable link between a hypostatized system of belief and a set of so-called sacred sites within which cosmologically important events are inferred to have occurred (see Berndt and Berndt 1985). But the problem with the Ngarrindjeri case was that no convincing case for this aspect of belief could be made. The "link" between an asserted belief and an attendant constellation of behaviors could not be made. Commenting on the absence of practises among the Ngarrindjeri with regard to Hindmarsh Island such as a restriction or "taboo" on visiting the alleged women's sacred site or sites:

> [Fergie]. And in any case it seems to me that the logical connection between the significance of a site and the assumption that it is going to have a taboo associated with it is actually—has no necessity. There is no logical reason why a site shouldn't have significance in knowledge, but necessarily have taboos in practice. So, I think we don't know if there were specific taboos in relation to this specific knowledge. But, at the same time—on the one hand, at the same time, it seems to me that even were there to have been such taboos, the experience of—in the Lower Murray would suggest that the maintenance of those taboos and the memory of those taboos might not have continued. That doesn't in and of itself negate the transmission of the knowledge. The knowledge about the significance of an area. (T: 5357–5358)

Religion, Belief and Action 91

A religious system that had been subject to as much destructive colonial impact as had that of the Ngarrindjeri since the early 1800s might very well have retained the belief in the religious importance of sites without having retained the practices, including the taboos alluded to by the anthropologist in the above testimony. But this hypothesis was directly contradicted by Doreen Kartinyeri herself, who explained in a media interview in 1994 that she always knew *what* the woman's business was, but it was only much later, in recent times, that she learned of its connection with the specific site or sites in question.[17] However, Kartinyeri's assertion, unlike that of the consulting anthropologist, is in line with what is more commonly the case in Australia: when subject to negative acculturative pressures, Aboriginal people first lose knowledge of the site while retaining for longer periods knowledge of the songs, myths and ritual practices that are associated with it (see for example Tonkinson 1970).

Peter Sutton, one of Australia's leading anthropologists of Aboriginal communities, who made a submission to the Federal Inquiry into the Hindmarsh Island Bridge Royal Commission, made the following observation which describes the nature of this scission between belief and knowledge somewhat differently. Here he draws attention to another component of the women's business, that it was linked with a myth concerning the Pleiades, or the "Seven Sisters," a common mythological motif throughout Aboriginal Australia, and invoked by the applicant Ngarrindjeri women as mythological justification for maintaining the separateness between sky and water:

> The 'content' of the Seven Sisters narrative has been withheld. There seems to be no problem with its standing as a tradition: it is attested to by a cross-section of Ngarrindjeri elders; the standing of such elders has been established; the fact that it is of spiritual importance to the relevant group seems very clear, and it has been cross-linked with a major prohibition. That is, its 'envelope features' indicate that it is the type of tradition which would normally be the basis of a threat of desecration to a place with which it is associated.

But Sutton goes on:

> Its link to the prohibition on the covering of the waters has not been explained. If such a link could be made out, would this be a case of content providing a rationale sufficient for a declaration? . . .
>
> It was also said that no 'rationale' had been given for the connection between the fact of the tradition and the rule that the area of the application must not be covered or further disturbed (Tr 26: lines 33–34). Two distinct kinds of rationale must be kept distinct here, however: that of someone who is a member of the cultural group concerned,

and that of an outsider interpreting that culture. I argue that there is no inherent reason why Ngarrindjeri women would have to be able to specify a logical link between the Seven Sisters and the prohibition on covering the waters, in order to make the link between the two. That is, the link may have been handed down minus its rationale.

In fact the holders of such traditions rarely, if ever, propose specific causal connections between the sacred details of a place and the specific taboos that surround it. When anthropologists ask for such whys and wherefors they are typically met with such statements as 'The Old People always said that would happen', or 'I don't know—it just is that way and always has been.' This is typical of the case of custom.

There are three usual reasons why such connections are not made explicit by members of the culture. One is that revealing such things is prohibited in certain contexts.

The second reason is simply that people are often not aware of the connections either because they are never brought to consciousness by anyone in the group, or because the people concerned have not yet learned about the connections.

The third reason, in my experience, is that people frequently regard the connecting symbolism to be obvious and it is thus unnecessary to make it explicit. To the outsider, however, this may not be the case. (Mathews 1996: 204–205)

There are two points I wish to make in regard to Sutton's compelling explanation. The first is that anthropological interpretation has been an inextricable component of the definition and identification of Aboriginal tradition for a long time. Anthropologists have been successfully describing and explaining Aboriginal kinship and land tenure systems in Northern Territory courts since the passage of the *Aboriginal Land Rights Act (Northern Territory) 1976*. With regard to other sacred site claims, anthropologists have acted successfully to explicate Aboriginal religious customs pertaining to sites in, for example, the case of Uluru (Ayers Rock) (see Layton 1986). Anthropologists have long been called upon to assess the significance of such indigenous statements and semantic and conceptual links between different cultural domains for the purposes of this type of legislative adjudication.

The second point is that insofar as the Aboriginal heritage protection acts are protecting "Aboriginal Tradition," this tradition in any anthropological version that makes sense cannot be made to reside exclusively in the cataloguing of sites. Nor, for obvious reasons, can the practices or myths or songs themselves, divorced from the knowledge of the sites that anchors them in the land, because these are no longer under threat and cannot be protected by law anyway.[18] The only thing that *can* be protected in both the legally and anthropologically sensible meaning of the term has to be *the relation between knowledge of a site and an associated mythological/ritual or symbolic/poetic complex*, because it was this relationship between practise and territoriality that uniformly constituted Australian Aboriginal ritual/ religious practices, however much this relation is controlled and concealed by different regimes of knowledge restriction. It is in the *relation* between the two terms that what we would want to call "cosmology," "culture" or "tradition" resides, at least for Aboriginal Australians. Again, it is the anthropologist who is called upon to make those connections between sites and their symbolism, meaning and knowledge that Sutton rightly admits are not always present in indigenous exegesis. As I have remarked elsewhere (Weiner 1997), I accept the position of the anthropologist as Victor Turner once characterized it, as an outsider who becomes privy to conceptual and other connections within a speech community that are concealed, by a variety of institutional mechanisms, from the insiders themselves.

We might then contend that we have been prevented from situating the belief as a total function of current Ngarrindjeri social behavior, since we were not given the information from which to make our usual symbolic equivalences between the "sacred" and the "material." We would therefore claim that in this case we could not find a path between the belief and social behavior. And if it is not sedimented in behavior, it is beyond the reach of the anthropological. As Kolig says:

> The cardinal question I am posing here is not what do Aborigines believe?—in terms of the corpus of their religious dogma, mythology, ethics, etiology, and so on—but rather, how do they believe? What is the practical side of their religious exercise, and how does this directly or indirectly shape their consciousness? (Kolig 1981: 7–8)

The anthropology of religion does not concern itself solely with the description of beliefs *as such*. It is not a version of theology. As Avery notes (n.d.: 125), echoing Needham's famous discussion (1972), the anthropologist usually infers the existence of beliefs from his/her observations of what people say and do. Moreover, he says elsewhere that in regard to the Aboriginal communities he has worked with:

> belief is not an important consideration in traditional knowledge ... I have never heard any Aboriginal person make a statement about their beliefs or be questioned about their beliefs about the facts of Aboriginal tradition. Aboriginal religion, to dramatize one aspect of tradition, is not a religion of belief, conscience or personal conviction. (n.d.: 8)

The Berndts, whose ethnography of the Ngarrindjeri in the 1940s provided the anthropological evidence for the absence of extensive gender-restricted knowledge among the Lower Murray Aboriginal populations, put it this way:

In most Australian Aboriginal groups there are, or have been, special words ... [that] relate to rituals which are usually described, in translation, by the terms 'religious' or 'sacred': *maraiin* in western Arnhem Land; *mareiin* or *duju* in north-eastern Arnhem Land, *daragu* (*darugu*) or *djudju* in the eastern Kimberleys; *tjurunga* among the Aranda. (Strehlow, 1947: 84–6). In many Aboriginal societies such terms refer to actions, persons, objects, or verbal material, rather than to belief as such: phenomena which can be seen or heard, rather than phenomena which must be inferred. ...

Looking at this kind of situation from the outside, we might say that there was no probing as to the nature of a person's belief, the degree to which this conformed with the beliefs of others. If he behaved in certain defined ways, at certain defined times, this seems to have been sufficient. We do not have enough information as to whether there were any consistent skeptics in the purely indigenous situation. Under alien impact, this is another matter. (Berndt and Berndt 1985: 228)

Thus, it was not the merely asserted right to secrecy and autonomy of beliefs, but the anthropologist's unwillingness (or, given the unacceptably short time she was given to assess the claim, the inability) to situate such secret beliefs (and beliefs in secrecy) within a total social regime of knowledge formation and practices, and also the unwillingness to subject the secret knowledge to what one could take to be normal procedures of anthropological interrogation that prevents other anthropologists from assessing the coherence and historical trajectory of the emergence of this constellation of beliefs.

What was missing from the consulting anthropologist's analysis of the Ngarrindjeri female or feminine cosmology is the same thing missing from Barth's account of Baktaman convention: what Tuzin has referred to as "cultural annotation" and which "accords with the tendency for meanings to be widely distributed in the cultural repertoire of ideas" (Tuzin 1992: 258). A cosmological proposition that purportedly was as critical and global as one which stipulates the separation of sky and water, or of estuarine islands and mainland, would, it seems, find expression across a range of Ngarrindjeri attitudes and theories regarding, for example, categorical definitions, spatial discrimination, geographical and geomorphic explanations, and corporeal dynamics, not all of which could possibly be restricted or secret in a marked sense, since they would presumably orient and diacritically mark much everyday activity and speech.

I subscribe to the moderate behaviorist position of Dewey as developed later in the century by Quine: "'meaning ... is primarily a property of behaviour'" (quoted in Quine 1968: 29). To put it in Richard Rorty's more contemporary pragmatist terms, belief is a gloss for a successful habit of action, or a habit of successful action.[19] I position this proposition against that of Geertz, which has spawned the formidable move towards idealism and voluntarism in contemporary ethnography, anthropological and otherwise: What prevents us from grasping what others are saying, Geertz maintains, "is not ignorance as to how cognition works . . . as a lack of familiarity with the imaginative universe in which their acts are signs" (1973: 13). I would, however, maintain that verbal and other behavior comprises the only data we have to infer the existence of this imaginative universe, and that the lack of familiarity that Geertz draws attention to is just as much a possible outcome of the exchange of utterances within a language or community as it is between them, as the dispute between the dissident and proponent Ngarrindjeri women showed so perspicuously.

CONCLUSIONS

Even though Von Doussa J stated (at 372) that "I do not think any useful purpose would be achieved by me endeavouring to assume the role of an anthropologist," he nevertheless made a number of pronouncements concerning the nature of Aboriginal tradition and belief in his judgement against the appeal of the Chapmans and Binalong Pty. Ltd. He first suggested (at 275) that a "tradition" can survive even if only one person knows about it. He also opined that "Spiritual beliefs do not lend themselves to proof in strictly formal terms" (at 391). In the face of Jane Mathews's assertion in the Federal Inquiry into the Hindmarsh Island Bridge Royal Commission that no compelling cultural or causative link could be made between the proffered spiritual beliefs and the cultural, physical and cosmological damage that would ensue if the bridge were to be built, von Doussa J said the following:

> It is apparent from the reports of both Dr Fergie and Professor Saunders that they had difficulty in comprehending the reason why a permanent link constituted by the bridge would have the devastating consequences asserted. . . . Where the reporter and the Minister encounter such a difficulty, of necessity they must proceed according to their perceptions of the depth and sincerity of the beliefs held by those seeking protection, and their evaluations of the importance of those beliefs as part of Aboriginal tradition. (at 396)

In response to this I repeat the main thesis here, which I have also discussed elsewhere (Weiner 2001): The existence of idiosyncratic beliefs is not at issue. The dilemma of the custodians of the Ngarrindjeri women's business is similar to that of Fredric Barth's Baktaman ritual adept. After a long period in which rituals have not been staged, a Baktaman adept who alone holds the associated restricted knowledge must nevertheless, when the ritual is finally scheduled, eventually *publicly* re-articulate it in a way that is acceptable to the community at large (see Barth, 2002). In neither

96   James F. Weiner

the Baktaman nor the Ngarrindjeri case am I making an issue out of the phenomenon of "fabrication." I do maintain that anthropologists must consider the public processes of judging the performative acceptability of utterances, propositions and/or beliefs, innovative or otherwise, that are alleged to be critical to the cultural repertoire of a community. The remaining topics all address this *social and practical* understanding of belief in anthropological terms.

THE QUESTION OF CHRISTIANITY

Because the dispute between the applicant and dissident women called into question the factual and historical basis for the sacred site claim, the arguments put forward by the applicant women and their advocates very quickly became phrased in mentalistic and voluntaristic terms, specifically in terms of the right to believe under an imputed liberal state regime of freedom of religion. The advocates for the case of the proponent women thus refused to distinguish between belief as a gloss for an imputed interior state, and belief as an anthropological shorthand for a nexus of intention, behavior, and conventionally established social effects. They must in fact jettison the latter in order to confirm the authenticity of the former.[20]

But authenticity is not the same thing as social saliency. From another perspective, there is a glaring blank space in our understanding of the trajectory of Ngarrindjeri spirituality this century, and that is their own experience of Christianity and the manner in which they have subjectively effected and experienced the fusion between Christian and Aboriginal eschatology. The thrust of the applicant women's claim, and hence the direction of the Royal Commission's cross-examination of it, was that this knowledge had been maintained and transmitted amongst a small group of Ngarrindjeri women who had retained their traditional female knowledge in the face of the comprehensive Missionization of the Lower Murray people since the latter half of the 19th century. The dissident women cast themselves as Ngarrindjeri whose upbringing was squarely located in the Mission station experience, who considered themselves Christian and yet who maintained that whatever continuity in Ngarrindjeri life had been possible had to have resulted from the coalescing of people on the Mission station at Port MacLeay (now called Raukkan). These women also had in some cases extensive records of promoting Aboriginal identity, culture and empowerment. In his doctoral thesis (1994), Clarke gives a detailed account of the social and geographic role of the Point MacLeay Mission in contemporary Ngarrindjeri life, but the Ngarrindjeri interpretive appropriation of Christianity is not examined. Nor was there any space in the Royal Commission or subsequent Federal Inquiry for its examination, no matter how authentic such an appropriation might have been made to look in anthropological terms.

THE LEGAL DIMENSION OF FREEDOM OF RELIGION

In the case of the claim of women's business on Hindmarsh Island, we were unable to assess the impact that Christian proselytization has had on Ngarrindjeri beliefs about personal power, totems and the spiritual efficacy of the landscape, all of which were implicated in the claim of women's business. This makes visible another dilemma: Because Christianity has an epistemic role within the religio-philosophical foundations of our own Western nation state, we can pose the following judicial problem: Citizenship may accord certain rights, but these rights are situated within a more encompassing, and ontologically prior constellation of obligations and responsibilities. They are ontologically prior because though our Western democratic philosophy begins with the sanctity of the individual, it admits that the expression of individuality is subject to the needs of the social contract. This view has been upheld in several landmark freedom of religion cases in the United States:

> With regard to upholding the Sunday Trading Laws, "although avowedly recognizing the 'religious origin' of Sunday Laws, the Chief Justice [Warren], in his four opinions, [asserted that] although the freedom to hold religious beliefs and opinions is absolute, what was involved in the cases at issue was not freedom to hold religious beliefs or opinions *but freedom to act*; and that such freedom, even when motivated by *bona fide* religious convictions, is not wholly free from legislative restrictions. (Abraham 1967: 203)

COMPARISON: THE CASE OF SIX RIVERS NATIONAL FOREST

Other cases in the United States which have put the First Amendment clause which ensures the free exercise of religious belief to the test in regard to indigenous American religion are also instructive here. For example, in the case of *Lyng v. Northwest Indian Cemetery Protective Association*[21] in 1987–1988, the United States Forest Service sought to build a road through a section of Six Rivers National Forest in California that "has historically been used by certain American Indians [of the Yurok, Karok and Tolowa tribes] for religious rituals that depend upon privacy, silence, and an undisturbed natural setting." It was maintained by the Native American plaintiffs that the disruption of the environment caused by the construction of this road would interfere with "training and ongoing religious experience of individuals using [sites within] the area for personal medicine and growth ... and as integrated parts of a system of religious belief and practice which correlates ascending degrees of personal power with a geographic hierarchy of power."[22] The case was initially upheld in a Federal District Court

[795 F. 2d 688], but was dismissed in a subsequent Supreme Court appeal in a decision of 5–3 with one abstention. The Supreme Court stated that it was simply unable to assess the subjective truth of the underlying beliefs that led to the religious objections to the road. This assessment was upheld by, among other points, that there was not a unanimity of opinion among Native Americans of the area that the construction of the road would be so destructive that it would imperil the religious practices in question. Here, the U.S. Supreme Court dealt with the same issue that Justice Mathews did in the Federal Inquiry into the Hindmarsh Island Bridge Royal Commission: what was the link between the asserted beliefs and the anticipated damage caused by the development in question? Although this connection seemed much clearer in the Six Rivers National Forest case, the Court still maintained that it was unable to satisfactorily establish this link. Furthermore, in another marked parallel with the Hindmarsh Island case, although the Native Americans were opposing the construction of the road, they did not object at the time to the area being used by tourists, other Native Americans, forest rangers and other visitors. In the Hindmarsh Island case, the issues of the barrages that already linked Hindmarsh Island and the mainland, and of the permission already granted to construct the marina, were cited in a similar way.

In the dissenting opinion, Justice Brennan first opined, in a decision that has important implications for Hindmarsh Island, that "Although few tribe members actually make medicine at the most powerful sites, the entire tribe's welfare hinges on the success of the individual practitioners." Therefore, the dissent goes on to later say, "the mere fact that a handful of the Native Americans who reside in the affected area do not oppose the road in no way casts doubt upon the validity of the lower courts' amply supported factual findings." It is important to emphasize that it was not the religious nature of the knowledge that the Hindmarsh Island Bridge Royal Commission cast doubt on. The Royal Commission rather expressed skepticism when confronted with the fact that that the community at large did not acknowledge that important religious knowledge (a) was restricted to a very few individuals, and (b) was buttressing the preservation in a practical sense of their cosmos.

The U.S. Supreme Court majority opinion in *Lyng* asserted that the "Free Exercise Clause" of the First Amendment "is written in terms of what the government cannot do to the individual, not in terms of what the individual can exact from the government."[23] In this case, the Supreme Court held, against the dissenting opinions, that it is unable to act as an arbiter of, for example, "what public lands are 'central' or 'indispensable' to which religions, and by implication which are 'dispensable' or 'peripheral'" (op. cit.).

> We would accordingly be required to weigh the value of every religious belief and practice that is said to be threatened by any government pro-

gram. Unless a 'showing of centrality' ... is nothing but an assertion of centrality ... the dissent thus offers us the prospect of this Court holding that some sincerely held religious beliefs and practices are not 'central' to certain religions, despite protestations to the contrary from the religious objectors who brought the lawsuit. In other words, the dissent's approach would require us to rule that some religious adherents misunderstand their own religious beliefs. (ibid.)

This opinion goes to the heart of the dilemma of Ngarrindjeri women's business that Sutton tried to solve in his submission to the Federal Inquiry into the Hindmarsh Island Bridge Royal Commission. In speaking of indigenous religion in terms of convictions and beliefs, rather than ritual or ceremonial action or mythology, the conditions are created under which the discovery of different and even opposed and contradictory beliefs within the same community becomes inevitable. Yet because of the adversarial dimension of these confrontations between indigenous communities and the state, which more and more is involving indigenous people themselves transmuting these beliefs into "cultural property" (see Brown, op. cit.), it is also strategically advisable for indigenous communities to be seen to be in agreement as to what this property is and what these beliefs consists of.

It thus appears that the U.S. Supreme Court has gone to the heart of the contemporary indigenous "sacred site" issue far more clearly and effectively that has its counterpart in Australia in recent times. The U.S. Supreme Court appears to recognize that in a situation of conflict over land, religious beliefs will be deployed by indigenous peoples in defense of that land and that in so doing, the Court will be forced to concede that the avowing of religious beliefs under such circumstances can have a political aim.

Of course there is nothing remarkable or bizarre about this fact in and of itself. But two anthropologically relevant observations can be made here: One is how frequently indigenous protagonists, such as those involved in the Hindmarsh Island Bridge dispute, deny that this is the case, although the ideological reasons why this is so are, again, understandable, at least to an external observer. Second and more generally, in both the *Lyng* case and the Hindmarsh Island case we observe that the Western legal system cannot satisfactorily assess an indigenous, non-Western religious system based on custodianship and care of mythologically important territorial sites, a system in which "ritual" has more analytical salience than "belief," and which is therefore contiguous with social and political processes within a particular indigenous community. The indigenous "masking" of the political dimensions (both internal and external) of their assertions of belief is in fact elicited by the Western courts' continuing commitment to the separation of religion and polity.

These two observations are both accommodated by a view of such court cases that accepts that *they are the contemporary form in which an indigenous politico-ritual custodianship of land is articulated and maintained in contemporary states* (see Merlan 1998; Weiner 1999). In order to return Hindmarsh Island to the anthropological fold, we must cease to linger over the question of *the existence* of women's business and concentrate on describing and analyzing *the conditions under which it was made to appear* (see Weiner 1995). This does no more than return to Sperber's outline for an epidemiology of beliefs, which would bypass at the outset the ideological contrast between religion and politics, and more importantly, would reveal at the same time the masking of religion's essentially political function by the indigenous protagonists in all of these cases. Such a treatment would begin by a more careful cultural and semantic excavation of the Aboriginal English term "business," which conflates social, political, territorial and religious communality.

By way of a coda, the last point I want to make concerns how the question of religious belief, Aboriginal or otherwise, as a testable phenomenon (legally, anthropologically and empirically) has been obscured by the politically more salient focus on racialism associated with Aboriginal beneficial legislation in Australia. Politically, the Australian Left has a stake in maintaining a racial approach to Aboriginal issues, because it wants to see Aboriginal cultural difference as a special sort of difference, consequently calling for affirmative protection of a special sort. The political Right in Australia these days advocates a more assimilationist approach to Aboriginal social, economic and political inequity, even though assimilationist policies of the past, particularly those that have come to recent public attention in the now notorious "Stolen Generation" report,[24] have been cast into disrepute by contemporary advocates of Aboriginal rights. The conflict between those who wish to help Aboriginal people maintain their cultural distinctiveness and those who favor some measure of assimilation within Australian national society has been a major dimension of the way the Australian debate over Aboriginal Land Rights and Native Title in particular has been phrased.

I want to argue here for a more general point, one that I have raised in other comments on Hindmarsh Island[25]: By accepting the terms and conditions of the beneficial legislation empowering their religion, culture and claims to land, Aborigines are already conjuncturally implicated—for which "assimilation" is just another gloss, however loaded it is in today's volatile political climate—in Euro-Australian society. But more to the point, by enacting beneficial legislation that is geared towards a particular racial group who define themselves in avowedly spiritual terms, the Australian government opens the door for the State to legislate on matters religious. Indeed, it cannot avoid doing so, given that it is Aboriginal spirituality which is said to constitute one of their chief dimensions of moral superiority as against secular white society (a sentiment that informs some defenses of Native American religion as well; for example Rasmussen and Smith 1995).

But as we saw in the Hindmarsh Island Bridge Royal Commission, and, more importantly, in the High Court appeal that the original applicants unsuccessfully lodged, as well as many other notable cases involving

Aboriginal religion such as Coronation Hill, it is thus inevitable that this spirituality will be defined and judged in Western and Christian (rather than Judeo-Christian) terms. This is because one of the problems with legislation that purports to protect cultural and religious difference is that the extent of difference it recognizes is limited. In our Western secularized Christian culture, we look upon religious freedom as a component of individual freedom, where people make choices and decisions concerning what to believe in, and what practices to engage in. In a multicultural society, the kinds of cultural and religious differences protected must, in a paradoxical fashion, be the "same kind of difference" for everyone (see Handler 1985: 171). What if, however, such rational and deliberate "deciding to believe" was not a function of the indigenous "tradition" in question, as the comments of the noted Australian Aboriginalists such as Berndt and Kolig quoted above suggest? Further, what if the post-Contact religious experience of indigenous people is enough at odds with their pre-Contact ritual life that they have already re-fashioned the basis of traditional mythico-ritual practice as one involving the freedom and conscious decision to believe? Indigenous people faced with this dilemma might find, as did the Ngarrindjeri proponent women, that their own goals were more practically met by phrasing them in terms of the moral necessity for racially beneficial legislation rather than protection of culture, religion or heritage per se. The manner in which Aboriginal beneficial legislation itself impels and elicits a certain particular version of Aboriginality, rather than passively "protecting" it, needs continuing anthropological investigation, description and debate in today's high-pressured politics of race, culture and indigeneity.

NOTES TO CHAPTER 4

1. The author is grateful to Peter Sutton, Francesca Merlan, Don Gardner, Tim Rowse, Ian Keen, Howard Morphy, Marlene Atleo and Adolfo de Oliveira for comments on earlier drafts of this chapter, and for the comments of the three anonymous reviews for the *Australian Journal of Anthropology*, where it was first published.
2. See Hanson (1989, 1991).
3. See for example §55 and §56 in "Report of the open-ended inter-sessional ad hoc working group on a permanent forum for indigenous peoples in the United Nations system," E/CN.4/1999/83, 25 March 1999. United Nations Commission on Human Rights, 55th session, agenda item 15. This point was also brought out effectively in Tonkinson's analysis of the Hindmarsh Island Bridge Affair (Tonkinson 1997).
4. Transcript of the Hindmarsh Island Bridge Royal Commission (T): 107. The entire public portion of transcript of the Hindmarsh Island Bridge Royal Commission can be found at the web site http://library.adelaide.edu.au/gen/H_Islnd/
5. See the web site http://www.foe.on.net/Kumarangk/
6. See *Tickner v. Western Australia* No. WAG 18 and 19 of 1995, unreported judgement of the Full Court of the Federal Court delivered 28 May 1996.

7. Hindmarsh Island Bridge Act 1997 (Cth).
8. *Kartinyeri v The Commonwealth* [1998] HCA 22.
9. *Chapman v Luminis Pty Ltd (No 5)* [2001] FCA 1106.
10. See Weiner (1995, 1997a, 1997b, 1999, 2001).
11. Early records and accounts indicate that coastal-dwelling Aboriginal populations of southern South Australia were depredated by renegade white whalers even before official contact had been made after the Adelaide settlement in 1836 (see Clarke, in press). I am grateful to the South Australian Museum for their help in making available historical and archival documents held there relating to the early Aboriginal history of South Australia.
12. The only word for "pregnancy" reported by the Berndts in their transcripts is *poliwolin* or *puluwolil*, literally "child-form" or "child-has."
13. "Q. Perhaps can I find this out. Did you see it as any part of your role, to accept or reject what you were told by Doreen Kartinyeri, or was it your role simply to hear it, understand it and then report on it.
A. And to see if it was in a sense resonant with what we had around it, if there was cause for saying, yes, this is reasonable, this is something which might fit our understanding of Ngarrindjeri culture. I mean, in an ultimate sense, what people believe can't be tested in this kind of a way, and neither me nor other anthropologists will purport to do that." (T: 5385).
14. This was essentially Needham's position: "The question of belief, confronts us, rather, with alternative linguistic conventions for classifying states of mind, pronouncing judgements, declaring expectations, and so on. When someone says that he believes he is resorting to a convention appropriate to a given situation (one given, that is, by a certain cultural past and the resultant ideology and forms of social life), but he is not reporting his experience of a distinct inner state or capacity. When we say of him that he believes, similarly, we are not observing any signs of a specific mental process but are describing a feature of that social situation as it is represented in a certain language" (Needham 1972: 132).
15. "Just as the observers' contradictions do not reflect contradictory empirical data *concerning the interior states of the Nuer*, so by contrast a complete accord on the equivalent of 'believe' in the Nuer language would still not supply evidence of an experience of belief" (Needham 1972: 31, emphasis added).
16. See Transcript, p. 5718.
17. The Adelaide *Advertiser*, 16 September 1994 (see Transcript, p. 4063).
18. That is, the threat they face is not one of eradication but its opposite—their copying and appropriation by non-Aborigines. The protection of Aboriginal artistic designs and other culturally vital representations is an important goal of proposed cultural property protection legislation (see for example Brown 1998).
19. Personal communication.
20. Diane Bell's recent *apologia* for the proponent women extends this argument (1998).
21. No. 86–1013, Supreme Court of the United States, 485 U.S. 439; 108 S. Ct. 1319; 1988 U.S. LEXIS 1871; 99 L. Ed.
22. Ibid.: App. 181. Cf. Id., at 178.
23. Quoted from *Sherbert v. Verner*, 374 U.S. 398, 412 (1963).
24. See the web site http://www.austlii.edu.au/rsjlibrary/hreoc/stolen/ for a complete text of the report on the Stolen Generation.
25. See Weiner (1997a, 1999).

REFERENCES

Abraham, H. 1967. *Freedom and the Court: Civil Rights and Liberties in the United States.* New York: Oxford University Press.

Avery, J. n.d. Chicken Hawk came to Badba. Unpublished manuscript in author's possession.

Barnes, B., and D. Bloor. 1982. Relativism, Rationalism and the Sociology of Knowledge. In M. Hollis and S. Lukes (eds.), *Rationality and Relativism.* Oxford: Basil Blackwell.

Barth, F. 2002. An Anthropology of Knowledge. *Current Anthropology* 43(1): 1–18.

Bell, D. 1998. *Ngarrindjeri Wurrawarrin.* Melbourne: Spinifex Press.

Berndt, R. 1947. Wuradjeri Magic and 'Clever Men.' *Oceania* 17: 327–335; 18: 60–94.

Berndt, R., and C. Berndt. 1985. *The World of the First Australians.* 4th Edition. Adelaide: Rigby.

Berndt, R., and C. Berndt. 1993. *A World that Was.* Melbourne: Melbourne University Press.

Bhaskar, R. 1979. *The Possibility of Naturalism.* Brighton: Harvester Press.

Brown, M. 1998. Can Culture be Copyrighted? *Current Anthropology* 39(2): 193–222.

Clarke, P. 1994. Contact, Conflict, and Regeneration: Aboriginal Cultural Geography of the Lower Murray, South Australia. PhD. thesis, Departments of Anthropology and Geography, University of Adelaide.

Clarke, P. (in press). The Aboriginal Presence on Kangaroo Island, South Australia.

Evans-Pritchard, E. 1937. *Witchcraft, Oracles and Magic Among the Azande.* Oxford: Clarendon Press.

Fergie, D. 1994. To all the mothers that were, to all the mothers who are, to all the mothers who will be. Report submitted to the South Australian Aboriginal Legal Rights Movement.

Geertz, C. 1973. *The Interpretation of Cultures.* New York: Basic Books.

Gell, A. 1980. Correspondence. *Man* 15(4):735–737.

Gellner, E. 1985. *Relativism and the Social Sciences.* Cambridge: Cambridge University press.

Handler, R. 1985. On Dialogue and Destructive Analysis: Problems in Narrating Nationalism and Ethnicity. *Journal of Anthropological Research* 41: 171–182.

Hanson, A. 1989. The Making of the Maori: Culture Invention and its Logic. *American Anthropologist* 91: 890–902.

Hanson, A. 1991. Reply to Langdon, Levine and Linnekin. *American Anthropologist* 93(2): 449–450.

Hocart, M. 1927. *Kingship.* Oxford: Clarendon Press.

Kolig, E. 1981. *The Silent Revolution.* Philadelphia: ISHI Press.

Layton, R. 1986. *Uluru: An Aboriginal History of Ayers Rock.* Canberra: Australian Institute of Aboriginal Studies Press.

Mathews, J. 1996. Report on the Inquiry into the Hindmarsh Island Bridge Royal Commission. http://www.aph.cov.au/library/pubs/bd/1996-97/97bd050.htm

Merlan, F. 1998. *Caging the Rainbow.* Honolulu: University of Hawai'i Press.

Needham, R. 1972. *Belief, Language and Experience.* Oxford: Basil Blackwell.

Quine, W.V. 1968. *Ontological Relativity and Other Essays.* New York: Columbia University Press.

Rasmussen, K., and C. Smith. 1995. Native American and Religious Freedom: The Case for a 'Re-Vision' of the First Amendment, presented at the Annual Meting of the Speech Communication Asociation, San Antonio. See http://www.paticafe.by.net/Athens/Acropolis/3976/Religion.html.

Sperber, D. 1996. *Explaining Culture: A Naturalistic Approach.* Oxford: Blackwell.
Strehlow, C. 1947. *Aranda Traditions.* Melbourne: Melbourne University Press.
Stephens, I. 1996. *Report of the Hindmarsh Island Bridge Royal Commission.*
Tonkinson, R. 1970. Aboriginal Dream-Spirit Belief in a Contact Situation: Jigalong, Western Australia. In R. Berndt (ed.), *Australian Aboriginal Anthropology.* Perth: University of Western Australia Press.
Tonkinson, R. 1997. Anthropology and Aboriginal Tradition: The Hindmarsh Island Bridge Affair and the Politics of Interpretation. *Oceania* 68(1): 1–26.
Transcript of the Hindmarsh Island Bridge Royal Commission. http://library.adelaide.edu.au/gen/H_Islnd 1995
Tuzin, D. 1992. Revelation and Concealment in the Cultural Organisation of Meaning: A Methodological Note. In B. Juilerat (ed.), *Shooting the Sun: Ritual and Meaning in West Sepik.* Washington, DC: Smithsonian Institution Press.
Weiner, J. 1995. Anthropologists, Historians and the Secret of Social Knowledge. *Anthropology Today* 11(5): 3–7.
Weiner, J. 1997a. 'Bad Aboriginal' Anthropology: A Reply to Ron Brunton. *Anthropology Today* 13(4): 5–8.
Weiner, J. 1997b. Must Our Informants Mean What They Say?. *Canberra Anthropology* 20(1–2): 89–102.
Weiner, J. 1999. Culture in a Sealed Envelope: The Concealment of Australian Aboriginal Heritage and Tradition in the Hindmarsh Island Bridge Affair. *Journal of the Royal Anthropological Institute* 5(2): 193–210.
Weiner, J. 2001. Strangelove's Dilemma: Or, What Kind of Secrecy do the Ngarrindjeri Practice? In A. Rumsey and J. Weiner (eds.), *Emplaced Myth: Space, Narrative and Knowledge in Aboriginal Australia and Papua New Guinea.* Honolulu: University of Hawai'i Press.

5 American Indian Sovereignty
Now You See It, Now You Don't
Peter d'Errico[1]

Sovereignty is an especially odd phenomenon. Everyone seems to want it. Those who claim to know it all tell us that sovereignty is just what we have, although some may have more of it than others. It seems to have been around for as long as anyone can remember. Even so, for such an established fact of life, and for such a cherished ambition, there is a disconcerting uncertainty as to what it is exactly, or where it is to be found, or who has it and who does not, or where it came from in the first place, let alone what is happening to it now. (Walker 1996: 16–17)

"DISCOVERY" AND "ENCOUNTER"

Another Columbus Day has come and gone. Another year, now more than five hundred since the Pope divided the world between Spain and Portugal, laying down the doctrine of discovery and conquest:

> INTER CAETERA, MAY 3, 1493. Among other works well pleasing to the Divine Majesty and cherished of our heart, this assuredly ranks highest, that in our times especially the Catholic faith and the Christian religion be exalted and everywhere increased and spread, that the health of souls be cared for and that barbarous nations be overthrown and brought to the faith itself ... [O]ur beloved son Christopher Columbus, [...] sailing ... toward the Indians, discovered certain very remote islands and even mainlands, [W]e [...] by the authority of Almighty God ... do ... give, grant, and assign forever to you and your heirs and successors, kings of Castille and Leon, all and singular the aforesaid countries and islands ...

An earlier Papal Bull had declared the legitimacy of Christian domination over "pagans," sanctifying enslavement and expropriation of property:

> ROMANUS PONTIFEX, JANUARY 8, 1455. ... [W]e bestow suitable favors and special graces on those Catholic kings and princes,

[...] athletes and intrepid champions of the Christian faith [...] to invade, search out, capture, vanquish, and subdue all Saracens and pagans whatsoever, and other enemies of Christ wheresoever placed, and [...] to reduce their persons to perpetual slavery, and to apply and appropriate [...] possessions, and goods, and to convert them to [...] their use and profit ...

We might look at these ancient documents with amusement or condescension, confident in the modern view that church and state are separate. This would be a mistake. These Papal Bulls are part of the fabric of U.S. and international law.

The fact that Papal authority is the basis for U.S. power over indigenous peoples is not generally understood, even by lawyers who work with federal Indian law. This is due in large part to the sophistry of John Marshall, one of the greatest figures in the pantheon of the U.S. Supreme Court. Marshall borrowed from Papal Bulls the essential legalisms needed for state power over indigenous peoples. He encased Christian religious premises within the rhetoric of "European" expansion:

JOHNSON v. MCINTOSH, 21 US 543 (FEBRUARY, 1823). On the discovery of this immense continent, the great nations of Europe were eager to appropriate to themselves so much of it as they could respectively acquire. Its vast extent offered an ample field to the ambition and enterprise of all; and the character and religion of its inhabitants afforded an apology for considering them as a people over whom the superior genius of Europe might claim an ascendancy. The potentates of the Old World found no difficulty in convincing themselves that they made ample compensation to the inhabitants of the new, by bestowing on them civilization and Christianity. (*Johnson v. McIntosh*, 8 Wheat. [21 U.S.] 572–73 (1823))

Steve Newcomb said it succinctly:

Indian nations have been denied their most basic rights [...] simply because, at the time of Christendom's arrival in the Americas, they did not believe in the God of the Bible, and did not believe that Jesus Christ was the true Messiah. This basis for the denial of Indian rights in federal Indian law remains as true today as it was in 1823. (Newcomb 1993: 309)

Johnson v. McIntosh has never been overruled. "Christian discovery" remains the legal foundation for United States sovereignty over indigenous peoples' lands. But it is concealed, as most foundations are, because *Johnson v. McIntosh* acts as a laundromat for religious concepts. After Marshall's opinion, no lawyer or court would need to acknowledge that land title claims in U.S. law are based on a doctrine of Christian supremacy. From that time on, in law and history books, "European" would be substituted for "Christian," so that schoolchild and lawyer alike could speak of the "age of discovery" as the age of "European expansion."

Marshall knew what he was doing. After writing that "Christian princes" could take lands "unknown to all Christian peoples," he admitted that the doctrine was an "extravagant . . . pretension" which "may be opposed to natural right" and may only "perhaps, be supported by reason." Nonetheless, he concluded that it "cannot be rejected by courts of justice" (*Johnson v. McIntosh*, 8 Wheat. [21 U.S.] 592 (1823)).

The "discovery doctrine" was not self-effectuating. It required force. As Marshall (*Johnson v. McIntosh*, 8 Wheat. [21 U.S.] 588 (1823)) wrote, "These claims have been maintained and established [. . .] by the sword." The (in)famous "Spanish Requirement" of 1513 is perhaps the most straightforward example. It was called the "requirement" because royal law required it to be read before hostilities could be undertaken against a native people. In Latin and/or Spanish, witnessed by a notary, the Conquistadors read:

> On the part of the king, Don Fernando, and of Doña Juana, his daughter, queen of Castile and Leon, subduers of the barbarous nations, we their servants notify and make known to you, as best we can, that the Lord our God, living and eternal, created the heaven and the earth, and one man and one woman, of whom you and we, and all the men of the world, were and are descendants, and all those who come after us . . .
>
> Of all these nations God our Lord gave charge to one man, called St. Peter, that he should be lord and superior of all the men in the world, that all should obey him, and that he should be the head of the whole human race, wherever men should live, and under whatever law, sect, or belief they should be; and he gave him the world for his kingdom and jurisdiction . . .
>
> One of these pontiffs, who succeeded that St. Peter as lord of the world in the dignity and seat which I have before mentioned, made donation of these isles and Terra-firma to the aforesaid king and queen and to their successors, our lords, with all that there are in these territories. . . .
>
> Wherefore, as best we can, we ask and require you that you consider what we have said to you, and that you take the time that shall be necessary to understand and deliberate upon it, and that you acknowledge the Church as the ruler and superior of the whole world. . . .
>
> But if you do not do this, and maliciously make delay in it, I certify to you that, with the help of God, we shall powerfully enter into your

country, and shall make war against you in all ways and manners that we can, and shall subject you to the yoke and obedience of the Church and of their highnesses; we shall take you, and your wives, and your children, and shall make slaves of them, and as such shall sell and dispose of them as their highnesses may command; and we shall take away your goods, and shall do you all the mischief and damage that we can, as to vassals who do not obey, and refuse to receive their lord, and resist and contradict him: and we protest that the deaths and losses which shall accrue from this are your fault, and not that of their highnesses, or ours, nor of these cavaliers who come with us. . . .

It is fashionable, especially around Columbus Day, to speak about the "encounter" of the "old" and "new" worlds, as a way of trying to forget exactly how bloody this event was. But, as Michael Shapiro wrote, "National societies that [. . .] have thought of themselves as a fulfilment of a historical destiny, could not be open to encounters" (Shapiro 1996: 56). And according to Michael Dorris,

> The pre-existent variety of Native American societies [. . .] has been consistently obscured and disallowed. Every effort has been made to almost existentially enclose the non-Western world into a European schema, and then to blame unwilling elements for being backward, ignorant, or without vision [. . .] Federal Indian policy was [. . .] shaped from the beginning at least as much toward deculturation as acculturation. (Dorris 1979: 75–76)

CONTEMPORARY NON-RECOGNITION OF INDIGENOUS PEOPLES

Over 300 million people on earth today can be said to be truly "indigenous"—living on lands which they have inhabited since time immemorial. In every instance, indigenous communities are legally circumscribed by one or more nation-states, within territorial boundaries drawn by government geography. These 300 million constitute an increasingly self-aware force for global rethinking of the nature of power. Their challenge is increasingly overt and serious to the world's political structure.

The United Nations' designation of The Decade of Indigenous People is a symptom of this challenge. The nature of the challenge becomes clearer when we consider the revision of the original designation, which referred to indigenous peoples. The plural form—"peoples"—triggered immense anxiety and successful resistance by member states of the UN, on the grounds that these 300 million people are individual citizens of states claiming jurisdiction over them, and not members of independent peoples.

"Peoples" in international law implies rights of self-determination, which the United States took the lead to challenge as not applicable to indigenous peoples. The United States argues that collective self-determination exists only through states, and that indigenous people are groups of individuals with shared cultural, linguistic, and social features, but without any internal coherence as "peoples." This argument contradicts the United States' claim that it deals with indigenous peoples on a "government-to-government" basis. Here is one example of "now you see it, now you don't."

In light of the history of treaty-making and with an eye toward restoring the sense of equality between nations that justified the treaty process to begin with, American Indians are—in concert with indigenous peoples worldwide—asserting a sense of their own "sovereignty." The United Nations Draft Declaration on the Rights of Indigenous Peoples is at the centre of this global struggle for self-determination. The Declaration is the product of twenty years of negotiating among indigenous peoples and UN bodies. Its very title draws the line of battle—rights of indigenous peoples.

FEDERAL INDIAN LAW

When we enter into the realm of "federal Indian law," we need to keep in mind that we are travelling in a semantic world created by one group to rule another. The terminology of law is a powerful naming process. In working with this law, we will use the names that it uses, but we will always want to keep in mind that the reality behind the names is what we are struggling over.

According to the theory of sovereignty in federal Indian law, "tribal" peoples have a lesser form of "sovereignty," which is not really sovereignty at all, but dependence. In the words of Chief Justice John Marshall in *Cherokee Nation v. Georgia* (1831), American Indian societies, though they are "nations" in the general sense of the word, are not fully sovereign, but are "domestic, dependent nations" (*Cherokee Nation v. Georgia*, 30 U.S. 1, 17 (1831)). The shell game of American Indian sovereignty—the "now you see it, now you don't" quality—started right at the beginning of federal Indian law. The foundation of federal Indian law is the assertion by the United States of a special kind of non-sovereign sovereignty.

In 1973, the federal district court for the district of Montana stated the underlying principle in the case of *United States v. Blackfeet Tribe*, 364 F. Supp. 192. The facts were simple: The Blackfeet Business Council passed a resolution authorising gambling on the reservation and the licensing of slot machines. A FBI agent seized four machines. The Blackfeet Tribal Court issued an order restraining all persons from removing the seized articles from the reservation. The FBI agent, after consultation with the U.S. Attorney, removed the machines from the reservation. A tribal judge then ordered the U.S. Attorney to show cause why he should not be cited for contempt of the tribal court. The U.S. Attorney applied to federal court for an injunction to block the contempt citations. The Blackfeet Tribe argued that it is sovereign and that the jurisdiction of the tribal court flows directly from this sovereignty. The federal court said:

> No doubt the Indian tribes were at one time sovereign and even now the tribes are sometimes described as being sovereign. The blunt fact, however, is that an Indian tribe is sovereign to the extent that the United States permits it to be sovereign—neither more nor less. (*United States v. Blackfeet Tribe*, 364 F. Supp., 194 (1973))

The court then explained:

> While for many years the United States recognised some elements of sovereignty in the Indian tribes and dealt with them by treaty, Congress by Act of March 3, 1871 (16 Stat. 566, 25 U.S.C. s 71), prohibited the further recognition of Indian tribes as independent nations. Thereafter the Indians and the Indian tribes were regulated by acts of Congress. The power of Congress to govern by statute rather than treaty has been sustained. United States v. Kagama, 118 U.S. 375, 6 S.Ct. 1109, 30 L.Ed. 228 (1886). That power is a plenary power (Matter of Heff, 197 U.S. 488, 25 S.Ct. 506, 49 L.Ed. 848 (1905)) and in its exercise Congress is supreme. United States v. Nice, 241 U.S. 591, 36 S.Ct. 696, 60 L.Ed. 1192 (1916). It follows that any tribal ordinance permitting or purporting to permit what Congress forbids is void. [. . .] It is beyond the power of the tribe to in any way regulate, limit, or restrict a federal law officer in the performance of his duties, and the tribe having no such power the tribal court can have none. (ibid.)

The fundamental premise of "American Indian sovereignty" as defined in federal Indian law is that it is not sovereignty. Federal power truncates "tribal sovereignty" in myriad ways too numerous to list here. Federal Indian law is perhaps the most complex area of United States law (including tax laws). In civil and criminal law both, the range and scope of "tribal sovereignty" is fragmented into overlapping and contradictory rules premised on one foundation: the "plenary power" of the United States. That such "plenary power" is nowhere stated in the U.S. Constitution is no more than a small nuisance to the judges who have declared its existence. Administrative agencies and Congress alike grasp firmly to their judicially created prerogatives of total power over their "wards," in whose "trust" they act as they see fit.

Federal Indian law is the continuation of colonialism. On the basis of a non-sovereign "tribal sovereignty," the United States has built an entire apparatus for dispossessing indigenous peoples of their lands, their social organisations, and their original powers of self-determination. The concept of "American Indian sovereignty" is useful to the United States because it denies indigenous power in the name of indigenous sovereignty.

In 1831, the Cherokee Nation sued the state of Georgia in the Supreme Court to protect Cherokee lands. The Court denied the Cherokee suit on the ground that an Indian nation is not a "foreign nation" entitled to sue a state in the Supreme Court. That decision has never been overruled and is cited frequently today. In June 1997, the Supreme Court decided that the Coeur d'Alene Tribe could litigate its land claims against the state of Idaho only in Idaho's courts. The Coeur d'Alene were claiming "aboriginal title," a subsidiary title subject to the "trusteeship" of the United States. They were trying to work within the limited concept of "American Indian sovereignty." In throwing the Coeur d'Alene suit out of federal court, the Supreme Court stated that the basis of its decision was that "Indian tribes [. . .] should be accorded the same status as foreign sovereigns, against whom States enjoy Eleventh Amendment immunity [citing Blatchford v. Native Village of Noatak, 501 US 775 (1991]" (*Idaho v. Coeur d'Alene Tribe*, No. 94–1474 (June 23, 1997).

The Cherokee were barred from suing in the Supreme Court because an Indian nation is not a foreign nation. The Coeur d'Alene were barred from suing in district court because an Indian nation is a foreign nation. You figure it out: "now you see it, now you don't."

Like every other colonial power, the United States early on found it did not have sufficient resources to maintain martial rule over territories it wanted to control. It resorted to "indirect rule" by puppet governments through the mechanism of appointed (and bribed) "chiefs." But it found that despite every attempt to make indigenous peoples disappear—including "allotment" of their lands and prohibition of their spiritual practices—indigenous peoples survived. By the 20th century, the condition of their survival was an embarrassment to the government. In 1934, the United States set out to "reorganize" indigenous peoples into elected corporate political structures—a formalised system of "tribal councils." The concept of "American Indian sovereignty" was used to justify sufficient authority in the "tribal councils" to maintain order within the "tribe" while denying these councils any authority beyond the territory which was "reserved" for them.

If we are honest about the legal history of the 1934 Indian Reorganization Act (IRA), we have to say that the "tribal council" system was intended as a more elaborate puppet government. The system was not the result of the treaty process, but rather the distortion of treaties in the direction that the United States wanted to interpret and apply them. The IRA was passed in part to stabilise the land base and social conditions of American Indians, which had been devastated by the 1886 General Allotment Act. The fact that some of the worst abuses of indigenous peoples were stopped by the IRA was some excuse for the act. But the act was also passed—as its title states—to "reorganize" the Indians, overthrowing traditional organisations and promoting a "democratic" tribal council system structured as a corporate business. The fact that some tribal councils still raise sovereignty issues is evidence of the resilience and continued existence of indigenous peoples.

Let me illustrate IRA "sovereignty" with the case of the Western Shoshone. In 1863, the Western Shoshone and the United States signed a Treaty of Peace and Friendship at Ruby Valley in the heart of Western Shoshone country. The treaty acknowledged Western Shoshone control over their homelands and provided easements across their land and some mining and related activities. Today, massive strip-mines ravage Western Shoshone lands and pollute and destroy the waters. The United States adds to this destruction by disposing radioactive waste in Yucca Mountain. Although Western Shoshone land title has never been proven to have been ceded or lost, the Supreme Court has ruled that they are precluded from litigating their title. Western Shoshone people who oppose the destruction of their lands as violations of their title are depicted as outlaws.

How did this come about? Was it through a denial of Western Shoshone sovereignty? No, it was through the affirmation of their "sovereignty"—that is, through the affirmation of the kind of sovereignty that the Western Shoshone have under "federal Indian law." As we have seen, this kind of sovereignty is not real self-determination. This sovereignty is the non-sovereignty of "councils" created by the United States government in the name of the Western Shoshone people under the Indian Reorganization Act.

In accordance with IRA principles, the federal government "recognised" various Western Shoshone "tribal councils" as the agents of Western Shoshone "sovereignty." The Temoak Band, one of the councils empowered to "govern" the Western Shoshone people and to "represent" them in dealing with the outside world, filed a claim under the Indian Claims Commission Act of 1946. This Act was intended to wipe out all Indian title for non-reservation lands by providing money compensation for such lands. The Act did not require that a claim represent all or even a majority of the Indians in whose name it was filed. As a result of the Temoak claim—which the traditional, "non-recognised" Western Shoshone opposed and the Temoak council subsequently tried to withdraw—the Commission told the Western Shoshone that their lands had been "taken" and that they would receive compensation.

The Western Shoshone refused to take the compensation and one family (the Danns) went to court to defend title against the United States. The Ninth Circuit Court of Appeals ruled that Western Shoshone title had never actually been litigated, that none of the claims made against it were sufficient to take it away, and that since the Western Shoshone had refused the Claims Commission compensation they still held title. The U.S. Supreme Court reversed the Ninth Circuit, stating that the Western Shoshone could not argue about their title because the compensation had been accepted on their behalf by the United States, acting as their "trustee"!

The Western Shoshone case is not atypical. Similar events have unfolded for many other indigenous peoples under United States law. The point is that "American Indian sovereignty" in federal Indian law is a tool for limiting the powers of indigenous self-determination and for allowing the United States to determine the structure of indigenous government. We need to remember always that "sovereignty" in federal Indian law operates in conjunction with so-called "trust" and "wardship" doctrines—two other concepts proclaimed unilaterally by the United States to assert power over indigenous peoples. "American Indian sovereignty" can only be understood in context of the whole complex of federal court decisions over the last one hundred and seventy four years of colonial and neo-colonial law.

The recent proposal in the United States Senate[2] to eliminate American Indian sovereignty as a condition for receipt of federal funds shows several important things. First, the struggle over Indian "sovereignty"—whatever it is—is far from over and is indeed a hot topic. Second, even the Congressional defenders of this sovereignty say that the United States could eliminate it if it wishes. Third, the notion that federal funding is rooted in treaty obligations, not in discretionary programs, is almost wholly forgotten. Fourth, the attack on Indian sovereignty can be packaged in a rhetoric of "helping the poor Indians." Indians have been the victims of "help" since the first missionary efforts.

"SOVEREIGNTY" IN INTERNATIONAL LAW

"Sovereignty" in "international law" is a power system originated in the 16th century by Christian European states in their dealings with each other and the Catholic Church. By the 19th century,

> [T]he European outlook upon the extra-European areas [. . .] became one which instinctively applied the concept of the sovereign state and the notion of international sovereignty to conditions in which these ideas remained alien. (Hinsley 1966: 206)

Sovereignty became "the dominant concept in the field of [. . .] political assumptions [. . .] the essential qualification for full membership [in] the international community." (Hinsley, ibid.: 214–215). The concept of "sovereignty" provided state power with an "inside" and an "outside." (Bartelson 1995: 53–54). States claimed supreme power inside what they called their "domestic" realms and defined other states' realms as "outside."

Now, as the 20th century ends, "It is fashionable to argue that sovereignty is changing and that states are losing their validity and meaning" (Denham & Lombardi 1996: 9), and discussing the decline of sovereignty has become a virtual cliché (Lombardi 1996: 153).

> [S]overeignty cannot be an accepted dogma either in terms of its theoretical utility or political sufficiency. The [. . .] elevation of sovereignty and statehood to universal supremacy is not just being called into question, but is being eclipsed by the press of events and ideas. (Denham & Lombardi 1996: 3)

It is an irony of history that "the expansion/imposition of the European state system during [the] decolonialization" of Africa and the so-called Third-World brought into question "the very idea of sovereignty" (Denham & Lombardi, ibid.). Decolonised peoples did not fit into the structure of the sovereign state. The result was (and is) extreme social dysfunction, as new states and their patrons tried to coerce peoples and fragments of peoples into sovereign allegiance. "[E]conomic development, an explicit goal of a sovereign state," brought on repeated episodes of violence with "highly politicized elites grasping for non-African models of governance that ultimately failed to fit African traditions and cultures" (Denham & Lombardi, ibid.: 7). Today it is clear that the failure of post-colonial states to be a vehicle for indigenous self-determination is not a momentary problem of adjustment to "liberation."

Other events and ideas are eclipsing the notion of sovereignty. Multinational corporations—entities dependent on and yet more powerful than states—dominate the world economy. The overall ecological failure of the system of state sovereignty—the destruction of the biosphere in the name of sovereign interests—is also becoming frighteningly obvious.

Thus, as Walker and Mendlovitz (1990: 1–2) put it, "[S]tate sovereignty offers only a misleading map of where we are and an even less useful guide to where we might be going." Such terms as "internationalization," "globalization," and "interdependence" "slip easily off the tongue, [. . .] but [. . .] [defer] all the hard questions. [. . .] What, for example, is it that is supposedly interdependent?" (pp. 2–3). "We [. . .] need to think about how we think about sovereignty, and about how it [. . .] constructs the non-options available to us" (p. 23).

The classical attributes of "sovereignty" already foreshadow the problem of applying this concept to American Indians and other non-state peoples: absolute, unlimited power held permanently in a single person or source, inalienable, indivisible, and original (not derivative or dependent). These are characteristics of power associated with divine right monarchy and the Papacy of the Christian Church. They are the core concepts of state power that arose around monarchs and church. They were the brainchild of western political theorists of the 16th and 17th centuries (especially Jean Bodin and Thomas Hobbes), as a solution to the problem of violent religious struggle. They are not the characteristics of power in non-state societies.

As Joseph Camilleri (1990: 14) wrote, "The emergence of the sovereign state was [. . .] the necessary instrument of Europe's colonial expansion." With this remark we see the need for an inquiry into the question whether

American Indian Sovereignty 115

"sovereignty" can become the instrument of liberation from colonialism. If "state" and "sovereignty" refer to a framework of "supreme coercive power," and such power is absent in "tribes," is this a justification for "domestic dependent nation" or *terra nullius*, or is it rather a challenge to state sovereignty as the organising principle of the world? Are we at the threshold of a new way of organising politics that will—like the state before it—rearrange everything from villages to the world?

Camilleri (ibid.: 35) pointed to "an increasingly powerful [. . .] desire to cultivate indigenous values, traditions, and resources that are often antithetical to conventional notions of state sovereignty." In a long passage, he described the potential for a new era of social organisation:

> The resistance to the present political and economic organization of society, expressed by the peace/antinuclear, ecological, communalist, consumer, feminist, gay liberation, human potential/self-awareness and other movements, cannot be overestimated. They represent a multidimensional response to the 'colonization of the life-world.' Their praxis may not yet pose a decisive challenge to the *status quo*, but it has already generated [. . .] a readiness to resist existing institutions and their life-eroding consequences. The point about these antisystemic movements is that they [. . .] are reaffirming the priority of [. . .] popular sovereignty over state sovereignty. For them the state retains a positive function only to the extent that it can be used as a vehicle for the realization of popular sovereignty. [. . .] Whether or not, and in what way, the state can be effectively integrated into the praxis of critical movements remains, however, a largely unanswered question. (Camilleri, ibid.: 35–36)

The conventional response to a suggestion that local politics might be the centre of global organisation is to dismiss it with the assertion that states are necessary because the functions they provide cannot be performed by smaller organisations. In a typical lecture, "the mere assertion of the state's necessity is enough to set the audience nodding in approval" (Magnusson 1990: 47). But,

> Why are we satisfied with such banalities? Why do we accept claims about the inevitability of the state, which, if posed in relation to capitalism or patriarchy, would be set aside in embarrassed silence? (Magnusson, ibid.)

One might expect local politics to be the most celebrated arena of democracy. Why is it that the conventional view denies the possibility of local autonomy, and instead offers suggestions for "citizen participation" in state institutions? In conventional discourse, the idea of local democracy—of popular sovereignty—"fades as an object of political theory" and along with it fade "the [. . .] communities that could sustain [. . .] it" (Magnusson, ibid.: 50). State sovereignty "encloses" local and popular sovereignty in "parties" and "interest groups," in "domestic, dependent nations," "wardship," and "trust relationships."

The concept of sovereignty was a response to civil war in the Christian world at the close of the Middle Ages. It spawned an era of centralising, territorial power that in our times—half a millennium later—is coming into question. Sovereignty—the notion of "absolute, unlimited power held permanently in a single person or source, inalienable, indivisible, and original"—is today a theory under siege. Indigenous peoples are only one of the besiegers, but their presence is felt worldwide. Who would have thought even a generation ago that such an "old" state as Canada would be threatened by indigenous peoples within its borders, or that the Australian high court would find it necessary to abandon the concept of *terra nullius*?

THE WAY TO SELF-DETERMINATION

Indigenous peoples around the world are attacking the supremacy of state governments. From an indigenous perspective, state sovereignty is a claim that violates their own pre-existing self-determination. Western jurisprudence has done a great deal to exclude "non-state societies" from the domain of law, because they lack hierarchical authority structures. If indigenous peoples follow the model of state sovereignty—which they are being told they cannot do because they are not states—they may find that when they attain this goal they have sacrificed the underlying goal of self-defined self-determination.

The critique of sovereignty jurisprudence is not just an academic matter. It is necessary to clear a space for "non-state" peoples to exist in the world. Can there be space—in the world and in discourse—for non-state societies, defined in their own terms? Is there a way to talk about indigenous self-determination without using "sovereignty"?

Tony Hillerman has commented on the anti-Indian legislative strategy of those in the U.S. Senate who want to strip "sovereignty" from American Indian tribes. He wrote that his friend, Navajo elder Hastiin Alexander Etcitty, "would say that the notion that any human, or group thereof, has sovereignty over any part of Mother Earth is a myth based upon the white man's Origin Story" (Hillerman 1990). Hillerman concluded that the problem of Indian sovereignty "involves more than how to save what they have from the whites who yearn for it. It can become an internal fight over values."

We are talking about the clarification of the path toward self-determination. What can we say about "American Indian sovereignty" that might help us imagine a way out of the political confusion of this post-modern age? For starters, we could be clear that there is a problem in working with a concept of "absolute, unlimited power held permanently in a single person or source, inalienable, indivisible, and original." Why should indigenous peoples choose a model of thinking, organisation, and development that was used to destroy non-state societies?

Ilyas Ahmad, in his discussion (1965) on the conception of sovereignty in Islam, suggested that a "realistic analysis" of sovereignty would discover "that the ultimate moving force which inspires and controls political action is a spiritual force—a common conviction that makes for righteousness, a common conscience" (Ahmad, ibid.: 67). This suggestion is startling because we are used to the Western notion of separation of church and state. Western discussion can speak of "common will," but gets nervous with the thought that this phrase only acquires meaning in spiritual terms. As we have seen, however, Western political thinking itself is grounded in theological concepts of "Christian nationalism." The notion of "absolute, unlimited power held permanently in a single person or source, inalienable, indivisible, and original" is a definition of the Judeo-Christian-Islamic God. This "God died around the time of Machiavelli. [. . .] Sovereignty was [. . .] His earthly replacement" (Walker 1996: 22).

For Bartelson (1995: 88), all significant concepts of the modern theory of the state are secularised theological concepts, not only because of their historical development, but also because of their systematic structure. Similarly, according to Lombardi (1996: 154), state sovereignty "is a 'religion' and a faith." Lombardi expands:

> The skilfully drawn borders that cartographers have provided for us are [. . .] spiritual and philosophical abstractions representative of a form of quasi-belief. They are [. . .] not detached maps of reality as proponents would have us believe. These geographies reflect an ardent desire to make (or impose) sovereignty a physical reality as natural as the mountains, rivers and lakes. (Lombardi, ibid.)

What does this mean for indigenous peoples, with a multitude of non-sovereign Creators and an entire Creation of sovereign beings? We are in need of a reassessment of political discourse, a terminology that will link postmodern politics and pre-modern roots of non-state societies. "Indigenous is nearly synonymous with diversity" (Barrerio 1977). The diversity of peoples' experiences and practices must be our focus, rather than the imposed "unity" of European experience and practice.

As Bartelson (1995), among others, recognises, the 16th century discovery of non-Christian forms of life in the Americas threatened the stability of Christian values:

> [T]he discovery of the American Indians [. . .] [t]he confrontation with something radically different from the Christian way of life raised the question of what kind of relations it is possible to entertain with

> this Other. First, to what extent is it possible to know the Indian except as something inferior? [...] Second, [...] to what extent is it possible to bring him into the framework of universal law by giving him the status of a legal subject? (Bartelson, ibid.: 128, 131)

The western response to this "discovery" was "an effort to ... [make] everything speak ... with one voice" (Bartelson, ibid.: 108). In this effort, non-state societies were given a "choice": to assimilate to the state system and give up their independent self-definition, or to maintain their self-definition and be denied a place in the world's legal and political order. The underlying assumption was that there is only one reality and it is western.

The problem of figuring out how to talk about indigenous self-determination without "sovereignty" is partially solved by learning how to talk about states and sovereignty accurately. Far from being an inherent and necessary aspect of self-determination, it appears that state sovereignty is but one form of self-determination.

"Sovereignty" is not an immutable "fact," but a political choice made under certain circumstances which may no longer be relevant. The eclipsing of sovereignty in today's world threatens the international order of states and raises the possibility of new ways of understanding what it means to be a people. Half a millennium of "sovereignty" theory has not fully eradicated the "other" against whom sovereignty theory was constructed.

The task before us is to understand the immense differences between states and stateless societies. We must not fall for the line that all societies naturally lead to state formation or that state formation is even a social desire.

> [T]he [...] emergence of the state reflects not the desire of a society for its kind of rule, but an urge in men to possess its kind of power [...]
>
> [T]he concept of sovereignty arises in the wake of the rise of the state [...] as an explanation of the basis of [its] rule. (Hinsley 1966: 10, 17)

Furthermore, as Walker and Mendlovitz (1990: 5–6) argue:

> The principle of state sovereignty formalizes a specific answer to questions about who we are as political beings that were posed in early-modern Europe [...] Yet while there has been considerable interest in the questions posed by the principle of state sovereignty, there has been much less reflection on the questions to which state sovereignty is itself an answer. Who are "we"? What is the political community within which we ought to be thinking about principles of freedom and obligation, justice and democracy? How ought we to understand the relationship between specific communities and other communities, and between specific communities and humanity in

general? [. . .] It is often tempting to minimize the significance of these questions.

These are spiritual questions. "What does it mean to be people?" is a spiritual question. The western, Christian, rationalist answer to this question is not the only possible answer. This is not the place to catalogue the ways in which indigenous peoples answer this question. Suffice it to say that the myriad versions do not require a concept of "state sovereignty." "Sovereignty," if it exists at all, is a quality of each Being in Creation. Beings join and part in myriad ways, none of them requiring "state sovereignty."

Indigenous answers to these questions are not some kind of creed or dogma. They are alive, "borne by [. . .] people[s]" (Ruiz 1990: 85) in the life of a community. The question "what does it mean to be people" is answered in "the giving and receiving of confidence and commitment between persons who recognise and affirm a common community." When a community has been fractured, the possibility of self-determination is undermined.

The most pressing problem for indigenous self-determination is the problem of "the people." Indigenous peoples who have been subjected to centuries of state violence in the name of state sovereignty face "a profound crisis of the meaning of community, a crisis of political identity" (Ruiz, ibid.: 86).

In this crisis it is tempting for a people to take on the ways of the state. These ways can be taught. They are in fact the most basic part of the curriculum of the modern state education system. It is not accidental that "education" has been a primary vehicle for destruction of indigenous peoples. "Education" defined by colonising states has aimed at the eradication of indigenous traditions, and at the destruction of "confidence and commitment between persons who recognise and affirm" indigenous communities. When such education is complete, it is safe for the state to allow a "recognition" of "traditions," because "traditions" have become static relics of the past, no longer part of everyday relations. "Ethnic diversity" then becomes window-dressing, decoration, new clothes for the emperor. The American state can tolerate and even promote the "diversity" of Irish-Americans, Italian-Americans, African-Americans, and, yes, Native-Americans. It would be possible for the American State to exist even if there were no "Americans" at all and everyone was a hyphen-American.

Ultimately, it is land—and a people's relationship to land—that is at issue in "indigenous sovereignty" struggles. To know that "sovereignty" is a legal–theological concept allows us to understand these struggles as spiritual projects, involving questions about who "we" are as beings among beings, peoples among peoples. Sovereignty arises from within a people as their unique expression of themselves as a people. It is not produced by court decrees or government grants, but by the actual ability of a people to sustain themselves in a place. This is self-determination.

Self-determination of indigenous peoples will be attained "through means other than those provided by a conqueror's rule of law and its discourses of conquest" (Williams 1990: 327). The "anachronistic premises" (ibid.) of the current system of international law—"discovery" and "state sovereignty"—must be discarded in order to understand self-determination clearly and see a way to manifest it. This is the real struggle of indigenous peoples: "to redefine radically the conceptions of their rights and status [. . .] to articulat[e] and defin[e] [their] own vision within the global community" (Williams, ibid.: 328). On the plus side for all of us, this struggle has the "potential for broadening perspectives on our human condition" (ibid.). As Phillip Deere said, "It is a mistake to talk about an American Indian way of life. We are talking about a human being way of life" (Deere 1979).

NOTES TO CHAPTER 5

1. This text was presented as the inaugural lecture in the American Indian Civics Project at Humboldt State University (Arcata, CA, USA), on October 24, 1997, sponsored by the HSU Center for Indian Community Development.
2. Senator Slade Gorton's rider to the appropriations bill for Department of Interior (H.R. 2107, *Department of the Interior and Related Agencies Appropriations Act, 1998* (Congressional Record—Senate—September 16, 1997)).

REFERENCES

Ahmad, I. 1965. *Sovereignty: Islamic and Modern*. Karachi and Hyderabad: The Allies Book Corporation.
Barrerio, J. 1977. First Words. *Native Americas*. Ithaca, NY: Akwe:kon Press (Cornell University) XIV #2.
Bartelson, J. 1995. *A Genealogy of Sovereignty*. Cambridge University Press.
Camilleri, J.A. 1990. Rethinking Sovereignty in a Shrinking, Fragmented World. In R.B.J. Walker and S.H. Mendlovitz (eds.), *Contending Sovereignties*. Boulder, CO: Lynne Rienner Publishers.
Deere, P. 1979. A Conversation with Phillip Deere. Videorecording. University of Massachusetts: Union Video Project. Available at University of Massachusetts/Amherst, W.E.B. Dubois Library, Audio-Visual Department.
Denham, M.E., and M.O. Lombardi. 1996. Perspectives on Third-World Sovereignty: Problems with(out) Borders. In M.E. Denham and M.O. Lombardi (eds.), *Perspectives on Third-World Sovereignty*. New York: St. Martin's Press.
Dorris, M. 1979. Twentieth Century Indians: The Return of the Natives. In R.L. Hall (ed.), *Ethnic Autonomy: Comparative Dynamics*. New York: Pergamon Press.
Hillerman, T. 1997. Who Has Sovereignty Over Mother Earth? *New York Times* (18 September).
Hinsley, F.H., 1966. *Sovereignty*. New York: Basic Books.
Lombardi, M.O. 1996. Third-World Problem-Solving and the 'Religion' of Sovereignty: Trends and Prospects. In M.E. Denham and M.O. Lombardi (eds.), *Perspectives on Third-World Sovereignty*. New York: St. Martin's Press.

Magnusson, W. 1990. The Reification of Political Community. In R.B.J. Walker and S.H. Mendlovitz (eds.), *Contending Sovereignties*. Boulder, CO: Lynne Rienner Publishers.
Newcomb, S. 1993. The Evidence of Christian Nationalism in Federal Indian Law: The Doctrine of Discovery, Johnson v. McIntosh, and Plenary Power. *N.Y.U. Review of Law & Social Change* 20 (2): 303–341.
Ruiz, L.E.J. 1990. Sovereignty as Transformative Practice. In R.B.J. Walker and S.H. Mendlovitz (eds.), *Contending Sovereignties*. Boulder, CO: Lynne Rienner Publishers.
Shapiro, M. 1996. Moral Geographies and the Ethics of Post-Sovereignty. In M.E. Denham and M.O. Lombardi (eds.), *Perspectives on Third-World Sovereignty*. New York: St. Martin's Press.
Walker, R.B.J. 1996. Space/Time/Sovereignty. In M.E. Denham and M.O. Lombardi (eds.), *Perspectives on Third-World Sovereignty*. New York: St. Martin's Press.
Walker, R.B.J., and S.H Mendlovitz. 1990. Interrogating State Sovereignty. In R.B.J. Walker & S.H. Mendlovitz (eds.), *Contending Sovereignties*. Boulder, CO: Lynne Rienner Publishers.
Williams, R.A., Jr. 1990. *The American Indian in Western Legal Thought*. Oxford: Oxford University Press.

ADDITIONAL BIBLIOGRAPHY

Anderson, T.L. 1995. *Sovereign Nations or Reservations?* San Francisco: Pacific Research Institute for Public Policy.
Fane, P. 1962. *Sovereign and Subject*. Kioto: Ponsonby Memorial Society.
Jouvenal, B. de 1957. *Sovereignty*. J.F. Huntington (trans.). Chicago: University of Chicago Press.
Landsman, G. 1988. *Sovereignty and Symbol*. Santa Fe: University of New Mexico.
Salmond, Sir J. 1930. *Jurisprudence*. 8th Edition by C.A.W. Manning. London: Sweet & Maxwell.
Spruyt, H. 1994. *The Sovereign State and Its Competitors*. Princeton, NJ: Princeton University Press.
Wunder, J. 1994 *Retained by the People*. Oxford: Oxford University Press.

6 A Possible Indigenism
The Limits of the Constitutional Amendment in Argentina
GELIND

In Argentina, the constitutional recognition of the rights of Indigenous Peoples took place with the 1994 amendment. The process leading to this recognition might be considered parallel to that which took place in other Latin American countries. It came about as a result of both the state's need to adjust itself to new conditions throughout the world, and the widespread agitation of Indian peoples and their organisations, a mobilisation favoured within the country by the return to the democratic form of government in the mid-1980s (see Iturralde and Guerrero 1997).

Before the reform, certain indicators kept suggesting that Argentina was becoming progressively aware of the international norms regarding Indian Rights. The issuing in 1992 of Law n°24071—which approved agreement n°169 of the International Labour Organisation (still to be ratified)—and the signing of the Agreement for the Formation of the Fund for the Development of the Indian Peoples in Latin America and the Caribbean (Indigenous Fund) constitute clear evidence of this awareness.

Moreover, it is necessary to say that, in regard to Argentina, there appears to be in the legislative production what Altabe, Braunstein and Gonzalez (1996) have called "inverted genesis" in the structuring of the specific legal order. That is, some provincial legislation on indigenous matters, limited to local realities, was later incorporated as the core of debate for constitutional reforms. Thus, a provincial law appeared first, then a national one (n°23302) was issued; and later the contents of such norms were incorporated in some of the provincial constitutions as well as in the national constitution.[1]

This chapter focuses on the analysis of legislative production regarding Indian matters. This process, which relies on the participation of different agents, builds interpretations based on public law that depict and limit certain specific features of (and for) "Indians." To do so, we concentrate on three texts that constitute significant steps of that process as the backbone of our research: Law 23302 of Indian policy; article 75 clause 17 of the National Constitution after the 1994 amendment; and, above all, Resolution n°4811, which regulates the achievement of legal standing for indigenous communities.

LAW N°23302 OF "INDIAN POLICY AND SUPPORT TO ABORIGINAL COMMUNITIES"

Passed in 1985 and regulated in 1989 by decree n°155, the aim of this law is to convert into "matters of national interest" "the attention and help given to aborigines and indigenous communities existing in the country as well as their defence and development." Its main purpose consists in achieving full participation of Indians in "the social, economic and cultural process of the Nation, while respecting their own values and ways" (art. 1).

According to this law, it is the state's responsibility to develop plans to allow Indians access to ownership of land, to foster Indian production, to preserve their own cultural features through public schooling, and to protect their health. However, the scope of the idea of "indigenous participation" is limited to their acceptance of state policies, rather than incorporating the possibility of developing and promoting their own policies and plans.

As regards the identification of individuals addressed by the law, indigenous communities are defined as "groups of families that consider themselves as such because they are descendants of the peoples inhabiting the national territory at the time of the Spanish conquest and colonisation, and indigenous people or Indians those who belong to these communities" (art. 2). Even though this definition seems to consider self-recognition as good enough a condition, the same law imposes ethnocentric barriers to a criterion that appears to be respectful of the autonomy and self-organisation of indigenous peoples. As prescribed by the law, the acquisition of legal standing paradoxically demands that Indian communities register themselves in the Register of Indigenous Communities, and base their organisation on criteria "ruled according to the resolutions of the law of cooperative associations, mutual institutions or any other form of association accepted by the laws at work" (art. 4).

Thus, the announced recognition can be achieved only in terms of a translation: Indian communities have to adapt themselves to the type of organisational legislation at work, that legislators presuppose close to Indian customary forms. Therefore, what is in fact expected of Indians comes to be in open contradiction with what is implied in article 1, so much so that the "values and modalities to be respected" end up being not those of indigenous peoples but those of the nation. Like previous legislation on indigenous issues, Law 23302 still defines asymmetrically the status of indigenous specificity, that is, as a difference to be incorporated and homogenised progressively within the national "us" in accordance with the peculiarities of the most inclusive (national) identity.

The recognition posed by the law is, in turn, far from being permanent. Aboriginality is seen as a condition which might disappear. As a result, the article stating the requirements for registration—which is to prove authenticity by means of showing continued existence or contemporary regrouping (art. 3)—also foresees that the legal standing can be cancelled when the conditions, which have determined its granting, disappear. On the one hand, self-recognition is not enough since it is "the authority in charge" who accepts or rejects the registration. On the other hand, the law not only anticipates the possibility of losing the acquired status, but is also ambiguous as to the agent that might cause the cancellation of such registration.

As the established way of tracing belonging was through the community, all Indians born or brought up outside a concrete location were excluded. In addition, the recognition based on the figure of "indigenous community" leaves aside the notion of Indian Peoples.

This law also predetermines the creation of the Instituto Nacional de Asuntos Indígenas (National Institute for Indian Affairs), NIA, a bureau with effective participation in and control of the decisions to be made by representatives of aboriginal communities grouped in a Co-ordination Council. Representatives of the Ministries of Education and Justice, Home Affairs, Labour and Finance would also comprise this council. The NIA is established as depending on the Ministry of Health and Welfare, which shows the ideology underlying the state's approach to indigenous affairs, an ideology linking indigenous matters with welfare offices. An Advising Council is also created, with members representing the Secretariats of Cooperative Action, Culture, Trade, the National Institute of Agricultural Technology and the National Committee for Frontier Areas. The Chairman of the NIA must be appointed by the Executive Office, which means that this council falls within the sphere of political action in the civil service.

NIA, whose functions are described in article 6, is supposed to fulfil both prescriptive jobs (such as deciding regulations) and planning and executive jobs (such as solving registrations and cancellations). Yet, while the law states that such a planning should be concerned with the "encouragement, promotion and development of indigenous communities," limits to decentralisation are nevertheless set, for the NIA resolutions can be appealed against in the Federal Court of Appeals.

In chapter IV, which refers to lands, the "awarding" of land ownership to Indian communities in the country is decided. Such land has to be "apt and enough" for agricultural, forestry, mining, industrial or craft purposes, according to the modalities of economic exploitation of natural resources each community has. The use of the term "awarding" is interesting because terms such as "restitution" or '"return" might have been used instead. This wording thus reiterates the state's role of "donor" in relation to Indian communities.

In addition, the interplay between concessions (arts. 9, 11) and duties (art. 12) limits Indian agency. Exemption of taxes, free character of transference, access to credit lines, impossibility to alienate property: the access to all these mechanisms has a price for indigenous communities. They have to settle on the "awarded" land and work the soil in person, not being able to sell, hire or transfer rights over the land or subdivide it or add pieces without prior authorisation. The state guarantees no changes on concessions made to indigenes, but Indians have to resign the right to use their property as regular owners do, if they want to go on being Indian owners. It therefore seems to be implied that, in case they refuse to resign the natural dynamics of ownership, their own aboriginality is liable to be cancelled. This ambiguity adds to the lack of precision as to who would decide when or how to ask for or implement cancellation.

Moreover, the recognition of indigenous communities degrades and submits to state agency the Indian capacity to control their own affairs. Concretely, the law states that "the counselling to aborigines ought to take into consideration their customs and techniques, complementing them with technological and scientific advances." Although the term "complementation" tries to convey a symmetric relationship, this clause states different kinds of asymmetry. On one hand, the desire, degree and modality of this complementation eludes an Indian agency which is again the object of policies generated somewhere else. On the other hand, Indian capacity is subordinated to the values of modernity inasmuch as it is limited to "customs and techniques." The underlying ideology of growth and development opposes "tradition" to "modernity", in terms of "customs" versus "scientific and technological advances." The way to incorporation and participation is still unidirectional: "Indians" are those who have to become modern, who have to adapt and improve themselves. This over-determines the meaning of the term "beneficiaries," which understands the subjects of this law as "fortunate" in several ways. This idea of "beneficiaries" indicates that the law involves a grant conceded by the state to the aborigines.

The way in which article 14 talks about education is also related to state-oriented ideology. Different issues treated by this law are depicted as matters of "national interest." Yet article 14 explains that "the intensification of educational and cultural services in areas where Indian communities are settled is a priority." If everything is a matter of national interest, this interest has its own priorities, as these are defined by the old national ideology, which believes that education redeems wretchedness. In this case the purpose is not to extend education to Indians in order to turn them into citizens (as was the aim at the end of 19th century), but to intensify this service. In one way or another, the lexical choice shows that what had been done in that area so far has not been enough. That is why article 17 mentions programmes which would help in a permanent process of turning indigenes into citizens, through education, literacy and post–literacy, educational compensation, and "whole-day" institutions.

The use of linguistic expressions in the stating of educational aims is significant. For example, "[t]o protect and promote the historical and cultural identity of each community, guaranteeing at the same time their egalitarian integration to the national society." The ideas of protecting and promoting imply that previous legislation may have perhaps lacked such a policy of recognition. The expression "at the same time" draws a horizontal line between the two scopes of organisation (Indian community/nation), whereas there is a basic ground-level asymmetry of appraisal. Hence the tension between "custom" and "modernity" reappears, embedded in the idea of "egalitarian integration." Thus, when article 15 sets educational contents, it also sets the conditions deemed necessary to protect and promote the historical and cultural identity. Integration could only be egalitarian if Indians learned "modern techniques for the working of the soil and the manufacturing of its products," how to build "communal or school farms or vegetable gardens" and organise "workshops for the preservation and dissemination of craft techniques," as well as "theory and practice of cooperative association."

On the topic of education, there is also a new provision, according to which the elementary school within Indian settlements will be divided in two cycles. The first—of three years—is to be delivered in the Indians' own language, developing the national language as a special subject. In the following years the learning adopts a bilingual modality. The lexical choice that distinguishes "Indian dialects" from the "national language" marks another case of asymmetry. In addition, since the teaching of Indian languages is limited to the first cycle, one may assume that bilingual education is seen but as a means of learning the national language.

In a country like Argentina where bilingual education was accepted only as late as 1985 and has yet to be implemented in most of the country, the aim of limiting the learning of the Indian mother tongue to the first cycle might seem simply "natural." But if the defence of Indian languages were a goal in itself, bilingual education would not be limited just to primary education. Hence such a restriction suggests it is merely considered as an appropriate means to guarantee literacy in the "national language."

THE NEW CONSTITUTION

For Altabe et al. (1996: 79) the constitutional amendment implied "the definite recognition of ethnic pluralism, which is understood as the possibility individuals have to identify themselves and behave as members of different peoples, although inserted within a national community."

In this sense, article 75 clause 17[2] shows both similarities and differences with Law 23302. As regards to similarities, such topics as bilingual education, recognition of legal standing, and the impossibility to seize, withdraw or transfer the land are retained.

However, the differences are relevant. First of all, there is the recognition of the ethnic and cultural pre-existence of Indigenous Peoples in relation to non-Indian settlers and their descendants. Second, the term "indigenous peoples" replaces that of community, though referred to as "Argentine" and not " in Argentina," an idea that strengthens the relationship of belonging and national fitting instead of that of extraneousness. Third, to promote and defend their identity is not enough: it must also be respected. Fourth, education should not only be bilingual but also intercultural. Fifth, the recognition of community possession and ownership of land instead of granting ownership according to the ways each community makes use of it (Law 23302). And, last but not least, the participation mentioned in the article, though limited to land management and related to their natural resources and other issues that affect their interests, also implies in a widest sense that Indigenous Peoples should be active participants in every affair that could affect their interests as peoples.

THE STATE OF INDIGENOUS POLICY AFTER THE CONSTITUTIONAL AMENDMENT AND RESOLUTION 4811

The terms adopted by the new constitution mean a significant step forward in the constitutional guarantee awarded to indigenous rights. It is thus surprising that this valuable legislative development subsequently made it as far as the Executive Office in the execution of its policies.

The decree (155) regulating the application of Law 23302 was never wholly put into practice. Nevertheless, there were two simulacra of NIA. The first one took place when the need for the constitutional amendment was at stake and several proposals for the contents of article 75 were being made by Indigenous Peoples and indigenist organisations. The second one took place when the Executive Office appointed an officer *ad hoc* instead of creating the proper office with indigenous representatives, as stated in the law.

Thus the inclusion of Indigenous rights in the Constitution was more the result of intensive indigenous mobilisation than of an official political programme. Therefore, the final version of this article is a combination of indigenous claims and proposals made by the constituents, a sort of forum for the production of indigenous policies, which was absolutely independent of the Executive Office. Nevertheless, the Constitutional amendment that changed the range of the Social Welfare Secretary to the State Secretary, granting it financial autonomy, reinforced the link between aboriginality and state assistance. Consequently, the National Institute of Indigenous Affairs, depending upon this Secretary, grew according to the rhythm of the contribution that international financial agencies offered for the development of indigenous communities.

Paradoxically, this growth made it possible for a national programme of indigenous mobilisation to take place during 1996–1997. The main objective of this Indigenous Peoples Participation Programme (IPP) was to promote the leading participation of indigenous peoples in the designing of the criteria and rules that the state should comply with in order to put article

75 clause 17 of the new constitution into practice. The organisers expected that the mobilisation could elaborate a legislative corpus encompassing indigenous claims as well as the political will of the lawmakers.

During IPP debates about key questions such as indigenous territory, legal standing, political organisation and participation, the Executive Office issued—through the Social Welfare Secretary and NIA—Resolution 4811 that establishes the conditions to be followed by indigenous communities to obtain their legal standing.

This regulation is doubly unconstitutional. Firstly, because according to article 75 clause 17 it is within the powers of Congress to accept the legal standing of indigenous communities. Secondly, since this resolution was designed without indigenous participation, the initiative of the Secretary contradicts the constitutional clause granting it.

This document came to light both when IPP was ending and an Indigenous national policy plan on land was being launched. On the occasion of President Menem's visit to native communities the government put on a neo-populist ritual to show off the land bequeath. Since this plan has not been put into practice so far, we infer that this land bequeath is mere make-believe.

According to its designers, this resolution would give a prompt answer to the specific needs of communities claiming the restitution of their land, until wider consultation was called for. Nonetheless, grounds for this resolution and the emphasis in forcing Indigenous peoples to submit it suggest, in our opinion, that it is one of the political strategies deployed by state officials to heed native claims only as long as indigenous people accept being part of an official indigenist agenda that greatly diminishes the strength of their claims.

Resolution 4811 states the "need" to "explain the criteria adopted in order to give instructions for the registration of communities." The text seeks its own legitimisation within the constitutional amendment introducing "deep changes to Law 23302." Furthermore, in taking into account the demands of some indigenous organisations by selecting the category "Indigenous Peoples inhabiting the Argentine Republic" as an equivalent to "Argentine Indigenous Peoples" mentioned in the constitutional amendment, it clearly avoids assigning them Argentine nationality.

Nevertheless, this is a partial echo because the expression "Indigenous Peoples inhabiting what nowadays is called Argentine Republic"—as these organisations refer to the historicity of the state in order to emphasise aboriginal pre-existence—was never used as such. In a way, the text tries to rebuild a link between Argentinity and Aboriginality through a national territory that has no origin and is eternal.

Immediately after this, although the writers of the Constitution placed the article 75 clause 17 within the Congress's powers and not in the section "New rights and guarantees," the resolution turns them into special rights related to "ethnic, cultural and historic identity, the legal standing of their communities, the possession and ownership of the land they traditionally occupy, the transmission of their knowledge by means of bilingual and intercultural education, the preservation of their heritage and existence by means of guaranteeing the impossibility to seize the land they inhabit, the granting of new land which should be apt and enough for human development, and their participation in management related to their natural resources."

In this list, the recurrent use of the possessive "their" marks the particular legal status of these subjects and makes it natural to associate them with certain objects and practices (identity, communities, knowledge, heritage, participation, natural resources) that could be demanded by them.

The attempt to control the political arena becomes evident through the elisions and partial inclusions of the texts of the preceding laws. When the phrase "and the other interests which affect them" as appearing in Law 23302 is elicited, the resolution restricts the spheres for indigenous participation. By including what was said in article 75, "to regulate the granting of more land [that is] apt and enough," and adding "future" to the word "grant," the constituent locates that act in the future.

Placing the constitutional recognition at the "highest range of priority as regards the application and interpretation of laws." resolution 4811 seeks to avoid any ambiguous interpretation that makes some of the prescriptions in Law 23302 appear to be 'relative' ones. For instance, the use of the term "indigenous communities" instead of "peoples." However, if the categorisation of Indians as Peoples could in fact pose a challenge to the claim of state sovereignty—an idea connoted by international law—this possibility is promptly neutralised when the declarer limits that category by using the possessive "our," thereby cancelling the possibility of foreignness among Indigenous Peoples and Nation. This strategy is reasserted through alleging that recognition of "the ethnic and cultural diversity of the Nation" is also derived from the same constitutional disposition. The declarer keeps for himself the place from which such diversity could be talked about as "ours," i.e., the nation's, thus sanctioning the idea of pluri-ethnicity, but not the claim of state pluri-nationality made by the most radical indigenous groups.

It is interesting that such recognition of diversity is stated as due to the constituents' good will: facing the past, as " an act of deep justice because of the historical reparation it means," and facing the present as "a clear recognition of the human, social and community rights of the original peoples that inhabited our homeland." It is significant that Indians are talked of in connection with the past ("inhabited") as if it were necessary—once again—to link aboriginality to the past rather than to the present.

The resolution includes several articles of Law 23302, which enable the NIA to work as an application agency, that is, one entitled both to decide the requirements for the registration of indigenous communities' legal standings, and grant, or reject, them as well.

The resolution quotes article 4 of Law 23302 in order explicitly to make a contradiction between the spirit of the law and the written words. Whereas the spirit of the law would be centred on "the respect to the historical identity of indigenous communities," these would be forced into "forms of association belonging to modern society, therefore completely estranged from the traditions and organisational forms each community has had throughout its history."

Resolution 4811, then, assumes a prescriptive role, stating that the indigenous entities "should, no doubt, be ruled by those proper historical, cultural or associative norms considered by the communities themselves to be the best in order to defend the interests they are involved with."

The granting of diversity disappears when we realise that the core of the question—the definition of the indigenous community—is kept untouched. Name, address, common origin, self-organisation rules and others, are kept as criteria, in spite of the variability of organisational forms. The so-called self-identification is now so greatly subjected to state scrutiny—self-identification in time and space as an utterly political body and document-bearer—that it inhibits the premises upon which this resolution is based: the legal one of "flexibility" and the administrative one of "simplification of requirements."

We suggest therefore that the so-called laxity in definition of an agency supposed to widen the range of the legal status of the Aborigine, only directs indigenous claims in a "politically correct" way within a specific indigenous agenda. Paradoxically, a text aimed at paying respect to cultural diversity and indigenous organisations becomes a kind of decalogue which, in stating the necessary requirements indigenous communities must fulfil to be considered as such, frames the landscape in which diversity can be accepted.

CONCLUSIONS

The analysis of Law 23302, article 75 clause 17 of the amended Constitution and Resolution 4811 has shown that compared to previous times during 1985 and 1996 relevant achievement took place regardless of the legal status of the indigenous subject. This has been achieved through two simultaneous political movements: on the one hand, an advance in the degree of recognition of Indigenous Peoples, and on the other hand, specification and restriction of the range of demands Indigenous Peoples are entitled to make.

The main axe that articulates all these movements is that of cultural diversity. It is, moreover, now creating a new political arena in which state officers, indigenous activists and other participants dispute over the orientation of politico-legal relations between the Argentine State and Indigenous Peoples.

As regards this analysis of these legal texts, inasmuch as they are routines that classify subjects and social relationships—the legal codification of which is conditioned by a so-called "sense of belonging"—they show that they not only limit the field of rights and duties of the "indigenous," but also act to reduce their potential demands within the wider frame of state lawfulness.

NOTES TO CHAPTER 6

1. Integral Aboriginal Law n°426/84 of Formosa Province; Law 6373/86 of Salta; Law 3258/87 of Chaco; Law 2435/87 (derogated and replaced by Law 2727/89) of Misiones; Law 2287/88 of Rio Negro; Law 3657/91 of Chubut; and Law 11078/93 of Santa Fe. The following provincial constitutional reforms also occurred: in 1986 Jujuy's (art. 50) and Salta's (art. 15); in 1988 Rio Negro's (art. 42); and in 1991 Formosa's (art. 79). In 1994, the National Constitution was reformed, as were, in 1994–1995, the provincial constitutions of Buenos Aires, Chaco, La Pampa, Neuquén, and Chubut.
2. According to article 75 clause17 of the amended National Constitution (1994), it is within the Congress's powers "to recognise the ethnical and cultural pre-existence of the Argentine Indigenous peoples; to guarantee respect for their identity and their right to intercultural and bilingual education; to recognise the legal standing of their communities and the possession and ownership of lands they occupy traditionally; to regulate the assignment of more land which should be apt and enough for human development; [to guarantee that] their lands cannot be alienated, embargoed or seized and sold, or the rights to them transferred; [and to] guarantee indigenous participation in all arrangements referred to as their natural resources and all other interests affecting them. Provinces can exercise these powers concurrently."

REFERENCES

Altabe, R., J. Braunstein, and J. Gonzalez. 1996. Indian Rights in Argentina: Reflections about Ideas and General Outlines Appearing in Article 75, clause 17 of the National Constitution. *Relaciones de la Sociedad Argentina de Antropología* XXI: 77–101.

Iturralde, F., and D. Guerrero. 1997. Demandas Indígenas y Reforma Legal: Retos y Paradojas. *Alteridades*. Itztapalapa: UNAM.

LEGISLATION

Integral Aboriginal Law N°426/84 of Formosa Province.

Law 6373/86 of Salta.

Law 3258/87 of Chaco.

Law 2435/87 of Misiones.

Law 2727/89 of Misiones.

Law 2287/88 of Rio Negro.

Law 3657/91 of Chubut.

Law 11078/93 of Santa Fe.

Law n°24071 (National).

Law n°23302 (National).

7 Strategies for Equities in Indigenous Education
A Canadian First Nations Case Study

Marlene R. Atleo

Providing strategies for indigenous people and existing leadership in educational organisations is expected to promote movement toward more respectful relationships in which partnerships are requisite "good educational practice" in a global social economy. In British Columbia the government has initiated a process to bring indigenous people and educational institutions into a better working partnership in education. While supported by provincial policy and leadership, this process must be forged in the communities through dialogues between educational professionals and indigenous people who are seeking an education that respects their culture and history. The forging of new relationships takes time and effort and often a baring of the heart as we move to new relationships between indigenous peoples and the settler societies.

The case study which follows comes from my experience of over thirty years in the indigenous community of the Nuu-chah-nulth as a woman, a mother, a wife, a fisher, a teacher, a social programme coordinator, and a recent Ph.D. graduate in educational studies. This study is offered to indigenous people and non-indigenous people as a model for "negotiating respectful new places to live and learn through education."

First, I describe the social process that contextualises the workshop presentation from which this chapter is developed. I am privileged to do this because of my personal development in which I was given "eyes to see" indigenous education in the Nuu-chah-nulth community. Next, I explore the aspiration for education of indigenous people like the Nuu-chah-nulth in the context of cultural content and process issues. These issues are presented in the light of strategies by educational experts in such areas as knowledge sets, multicultural educational leadership, issues of recruitment, retention and curriculum, the institutions that serve First Nations people, and, finally, conceptual strategies centred on instructional design. This case study is not meant to be exhaustive but merely an introduction to the complexity of the problem area and opportunities to make headway toward equities in indigenous education. The terms indigenous, aboriginal, and First Nations are used interchangeably throughout.

SITE

The material in this article was first presented at a small Northwest coastal college, whose educational system is articulated at various sites in the territories claimed by indigenous First Nations of the Wakasan linguistic groups of the Nuu-chah-nulth, as part of a cultural awareness workshop. Nuu-chah-nulth are a group of about 7500 people living mainly on the West Coast of Vancouver Island, British Columbia, Canada. The workshop location was in Port Alberni, Barkley Sound, where the Nuu-chah-nulth Tribal Council has its headquarters and where the closest college is located. Initiated by the North Island College (NIC) administration in response to a three-phase provincial strategy (Province of British Columbia 1998) to better recruit, retain and realise more relevant curricula, the workshop programme aimed to provide operational, administrative and academic personnel with First Nations cultural awareness to promote a better orientation to the bulk of First Nations students that are currently attending and have the potential to attend.

After a prayer asking the Creator for good communication for the group, offered by a respected Elder, a representative of the Hupachasaht chiefs of the original occupants of the territory situated in Port Alberni, the programme got underway. The elected Chief of Hupachasaht First Nation and Main Table Treaty[1] Negotiator for the Nuu-chah-nulth First Nations, Dr Judith Sayers,[2] spoke first about the Treaty process issues, sociohistorically contextualising the communication issues worked out at the treaty table. The second topic, residential schools and their intergenerational effects, looked at how children, families and communities suffered grievous losses of cultural and familial opportunities because of the government policy of taking children away from their parents for schooling (see Miller 1996). Dr Sayers recounted her personal experiences in the educational system through schooling in the Alberni Valley and as an undergraduate at Brigham Young University, Utah, USA, and the Faculty of Law at the University of British Columbia (UBC). She spoke candidly of her experiences of inclusion, based on religious principles at Brigham Young, as well as of exclusion and discrimination based on perceptions of "special" treatment by other students in the Law Program at UBC.

A Hupachasaht linguist spoke about his own experience at the Alberni Indian Residential School (AIRS) in Port Alberni, as a witness of the effects of government and church policy to eradicate aboriginal culture through the socialisation of children away from the influences of their parents and extended families. Finally, a Hupachasaht youth, a North Island College student and member of the Community Advisory Board, talked about the continuing legacy, that affects present and future generations, of the policies and practices enacted through the residential school. Throughout, questions from the participants were answered candidly (Miller 1996; Nuu-chah-nulth Tribal Council 1996).

As the first speaker of the afternoon session, my intention was to draw together that which the attendees had witnessed and frame it in such a way that it might be personally relevant to them. The intention of this strategy was to provide another insight to educational issues through a personal account of my education into Nuu-chah-nulth culture. This strategy compares and contrasts indigenous First Nations perspectives with that of non-indigenous perspectives, provides strategies for learning to respect First Nations perspectives and provides instructional strategies to provide educational leadership for indigenous First Nations post-secondary education.

In the protocol of thanking, in which I showed my respect to the people who made the event possible,[3] I also acknowledged my partner of thirty-two years, Dr E. Richard Atleo, founding instructor of the Arts One First Nations Program and First Nations BA program at Malaspina University College, Chief Umeek, of the Ahousaht First Nations. Richard had initially been asked to participate but suggested that they ask me in his stead. In Nuu-chah-nulth tradition, chiefs did not usually speak for or about themselves but appointed an official speaker to represent them. The speakers were in effect the public voice of the chief. The office of speaker was often also a hereditary position. Speakers today are frequently confused with the chiefs they represent because these nuances of cultural tradition are little understood by non-Nuu-chah-nulth. I, in the tradition of Umeek, the whaling chief, was the partner who had been a witness to, and a participant in, the secret and public travail of the whaler. Thus, I became the "witness" to recount the events in the ritual of cooperation on the beach (i.e., in public).

NUU-CHAH-NULTH EDUCATION INTO CULTURE

Umeek (Richard) had encouraged me to relate the experience of my formal education into the culture of the Ahousaht First Nation, Nuu-chah-nulth. My first experience with First Nations people was here in Port Alberni, where my family had moved in the early 1960s. The National Employment Canada Register had recommended my father, a naturalised Canadian citizen, take a "low stress" job at the Alberni Indian Residential School (AIRS) after a heart attack at the age of forty-two. Consequently, I lived in Alberni and attended a local junior high school.

My father had been a non-military prisoner of war (POW) for seven years in Canada during the Second World War, with many pro-Nazi and Fascist Canadian prisoners. His imprisonment occurred in 1939 because when he was nineteen, his father, a social democrat living in Nazi Germany, sent his only son off to the merchant marine with instructions to "find a safe place to stay for the duration of the conflict." My father had "jumped" ship in Union Bay on Vancouver Island, British Columbia. Caught by the Royal Canadian Mounted Police, he was imprisoned at Kananaskis, Alberta, and the first in a series of work camps across Canada. At the residential school it did not take him long to see the parallels between what the children were experiencing and how they were being treated, and his own traumatic imprisonment. The memories that were triggered precluded his remaining in that job because he felt an overwhelming powerlessness to help the children in his care (see Miller 1996; Nuu-chah-nulth Tribal Council 1996). He worked there only three short months, but the experience changed my life forever.

My father's low wages and nights away from home in dormitory supervision created hardship for the family, which he tried to ameliorate in a variety of ways. When there was not enough to eat at home he took us up to the school to eat with the rest of the children or brought home leftovers. When there was no money for movies we went to the screenings at the school. Because he drove the students to after-school events he sometimes brought them to our house for a meal afterwards. Coffee and fresh bread were favourites, as were the huge coffee cakes my mother made from grapes that grew in the back yard. Nearby was the elementary school to which the children from the residential school were bussed daily, and my mother could not believe how often they would lose their white-bread and bologna lunchtime sandwiches, so as to come to our home with my brothers for sandwiches of fresh homemade bread with peanut butter and jam and coffee. We came to understand it was a "taste of home."

While I had made some friends in the neighbourhood, their interest soon waned when they realised I was "chumming" with the AIRS children and having them over to our house. The non-Native kids soon shunned me because I was violating social rules about with whom to associate. One night, a couple of non-indigenous neighbourhood friends were walking home with me over the railway trestle between Port and Alberni when they grabbed and dangled me over the side as a means of showing their superiority because we had just been talking about the "residential school kids" and I was not complying with their perspective.

Our family moved back to the mainland of British Columbia at the end of the school year, but by then the friends from the residential school had become significant. I remained in contact with several for years afterwards, exchanging letters with them or meeting them when they passed through Vancouver. When I was a high school senior, one of those friends, who was attending UBC at the time, introduced me to one of his fellow students, who was also his nephew. As an immigrant, I was ignorant of the Canadian cultural stereotypes of "Indians" except from TV. The "Indians" I knew did not match any of that "objective" information. How could I know that these two young men attending UBC were an anomaly when they were the only ones I knew? I eventually married that nephew, E. Richard Atleo.

By marrying him, I became a legal Indian under the Indian Act, without even knowing it. I married the hereditary third chief of the Ahousaht First Nation. At eighteen, I had no way of knowing what it meant. I was clueless. The first summer, after we married, I flew to Tofino in Clayoquot Sound from Vancouver with my new baby. My husband met us, took us to the wharf, and down into the cabin of a tiny fish boat for the two-hour trip to Ahousaht on Flores Island. This is not a romantic "captivity story" because I was a willing participant. But I was a curiosity in that village. I was the first non-indigenous woman to marry one of their boys and come home to live. People respectfully called me "Mrs. Richard."

We lived with Richard's grandmother Nan and her partner, Teddy George. They were warm, welcoming and inclusive. Cold running water was the only amenity. My first job was to learn to dump "honey buckets" into the water on the beach without getting the faecal backwash in my boots. I was learning to live from a "cultural ground-zero." The female elders would come to visit, sit and watch me work around the house and tend my baby. They would talk to each other about me in Nuu-chah-nulth and would sometimes tell me what I should be doing. Nan would explain what was happening. She taught me to weave baskets with designs that were mnemonics for traditional stories and myths. She taught me how I was related to Richard's relatives so I could weave my children into their network of relations. She taught me what was expected of "Mrs. Richard." She told myths as well as family and personal stories. We played cat's cradle, at which she was inventive and hilarious. The string-figure bear hunched on a log *schuu-mapt*, defecating, was hilarious. She showed me berry patches near the village. She showed me different ways to cut different fish for different uses. The variety was intriguing and engaging. She introduced me to the cultural rhythms of which I was to become a part.

I was only one of generations of women over millennia that had married into a Nuu-chah-nulth family, moved into their locale and needed to be taught their ways. I was to be made to feel welcome by my husband's family members, to feel "at home," comfortable and familiar. The elders would correct me if I did something that violated local custom. People gossiped about me as a means of social control, demonstrating that they were treating me as one of their own, part of their social milieu. People interacted authentically with me and it was not long before I was getting the message. I participated with them to reshape myself to fit into Ahousaht spaces for an Ahousaht woman.

A large gathering was held for our baby son because he was an heir apparent to a chieftainship. The village adults and elders wanted to meet him although he was only six months old. Everyday I was amazed at the different way that Ahousaht people thought and acted and understood the world. But I was also confused. The man that I met and married, who had completed four years of university, was "at home" a man of the village who acted as part of the village and expected me to also learn to be part of his people. Then, when we were denied hotel and motel rooms in the local villages of the West Coast where there were vacancy signs, my confusion increased at such discrepancies between "objective cultural realities."

Such was the beginning of my formal education into Nuu-chah-nulth culture and social expectations in the context of the larger society of the West Coast. This provided me with a template for understanding what was to come and for growing in that knowledge to the point where it became second nature, a point of personal identification for me. In the last ten years, I have returned to university to attempt to articulate some of my experiences and share some strategic understanding with indigenous First Nations about ontology and epistemology that provide foundations for professional practice and with non-indigenous professionals who interact with First Nations people. I claim that I went back to formal schooling in self-defense, so my children and grandchildren will not have the experiences that Richard and I had to endure.

NUU-CHAH-NULTH EDUCATIONAL ASPIRATIONS

The aforementioned indigenous "awareness" workshop at NIC was designed to help the faculty, administration and staff move towards an understanding of Nuu-chah-nulth educational aspirations in the light of history and future expectations. There was a welcome by the traditional representatives of the territory in a show of cultural courtesy and respect. The stories of past experiences were told in the firsthand accounts of survivors of the attempted "civilisation" of the "savage" through formal institutional socialisation called education. A glimpse was provided into First Nations perspectives about socio-technical or legal aspects of institutional oppression, repression, and disruption of cultural transformation.

The dancers of the Haa-huu-pay-ak cultural school provided a demonstration of cultural persistence and logic in their performance. The presentations and performances provide a frame for my words. While my words are nested in that frame, my message is in the dialectic between First Nations frames and those of Canadian professional educational practice. While the latter makes the statement that the *status quo* maintains barriers First Nations cannot ourselves dismantle, the performance of our First Nations children demonstrates that identity and cultural persistence are not discontinuous with educational, economic and social achievement of the larger society from a Nuu-chah-nulth perspective. My role in the workshop, as a person with formal and informal experience of the Nuu-chah-nulth culture and community but who was not "indigenous," was to try to make some sense of this by moving from themes of past First Nations educational experiences and failure in the non-Native systems, to ways in which local colleges can participate with Nuu-chah-nulth in our vision for the future through professional orientations, institutional learning, and instructional technologies.

Hermann Hesse said, "It is not our purpose to become each other; it is to recognise each other, to learn to see the other and honour [respect] him [her] for what he [she] is." *Issak*—Respect—recognising the culturological ordering of the lifeworld is the key. First Nations aspire to maintain their core cultural identity as individuals and a group while participating in a Canadian future. In the Delgamuukw decision the Supreme Court of Canada concluded with the remark that "We are all here to stay." Nuu-chah-nulth, in their treaty negotiations and partnerships with institutions of the larger society, acknowledge that as a fact. The terms of how we are going to do that were the theme of the workshop, and are to be worked out in harmony with International Human Rights and the Charter of Rights and Freedoms. The history of the Charter suggests that Canada, which was "(e)stablished by two historically opposed peoples, enriched by various cultures, languages and religions as well as the Aboriginal peoples, and marked by a geography itself highly diversified, could not help but be a land of compromise. 'Unity in diversity' could become Canada's motto. The Spirit of moderation and tolerance characterizes the Canadian federation and assures its survival" (Government of Canada 1998). In some ways, this suggests that to assure survival, that Spirit needs to be embraced. It suggests that "unity in diversity" (Tully 1995) is labour intensive and demands cooperation. For example, in the document summarising discussions of the Roundtable on Population Health there is the comment that it was no longer acceptable to agree to disagree, and it declares instead a national mandate to "work something out."

NUU-CHAH-NULTH FIRST NATIONS APPROACHES

Indigenous First Nations such as Nuu-chah-nulth have a very long history of experience with unity in diversity as part of a long sociopolitical history. The highly complex protocols that were and continue to be a part of Nuu-chah-nulth social and political activity reflect the highly structured means for the respect of diversity and the creation and recreation of unities in diversity. It sounds like Canadian non-Native people are now at a place previously experienced by Nuu-chah-nulth. The transformation of career scripts in changing contexts is not new to Nuu-chah-nulth while maintaining sociohistorical integrity (Golla 1989). For example, the Atleo chieftainship, of which Umeek is the head, has a historical mandate to reduce the bloodshed and suffering among our Nuu-chah-nulth people. It is a mandate that our lineage takes seriously. For many of us, that mandate serves as an underlying thread for career scripts. Some of the ways we enact that mandate is through our work. Members of our family hold such positions as elementary school teacher, college instructor, programme/workshop/curriculum developer, licensed psychological counsellor, RCMP (Royal Canadian Mounted Police) officer, school liaison worker, treaty negotiator, private educational institution owner and operator, educational consultant, lawyer, computer network technician, electrician, information systems consultant, social programme coordinator and developer, teacher aide, health care consultant, and education and social science researcher.

The people of the lineage thus carry on in the cultural work of the ancestors in the present.

An example is my master's degree research (M.R. Atleo 1993), in which I looked at the effects of social role attitudes and the planning behaviour of First Nations mothers. I "knew" from experience that Ahousahts planned, in the face of contradictory anthropological evidence and theory. I had never been to so many planning sessions before joining that family and village. I needed to articulate a narrative of planning that situated First Nations mothers and did not deny their basic human competencies as Justice Addy had denied them in a treaty judgement against the Dunne-za/Cree based on the anthropological and sociocultural myth that these people could not plan or save because of the supposed nature of a native culture founded on, among other things, sharing, acting on instinct and spontaneity (Goldthrope and Ridington, in M.R. Atleo ibid.). The Canadian government through the Department of Indian Affairs had indeed usurped strategic planning activities, but that did not preclude the planning in deep time that over which government had no control. In fact, the recent settlement wherein Dunne-za/Cree were compensated for mineral rights denied in the same era suggests that a long-term perspective may have some advantages. My current research looks at the Umeek narratives about an ancestor of our lineage in order to understand the learning models of Nuu-chah-nulth, how they are embedded in social and economic resource structures and how they are transformed culturally in response to change. Nuu-chah-nulth have been on the West Coast for at least 4,500 years (Marshall 1993). Nuu-chah-nulth culture is a highly evolved oral tradition, characterised by a narrative mode of thought, giving rise to complex sociopolitical institutions that are just beginning to be articulated and explained by Nuu-chah-nulth people. My Nuu-chah-nulth name, ?eh ?eh naa tu kwiss, means "a person that can say the same thing in many ways" or "a person who can speak in metaphors/similes." It speaks of a culture that revels in diversity and consists of means to enhance diversity as a strategy of sustainability. It is a culture that simultaneously nurtures diversity and sustainability. My e-mail signature includes the statement: "In celebration of the artifice that the artifact can only hint at," which is about seeing beyond the material, with the eyes of spirit, as I was taught by Nan and a host of Nuu-chah-nulth people over the years. While I was taught by immersion, I have tried to *hamatsup*—show or demonstrate—"cultural content and processes" that may help non-Native educators better "see" First Nations students that look for educational leadership.

CULTURAL CONTENT AND PROCESSES: TECHNICAL VIEWS

I now move on to look at non-Indigenous "cultural content and processes." Because it is very difficult to become culturally "self conscious," to understand what I am going to talk about I need to be seen, not with the textual mode of inductive/deductive logic, but with eyes that are looking for a brand new thing that has not been seen before. The three-dimensional pictures or stereograms that were a fad recently provide some clues to the type of "seeing" to which I am alluding, in which one or more figures are embedded in a thick context (Magic-eye 1998; N. E. Thing Enterprises 1995). Few people can see the embedded figure, especially if, to begin with, they do not know what it is. Of those people who can see the embedded figure, many are unable to keep it in focus or dominant. That process is a metaphor not only for what it is like for Nuu-chah-nulth adults to try to deal with non-First Nations ways of seeing, but also for how it is for non-First Nations trying to see Nuu-chah-nulth ways. As an instructor, imagine your student could only see the hidden figure and you yourself could only see the field in which it was embedded. Imagine that you were trying to help the student agree with yourself about aspects of "the picture." This illustration seems extreme but is germane to people with cross-cultural experience. The "ground" can be organised into more than one phenomenological field. If we think of North West Coast art we may think of the embeddedness of figures and the dynamics of the art. I would suggest that this is an illustration of a bi-stability of gestalt and cognition in bi-cultural functioning.

Apter's (1982; 1989; 1993) "reversal theory" shed some theoretical light for me on this phenomenon, which I am just beginning to explore with the view to applying it to adult education (M.R. Atleo 1998). Reversal theory is a structural phenomenological theory about motivation, emotion and personality. This meta-motivational model challenges Hebb's (1955) equilibrium theory of arousal, maintaining that it provides only part of the picture. Apter's re-formulation reveals Hebb's formulation to be the interactional effects between two different modalities of motivation, the telic and paratelic. The telic mode is a goal-focused motivational modality, the paratelic mode an activity-focused one. By looking at these two modalities at equilibrium, Hebb only reveals half the motivational picture. The other half is the ability to move between goal-centred (telic) and activity-centred (paratelic) modes. Aboriginal people ideally seek motivational balance as a cultural strategy, a studied ambivalence that permits a transcendence of the usual liminal ranges. Perhaps this is what Patti Lather (1991) calls upon in her recommendations for sound research, that there be a studied ambivalence, a bi-stability, through which we can see more. Traditional Nuu-chah-nulth were always on the "look out" to see more!

But First Nations are not having their cultural and cognitive ways recognised because education is culturally constructed from a non-Native perspective, which has relied on an immature scientific tradition that has spurned cultural ways of knowing as a variable in its behavioural incarnation. Michael Cole (1996) informs us of the history of the schism between universalist and culturalist ways of establishing "truths" and more sophisticated methodologies, which are allowing the formulation of a scientific cultural psychology that recognises cultural cognitions in contexts through the melding of Piaget and Vygotsky's works. John Berry (1990) has done much groundwork from a classic psychometric perspective. His findings, like those of Ogbu (1982; 1983; 1992), distinguish between immigrants and First Nations and also between First Nations on a cognitive basis. For example, according to McShane and Berry (1988), cognitive orientations are enduring but vary between aboriginal groups. First Nations psychologists (Chrisjohn, Towson and Peters 1988) suggest that it is the context that shapes the cognitive orientations and especially the hostile context of non-aboriginal educational institutions. The Canadian multicultural project has fuelled research in this area, with Art More (1987) working on the problem of learning styles for several decades now, beginning with the Native Indian Teachers Education Programme (NITEP) (First Nations House of Learning 1998) at UBC in the 1970s. The widely assumed "psychological unity of mankind" is being challenged by the facts of cognitive pluralism, the endurance of such orientations based in diverse development, cultural history, technological exposure, and institutional factors. The fact of cognitive pluralism or diversity of rationality has only recently filtered down into instructional design and cognitive science. Surely, if we are valuing biological diversity as a means to sustainability, then we can acknowledge diversity of rationality, not as chaos, but as a means of the creation of new knowledge communities, new meaning-making for unity in diversity. "Attention must be paid to the social rules that mediate the way the artifacts [of culture] mediate social relations" (Cole 1996: 297) when considering the role of culture in developmental psychology which forms the basis of educational curriculum and practice.

Educational practice can be informed by the likes of Olson and Torrance's exploration (1996) of how history, anthropology and education are products of culture, and how the same affects cognition. For example, Oatley (1996), supplying us with some clues when he talks about the relationship between narrative and scientific thinking, maintains that the former provides the conceptual ground and the latter the conceptual figure that we elicit from the ground. The First Nations narrative provides a different ground than that of the narrative of the non-aboriginal person and *vice versa*, even if both parties are speaking English. The logic that is used for narrative thinking is different than that used in scientific thinking.

Also, the logic of scientific thinking is generally formal logic for which proofs lie in inductive and deductive dialectical inference. Oatley (ibid.) cites Pierce's assertion that there is actually another dimension of inference, namely, abduction or guessing or hypothesising. Experiments that test hypotheses include abductive logic (reasoning from rule to result to case logic, which has been called "informal logic"), which is the best guess from the narrative of the literature tested with the dialectic of induction (case to result to rule logic) and deduction (rule to case and result logic). Now if First Nations are not a part of the narrative by exclusion (not being a part of the sample, etc.), then there is no point in inducting or deducting because no guess can be made since First Nations people are not part of the picture. How can you guess at something if it is out of your experience/narrative? I remember watching a Grade 2 teacher in the school at Ahousaht asking a little girl, who was being kept after school, to read a word. The little girl took some wild guesses, to which the teacher reacted negatively, strongly and harshly. The little girl made another couple of attempts. Rather than helping her sound it out or provide any clues, the teacher finally shouted the word at the child and dismissed her to talk to me as I had been waiting at the door. While I do not remember what the object was, I do remember thinking, that child has no experience of the word. How can she "relate" (envision and match the experience to the word) to it?[4]

Usually the way such a guess is made is through a process of "metaphorical mapping" of a familiar source figure (of speech) onto a new target space (Lakoff and Johnson 1980; Turner 1998). This becomes a natural way of "relating" to other persons/objects/situations and across domains. But if we are familiar with only one domain, or do not understand the way the "game" works, the "guessing" is ineffective. When the rules of the game are hidden because the abductive (or informal) logic of the culture is not taught, then the game becomes impossible to learn. Remember that it was the "game" that Nan taught me first, not the rules, not the penalties, but the rhythms, the cultural process frames, the spatial frames in an atmosphere of inclusion and compassion so typical of education by aboriginal elders (Akan 1993; Lightning; 1993).

SHIFTING PARADIGMS—CULTURAL SLIPPAGE

Experienced educational leaders are likely aware of the paradigmatic shifts of this postmodern era, which are permeating the deep structures of the education system at this present time, and that is why it feels like institutions and people are being challenged at their very core. I am using "paradigm" to mean sets of ontological and epistemological assumptions as defined by Schultz and Hatch (1996). While Kuhn's (1962) early response to paradigmatic shifts was to label them "revolutions," his later take was a much gentler rendition, a frame theory, by which incommensurabilities, irreconcilable discontinuities in knowledge paradigms, are in fact worked through in the transformation of frames through which we apprehend our realities. In our era, we are becoming more aware of the many frames actively in use in our society, institutions, academic theory, professional practice, etc., and how they affect our personal and professional interactions, e.g., the contrasting frames of men and women (Gray 1995) or at play, and in conflict, in family violence and in war.

Postmodernist approaches may be understood as overlapping frames that are unarticulated wherein there seems to be chaos and movement that cannot be held still. This seeming cognitive and affective chaos is how the social interaction with non-Natives has seemed for First Nations for more than one hundred and fifty years in the Alberni Valley of British Columbia. Bracken (1997) analyses correspondence to demonstrate how colonial administrators were trying to figure out what the Native people were doing and then legislating what they thought Natives should be doing. Right at the beginning, Sproat (1868) told First Nations people in the Alberni how it will be, and First Nations people spoke back saying that was not how they saw or wanted it. Sproat (ibid.) even went so far as to write about how Native people mispronounced their own language. So the frame we are collectively presently presenting is the First Nations response to the legacy of the likes of Sproat. Historically, the non-aboriginal institutions have a legacy of annihilation of First Nations through assimilation, whereas First Nations have a legacy of persistence through resistance. Now Nuu-chah-nulth are looking to the institution of North Island College (through its faculty and staff) to find a new way to reverse this destructive behaviour and move forward in collaboration and cooperation, dispelling incommensurability.

While Kuhn (1962) suggested incommensurability in his initial formulation of "Scientific Revolutions," his later version suggested a working out of conflicts bit by bit. For educators, for example, this has meant moving from a cultural-assimilationist perspective to a multicultural perspective to a cultural-relativist perspective. Due to law and public policy, these shifts, based on research and political change, challenged professional practice where those abstractions are worked out "on the ground" between people. In a cultural-assimilationist perspective, professionals perpetuated the values of a dominant sociohistorical perspective, bringing others into that view through the legal and moral authority of the state. The policy of the state changed to a multicultural perspective requiring that professional practice move to valuing voluntary minorities that were both assimilating and accommodating to Canadian culture. In response to current policy and law under the charter (Secs. 15.1 and 15.2) (Government of Canada 1998), the provision of equities to involuntary minorities such as First Nations in Canada becomes a professional requirement to promote inclusivity. How does one begin to professionally value the culture and perspective of a minority that historically has been formally and publicly derided and oppressed? How can professionals from the majority or even an immigrant perspective begin to speak to that need if we do not understand some of the implications of Ogbu's (1982; 1983; 1992) claims that involuntary minorities are motivationally different from voluntary minorities such as immigrants? Consequently, the particular barriers faced by students from involuntary minority populations must be understood more particularly.

KNOWLEDGE SETS OF INSTRUCTIONAL EXPERTS

On of the greatest barriers I would suggest is the lack of reflectivity by the teachers and instructors about the cultural processes underlying their own practices. The types of knowledge that practitioners manage in their instruction and student interaction are pedagogical and discipline-specific, but that knowledge is also nested in other knowledges that are culturally constructed, as shown, for example, in Glatthorn's (1997a, 1997b) summary of teacher effectiveness, based on Shulman (1987), which identifies seven types of knowledge acquired by experienced teachers/instructors:

1. Content knowledge (e.g. knowing genetics).
2. Pedagogical content knowledge (knowing how to make genetics understandable and interesting to young adolescents).
3. General pedagogical knowledge (knowing strategies for managing student behaviour).
4. Curriculum knowledge (knowing the content of the district and state curricula).
5. Knowledge of learners and their characteristics.
6. Knowledge of educational contexts (knowing how schools and classrooms work).
7. Knowledge of educational aims, values, and their philosophical and historical grounds.

While both content knowledge and pedagogical content knowledge have been shown to be essential for teaching effectiveness (Grossman 1991), we know that post-secondary instructors are usually hired for their content expertise and rarely have pedagogical or androgogical training, which creates a rather large knowledge systems gap between the student and the instructor (Mezirow et al. 1990; Mezirow 1991a; 1991b; 1992; 1996; 1997). Other experts in the field have emphasised varied foci for teachers' professional development, including the following. (The list is not intended to be either exhaustive or prescriptive, and only selected sources are noted for each).

- The changing family and the special needs of children (Katz 1991; Pallas et al. 1995).
- New knowledge of human development (Sigel 1990).
- Multiculturalism and student diversity (Abi-Nader 1993).
- New and more effective methods of teaching (Elmore et al. 1996).

- Problem-solving strategies for improving schools (Joyce and Showers 1995).
- Problems and possibilities of teacher leadership (Wasley, 1991).
- Improvement of student learning (Renyi, 1996).
- Teacher's role in curriculum (Glatthorn, 1997).
- Technology and schooling (Meyrowitz, 1996).

Little can be taken for granted in a swiftly changing world where teaching is about mediating knowledge systems to and for students. The complexity of those systems suggests that good mediation requires a teacher/instructor not only to be fully grounded but also to be able to understand the students' ground and the interactional forces between those two positions to create multiple opportunities for learning.

MULTICULTURAL EDUCATIONAL LEADERSHIP—A LEARNING SITE FOR PROBLEM ANALYSIS

The challenge of speaking to educational leaders such as college instructors, who have both diverse academic backgrounds and the common purpose of providing educational leadership, brought me to the work of Dr Edwin D. Bell (School of Education, University of East Carolina), who teaches educational leadership at a postgraduate level and supplies a model for educational leadership development in multicultural teaching. Available on a website (Bell 1998), Bell's course on multicultural education provides syllabus, outline, bibliography, simulations, a reflection exercise and the Keirsey Temperament Sorter that allows you to take the test online and get a temperament classification for your results. This site gives us some idea of expectations of criteria for school and community cultural understanding for educational leadership.

Bell's instructional strategies include case studies, simulations, lectures, discussion and writing. Course objectives include discussion about the impact of culture on social and organisational interaction; identification and analysis of individual and cultural differences that affect teaching and learning; identification and analysis of instructional concepts and strategies for multicultural classrooms; identification and assessment of the elements of organisational culture. Competencies to be demonstrated are the ability to develop and implement a lesson plan with multicultural strategies; to diagnose the organisational culture of the school/college; to develop and implement an action plan to modify the culture of a school/college; to use Internet searches for instructional information, and to use e-mail; to use a spreadsheet to summarise, analyse and display data. For the practitioner, Bell's "reflection exercise" (based on Hidalgo's work on multicultural teacher introspection) presents some interesting questions (fifteen in all) designed to elicit reflection on how pervasive culture is as a perceptually and conceptually organising process.[5]

In his course content, Bell sets a high standard for educational leadership in the classroom in which the complexity of the problem is fully explored. Also, the personal interactional nature of the problem is investigated. Bell's bibliography demonstrates the depth and breadth of the issues, which include diversity, poverty, gender, developmental differences, individual and organisational levels, theory and practice, teaching methods and learning processes, organisational climate, institutions as collaborative cultures, restructuring, de-culturalisation and the struggle for equality, programme evaluation, etc.

FRAMES THROUGH WHICH TO "SEE": RECRUITMENT, RETENTION AND CURRICULUM

I have used Bell's course as an example of the depth and breadth of the problem as a means of analysis so that we can understand that it's not just a little tinkering with curriculum or a better transition programme or another First Nations (FN) instructor that will do the job. The complexity of the problem was recently addressed at a Western Canada First Nations Health Careers Symposium (UBC), involving academics, students, administrators, FN advisory committee members, provincial representatives from the ministry of skills, training and labour, federal government representatives from the ministry of health, and FN national and tribal representatives in an exercise that identified the barriers to FN health professional development and strategies to overcome barriers to recruitment, retention and curriculum. Issues discussed covered institutional culture, academic culture, programme structuring, curricular content, delivery methods, and structuring. The results of those discussions seem generalisable for the most part to post-secondary education. We will now look at issues of First Nations participation through the lenses or frames of recruitment, retention, and curriculum.

Recruitment

Recruitment of aboriginal students is a challenge of interest to the First Nations community and educational institutions. The population dynamics of First Nations make it the fastest growing and on average, the youngest group in Canada. First Nations are swiftly growing a potential pool of students for the local community colleges. This First Nations baby boom is occurring at a time in history when Canadians are institutionally short on money but long on the social capital of the non-Native baby boom. Understanding and meeting the needs of First Nations is a challenge for the existing social capital of the post-secondary education system. The manner in which those needs can be met through recruitment is illustrated by the examples briefly summarised below. The programmes are "the economy model," the Adult Education Program at Haa-huu-pay-ak, and "the deluxe model," the Faculty of Medicine of the University of Alberta. North Island College (Port Alberni) would most likely fall somewhere in between.

Adult Education Program at Haa-huu-pay-ak

The Adult Education programme at Haa-huu-pay-ak (1998) uses Open Learning Agency materials for Math and English in a setting of, by and for Nuu-chah-nulth (Ha-shilt-sa 1998). The social context and process underlying the academic work rests on the practice of the 4 R's: Reverence, Respect, Relevance, and Reciprocity (Archibald 1997; M.R. Atleo 1998), i.e., reverence by acknowledgment of the Creator; respect by cultural courtesy and acknowledgment of hereditary system; relevance by the embeddedness of the students in the learning activities; and reciprocity through sharing between segments of the community, age groups, First Nations of Nuu-chah-nulth and Coast Salish, institutional resources, etc. Some key programme features include visits by elders to pass on their cultural knowledge, use of local community resources (e.g., computer training), inclusion of families on site in social activities, integration of students into other institutions by taking courses at NIC, help to students in funding application, and sensorimotor learning of traditional crafts to link participants back to traditional resource use, with input from an indigenous East Coast healer/artist. Further, presentations by a Nuu-chah-nulth member who has gone through the educational system and developmental process allow students to apprehend normative expectations for their own transformational process. Similarly, there are talks by past graduates describing their personal experiences of academic success and describing the work they now do. These and similar items detailed in Ha-shilth-sa (1998) provide an emic perspective on Nuu-chah-nulth education, ideas, and strategies in the development of a Nuu-chah-nulth narrative about transformation into non-traditional modes of thought and occupations.

Aboriginal Recruitment Strategy—Faculty of Medicine, University of Alberta

The aboriginal programmes administrators at the University of Alberta employ some aggressive recruiting and retention strategies based in a national recruitment policy (1998), focusing on post-secondary students. According to the programme coordinator, admissions policy is key in that while complying with faculty policy it provides a flexibility and openness that allowed the greatest opportunity for applying First Nations people. A FN scholarship provides funding that can be used for admissions, and a whole host of services (programme planning, advocacy, personal counselling, referrals, assistance in finding summer jobs, etc) are geared for the FN student. The recruitment policy includes extensive promotional and marketing activity, career fairs and workshops. There is also intense networking, not only through aboriginal liaison workers but also interested faculty, to identify and enrol potentially promising applicants.

Such recruitment provides a legitimating framework in which to demonstrate the institution as an inclusionary context, to counter Chrisjohn, Towson and Peters's (1988) assertion that FN students generally find educational institutions "hostile" environments. However, E.R. Atleo's (1989) conclusion was that there was a need for a "theory of contexts" to explore the manner in which more inclusivity can be demonstrated institutionally to foster more student success. The lingering distrust by the indigenous community cannot be discounted. It is still preferred that programming be developed in indigenous settings and that the aspirations for self-governance include education.

Retention

The drop-out-drop-in pattern of educational participation that indigenous First Nations populations exhibit can be understood from a cultural perspective as differences in life-path trajectories. The timing of transitions through different cultural institutions regulates their articulation with the institutions of the larger society. The historical lack of cross-institutional mechanisms to bridge this gap has not yet been overcome because of its depth and breadth. E.R. Atleo (1989), using a time-series analysis of enrolment data for status Indians of the province of British Columbia, historiographically tested the hypothesis that as the educational systems and Canadian society in general became more inclusive, so FN enrolments and hence participation would increase. The findings were statistically significant. In the First Nations community such statistical significance can be seen in the social significance of the numbers of participants in post-secondary education. Chandler (1997) and Chandler and Lalonde (2000), in their epidemiological study of FN adolescent suicide, found an inverse relationship between the efforts of FN in the self-government process and adolescent suicide. Communities with greater involvement in land claims, self-government, local control of education, etc. were found to have lower adolescent suicide rates. E.R. Atleo's (1993) First Nations education study found that children who had a good sense of connectedness to their "historical selves" were more likely to do well in school. The complex relationships between First Nations communities, their past, the social institutional inclusion of the larger society, and the educational participation of First Nations students play themselves out ultimately in the classrooms between the instructors and the students.

As we understand the asynchronicity between indigenous life career trajectories and the non-indigenous sociohistorical career trajectories that shaped current educational institutions, we may better understand how to make such institutions more inclusive of life career trajectories that can accommodate diversity of more than one culture. E.R. Atleo (1989) pointed out that historically poor First Nations educational performance may (Ogbu, 1992) be related to perceptions of cultural threat or oppression. First Nations operating in a narrative mode of thought would perceive exclusion in the context of exclusively scientific thought in which their history is denied, denigrated, and devalued. Immigrant performance, on the other hand, may be better because their perceptions are that their culture is being enriched or enhanced by the scientific thought valued by school culture.

Barriers to educational participation identified in the First Nations Health Symposium (1998) coincided with Atleo's (1989) "theory of context" conceptualisation of "perceptions of inclusion." That one is excluded from another groups' activities until one is formally included through a show of respect may be at the heart of this issue. Barriers identified at the symposium included institutional culture, institutional system timing, sequencing, scheduling, administrative protocol, interpersonal social barriers between FN students and other students and between FN students and staff/faculty with heightened perceptions of power relations. Barriers originating in the FN community were also identified as lack of bi-cultural functioning, attitudes towards the education system as a legacy of residential school experience, Indian Act historical equation of "Indian status" and "primitive developmental state"; i.e., Indians who became professionals were automatically disenfranchised because now they were "civilised"!

Family and personal system developmental issues of the student can be seen as a barrier. Why try to keep indigenous students when they do not seem to be there? Helping to break down the cultural barriers of the institutional system is a place to start.

Curriculum

We have touched on inclusive dimensions that are social. How do those inclusive dimensions become part of the psychological process whereby knowledge is mediated and developed and exchanged? Consequently, I looked to the key to transmitting such through curriculum. As I seek to acknowledge the cultural aspects of cognition that impinge upon learning, there is a natural tendency to revisit the cultural meanings of words through etymological investigations going beyond the scientific surface of meaning, much in the way research is conducted. So, what is "curriculum"? The Oxford reference dictionary says that it is a "course of study." "Course" is further defined as: 1. An onward movement in space or time; a direction taken or intended; the direction or channel followed by a river; 2. The successive development of events, the ordinary sequence or order; a line of conduct or action; 3. A series of lectures, lessons, etc., in a particular subject; a sequence of medical treatment; 4. Each successive part of a meal. 5. A golf course, a race course. 6. A continuous row of masonry at one level in a building. And "study" is defined as: 1. To give one's attention to acquiring information or knowledge, especially from books. 2. The object of this; a thing worthy of study. 3. A work presenting the result of investigations into a particular subject; a preliminary drawing; a written or other portrayal of an aspect of behaviour or character, etc. 4. A musical composition designed to develop a player's skill. 5. A room used by a person for reading or writing, etc. (verb:). 1. To make a study of; to examine attentively; to apply one's self to study. 2. To give care and consideration to. 3. To deliberate carefully; to be intentionally contrived.

Thus, through this etymological exploration, we can see that while we have a tendency to "see" the word textually, it has spatial and temporal aspects, and the organisation of the perceptual field is very holistic. By convention English speakers associate "curriculum" with formal textual institutional processes organised in an orderly linear fashion. But when we look at the phenomenological field that the whole of the "definitions" organise there is room for many different ways to understand "curriculum."

The organisation of the phenomenological field that is usually dealt with only at the level of curriculum must be seen also at the larger levels of organisation. Marshall McLuhan said, "The medium is the message" (Meyrowitz 1996). For Indigenous students the curriculum begins with the spatial and temporal ordering of knowledge in a culturally relevant way. Thus, we can look at institutional strategies, programming strategies (intercultural and comparative), and instructional design strategies.

INSTITUTIONAL STRATEGIES

The development of a Canadian First Nations College system mimicking the Tribal College system in the United States is certainly an option in this day of virtual classrooms. Tribal Colleges are an educational strategy that has proven to be very successful for Native Americans in providing professional development and graduate school preparation. While there are some stand-alone First Nations post-secondary institutions, there still needs to be cross-institutional articulation within British Columbia. Even if stand-alone First Nations institutions increase, governance requirements such as course transferabilities will still require inter-institutional networking and cooperation.

PROGRAMMATIC STRATEGIES

The programmatic level strategies presented here are an intercultural curriculum strategy from an intercultural perspective, in which the Western biomedical model is privileged, and from a comparative perspective, in which Western and First Nations perspectives are both valued to provide a space in which First Nations students develop perspective resilience to deal with mainstream programming that privileges the Western scientific perspective.

Intercultural

One way of thinking about one curriculum and more than one culture is as intercultural curriculum. At the First Nations (FN) Health Careers symposium (First Nations House of Learning 1998), a microbiologist proudly presented the FN component of his faculty of medicine. They had managed to greatly increase the number of hours of FN Traditional Medicine into an expanded course on "Complementary Medicine" as part of a curriculum revision for MD qualifications. The First Nations medical and health career students were furious as a result of his presentation. The strategy looked acceptable in the context of privileging a biomedical model varying with local contexts. The microbiologist was perplexed. He had taken great pains to explain that, being from Northern Ireland with international teaching experience, he was very sympathetic to First Nations needs and aspirations. It was obvious that he had taken great effort to promote the integration of an FN component into this course that had only grudgingly been approved by the University Senate. In the curriculum, the integration of the FN component had effectively relegated the whole of the FN worldview and medical tradition into a technology that was complementary to the Western biomedical approach. Several aboriginal attendees, including a new medical doctor, a couple of masters of science entering medical school in the fall, some undergraduate students in science, and a psychologist, exclaimed that it was not substantive enough from a First Nations perspective. The content was not sufficient to ground FN students or to orient non-FN practitioners. A little smudging and sweat lodge experience combined with elders' talks does not, in the estimation of the students who had gone through such programmes, begin to prepare non-aboriginal professionals to deal with FN cultural products. They recommended a compulsory introductory course, including a sociopolitical history for the health careers field as a whole, especially in light of biomedical manifestations in oppressed populations of "diseases of civilisation" at epidemic levels, as well as contagious diseases. The ontological and epistemic barriers had not been overcome in the intercultural approach. For the newly developing UBC programme it was recommended that there be an FN Health I course modelled on the Malaspina Arts-One First Nations.

Comparative

The Malaspina University College Arts-One First Nations (1998) is a programme that allows First Nations students and non-Native students together to experience a comparative curriculum, which helps to make explicit the paradigmatic assumptions with a narrative approach that examines the ontological and epistemological issues right at the beginning of the students' college careers. The mainly narratorological approach allows students comparative experience with First Nations and non-First Nations perspectives through literature, stories, writing, elders' presentations and visitors. The programme includes elders in residence. First Nations cultural practices are used in the classroom as a part of the pedagogical approach. The development of textual skills and dvelopment of oral presentations skills are equally weighed in this programme. In the first year, the students developed, choreographed, and wrote lyrics, poetry and prose as part of a final production. The initial retention rate of the program was more than 90% because of the social solidarity that the programme encouraged, which resulted in high levels of peer support, faculty support, elder support and instructional support. The supports developed in this setting then provide a foundation for other courses.

The Arts-One First Nations Program was intended as a stand-alone programme providing transition into the college. Since the second year has no First Nations programming, second-year students clamoured for more programming with the comparative academic core and cultural support that allowed their successful development in the other courses. Consequently, after both teaching Arts-One First Nations for two years and student pressure, Richard Atleo worked to implement the FN core of the BA First Nations programme by providing a First Nations Traditional Ecological Knowledge and Resource Management component in the third year, and in the fourth year First Nations Families and Governance, with a BA essay a requirement for graduation. The first graduating class (1998) consisted of eight students.

The instruction approach is team teaching accomplished by matching First Nations instructors with non-First Nations secondments from other departments. The teaching team models different worldviews in their daily interaction. They model two different perspectives about content and two different cultural value systems in an atmosphere of academic and personal respect. The elders provide a moral frame and counsel for the teaching team and the students.

CONCEPTUAL STRATEGIES—INSTRUCTIONAL DESIGN

There are a couple of other approaches I want to identify that fall short of institutional and programme revision. They have to do with conceptual approaches to instruction through instructional design and a "levels of learning" approach to conceptual development. These approaches provide variety for the diversity found in the classroom. A reminder here may be appropriate about the diversity within the FN community in Port Alberni, which is a product of developmental histories and, consequently, the need for a range of strategies for instructors.

The material on Cognitive Teaching Models that I favour is borrowed mainly from Wilson and Cole (1996). As I mentioned at the beginning, there has been a development in the relationship between psychology and instructional design or curriculum development from the 1960s to the 1990s. Wilson and Cole (ibid.) divide this development into three eras, by the dominant paradigms, status of instructional design, status of instructional aspects of psychology, and the relationship between instructional design (curriculum development) and instructional (learning) psychology. Instructional psychology has developed in research on the process of instruction and learning and is not merely basic psychology applied to education. Only recently have psychologists and instructional designers begun to develop a substantive dialogue around situated cognition and constructivism. Some of the models identified are Cognitive Load Theory, Contextualized Instruction and Cognitive Apprenticeships, Problem-Based Learning, and Tools for Knowledge Building Communities. What follows are notes taken directly from Wilson and Cole's (1996) work and my commentary.

Traditional First Nations narrative learning and sensorimotor model development organises knowledge in ways that use mnemonic devices and culturally contextualised learning strategies. Moving into a different cultural context requires the development of a whole new schematic repertoire that must be learned from the bottom up. One of the most basic problems is that of cognitive overload that has no cultural experiential support. Consequently, the issue of cognitive load becomes an important limiting factor that needs to be understood and dealt with in instructional design.[6]

1. Cognitive Load Theory (CLT)—improving traditional instruction: information processing concepts of memory, schema development, and automaticity of procedural knowledge.
   - Limited working memory poses constraint on performance and learning capacity.
   - Mechanisms to circumvent limits are: schema acquisition (chunking) and automation of procedural knowledge.
   - For example, Sweller's (1989) model of Instructional Design.
   - Limited working memories make assimilation of multiple elements of information simultaneously difficult.
   - When multiple information elements interact they must be processed simultaneously creating heavy load.
   - High levels of element "interactivity" and resultant cognitive load may be inherent in content—weak methods of presentation and instruction may result in unnecessarily high overload.
   - Simple content best. If demands of content exceed limits of learner's working memory, learning does not occur (Sweller and Chandler 1994).
   - Instructional prescriptions: Analyse attentional demands of instruction; use single, coherent representations; eliminate redundancy.

- Provide for systematic problem space exploration instead of conventional repeated practice.
- Present animation and audio narration/text descriptions simultaneously rather than sequentially.
- Provide worked examples as alternatives to conventional problem-based instruction.
- Worked example: conventional—principle, concept, rule—followed by extensive practice on problem by applying rule.—"learning by doing" but CLT says "may hinder understanding of subject matter."—worked examples redirect attention from problem goal and toward problem state configurations and their associated moves (Sweller and Cooper 1985: 86) based on:
- Both schema acquisition and rule automation are blocks of skilled problem solving.
- Focus on problem solving not best way to acquire schemas or facilitate rule automation because inappropriate focus and heavy cognitive load.
- Alternatives to conventional problem solving must be carefully analysed and modified so they do not impose new problems.
- Format of instructional materials should be organised to minimise the need for students to attend to and mentally integrate disparate sources of information.[7]

Because traditional education was not "schooling" but delivered in the context of social life and development, the understanding of contextualised instruction and cognitive apprenticeships is a vital way to mediate the knowledge systems of non-Native culture and content to First Nations students.

2. Contextualized Instruction and Cognitive Apprenticeships.
   - Teaching tacit, heuristic knowledge as well as textbook knowledge.
   - Situated learning: teach knowledge and skills in contexts that reflect the way the knowledge will be useful in real life.
   - Modeling and explaining—show how a process unfolds and tell reasons why it happens that way.
   - Coaching: observe students as they try to complete tasks and provide hints and helps when needed.
   - Articulation—have students think about their actions and give reasons for their decisions and strategies.
   - Reflection: have students look back over their efforts to complete a task and analyse their own performance.
   - Exploration—encourage students to try out different strategies and hypotheses and observe their effects.
   - Sequence—present instruction in an ordering from simple to complex with increasing diversity and global before local skills.

- Sherlock—computer-coached practice environment developed to promote trouble- shooting skills of Air Force electronics technicians. Central feature is intelligent hyper-display—dynamical diagrams of the expert system in which the learner is working. Based in research on expert–novice differences.
    a. knowledge organisation and structures
    b depth of underlying principles
    c. quality of mental models
    d. efficiency of procedures
    e. automaticity to reduce attentional demands
    f. procedural knowledge
    g. procedures for theory change
    h. meta-cognitive skills
- Goal-Based Scenarios—combines elements of simulation, case-based reasoning and traditional Intelligent Tutoring System modelling techniques.
    a. Student given role to play.
    b. Student engages in simulation in order to solve the defined problem or achieve the goal interacting with agents and object in simulated environment.
    c. When student gets stuck a tutor is available to offer advice, tell stories, etc.
    d. Goal-based scenarios have been developed: Broadcast News, Sickle Cell counsellor, Yello.[8]

Moving from developing contextual maps and learning models from "expert" teachers and instructors who are intimately knowledgeable with the territory of the issues leads into the movement through such territories with problem solving by defining and structuring emergent domains.

3. Problem-Based Learning—to address ill-structured problems and/or ill-structured domains (or, I would say, "emergent domains") with the following characteristics:
    - Defining problem requires more information than initially available.
    - Nature of problem unfolds over time.
    - No single, right way to get the information.
    - As new information is obtained, the problem changes.
    - Decisions must be make in the absence of definitive knowledge.
    - There may never be certainty about having made the right choices.
    - Medicine, business, education, architecture, law, engineering, and social work are using this model as well as high school—in medicine because ill-structured problems in ill-structured and ever-expanding domains require life-long learning skills.

- Students work cooperatively in small groups working on both content (science knowledge) and skills (examining/diagnosing patients, meta-cognitive skills such as self-monitoring, reflections, and resource allocation). Authenticity is critical in motivating students. Process:
  a. problem formulation—isolation of important facts
  b. self-directed learning through group membership
  c. problem re-examination as group members reorient
  d. abstraction—articulation of comparisons and contrasts
  e. reflection—debriefing and identifies areas for improvement
4. Tools for Knowledge-Building Communities—three metaphors for communication:
  a. as transmission of information—a message over time and distance conveyed from one person to another,
  b. as ritual—where the content is less than the manner in which it is presented,
  c. as transformation—in which the sender and receiver are transformed as they share goal of learning and knowledge generation.
- Epistemic games—culturally patterned—generate new knowledge by participating in certain defined cultural patterns or forms—epistemic forms: contain new knowledge and adhere to defined structures accepted by the community. Generating these forms is called epistemic games in which a set of rules or conventions allows the generation of a given epistemic form: Three types:
- Structural analysis—what are the components of a system?
    Lists; spatial decomposition; temporal decomposition; compare and contrast; cost-benefit analysis; primitive elements; cross products; axiom systems.
- Functional analysis—how are the elements in a system related to each other?
- Critical-event—identify causes leading to event or consequences from event.
- Cause and effect—distinguish between causes and preconditions.
- And/or graphs—break an event into problems and actions to solve.
- Form and function—distinguish between objects, structure and purpose.
- Process analysis—how does the system behave?
- Systems-dynamics—model a system showing how variables +/-; feedback.
- Aggregate behaviour—model a system showing how interactive events affect system.
- Situation-action—model a situation by a set of rules to apply in various cases.

- Trend/cyclical—model the relationships between variables to show change over. time—linear, exponential, cyclical or growth.

Morrison and Collins (1995) argue apropos epistemic games:
a. Eurocentric culture supports numerous way of constructing knowledge.
b. Ways of constructing knowledge are culturally patterned.
c. Different contexts (communities of practice) support different ways of knowing and different epistemic games.
d. Goal of education is to become epistemically fluent.
e. Does the environment foster or inhibit epistemic fluency?
f. Playing of epistemic games exhibits following:
(a) Constraints to playing; (b) entry conditions; (c) "allowable moves"; (d) players may transfer; (e) game playing results in the generation of a defined epistemic form.
- Utility to teachers: (a) useful as diagnostic/interpretive device; (b) targeting game-playing as a learning device.
- Computer supported intentional learning environments (CSILE).
Designed to support the high-level, knowledge-generating activity resulting from question-asking process where students can learn and exercise meta-cognitive skills.

Summary

Design and implementation are inseparable. Choosing a model is closely tied to the curriculum question–learning goals, which requires that consensus on the kind of learning to be sought between sponsors and members of the learning community itself. Deciding upon a teaching model and making decisions within that framework is a highly situated activity. Each teaching model is a particular blend of costs and outcomes. Instruction should support learners as they become efficient in procedural performance and deliberate in their self-reflection and understanding. Successful programmes must seek to make complex performance doable while avoiding the pitfalls of simplistic proceduralisation. Scaffolding—a key problem that is not yet well understood. Appropriate and wise scaffolding helps to keep learners in the critical development zone (Vygotsky, 1978). Implementation of teaching models must also be supported so the model does not do violence to the situation. A constructivist agenda and authentic, meaningful tasks bring into focus the novice performance within a complex environment. Values of the cultures of individuals and groups are a major challenge that goes to the very root of educational thought and practice. The need to deal with the order of business that has been presented requires us to reach deep, and that is a challenge. And yes, it will undoubtedly require a shift of some sort. But what sort of a shift is the question.

EPISTEMIC STRATEGIES—META-THEORETICAL THEORISING

New theory that organises previous theoretical formulations in ways that suit current purposes can promote a paradigmatic shift. The neo-piagetian work of interactionists and constructivists come together in the work of Campbell and Bickhard (1986) in a "Knowing Levels" framework in which reflective abstraction allows a type of bootstrapping to new levels of thinking. This perspective takes us well beyond Bloom's taxonomy. Especially when we are dealing with adults who are functioning at high levels in one domain but lower levels in other domains, this conceptualisation allows us to understand the "bootstrapping" process between domains and to participate in the scaffolding process that will lead to student success.

This concept is nicely presented in Bereiter and Scardamalia (1992) for those that want a technical explanation of the phenomenon of helping others move to higher levels of knowing, based in the Knowing levels approach by Campbell and Bickhard (1989). I come at it from a more narrative approach, namely, from the perspective of the discourse of elders providing a post-formal operational level or Level 7 as a "way of knowing goal." At Level 7, knowledge is a semi-autonomous artifact. "Students recognise that knowledge objects, like other constructed objects, can take on a life of their own and may be considered independently of their personal relevance. Thus, at this level, knowledge objects become things that one can relate to, use, manipulate, judge in various ways, and have feelings about—just like other things in the real world." At Level 6, knowledge is an improvable personal artifact. "A theory or other knowledge object is viewed in terms of what it can and cannot do, what its virtues are and where it is in need of improvement, although still viewed as a personal possession." At Level 5, knowledge is a personal artifact. "Although constructivism is widely endorsed by teachers, it is not common for young students to view themselves as constructors of knowledge. Viewing oneself as constructing knowledge is a large step beyond viewing oneself as constructing knowledge representations." At Level 4, knowledge is viewable from different perspectives. "Students see that the same knowledge can appear in different contexts and can be viewed from different perspectives. This is an important step toward objectification." At Level 3, knowledge is representable. "In trying to communicate what they know to a reader, students take into account what the reader already knows and is in a position to understand. Thus knowledge is no longer just something in the head to be expressed but is something to be represented, shared, interpreted by others." At Level 2, knowledge is an itemisable, mental content. "Children can relate things they know about a topic and often delight in doing so. Thus, implicitly, knowledge consists of sortable items." At Level 1 knowledge is an individual mental state. "Children realise that one person may know something that another does not. Thus, implicitly, there is some entity—a fact—which a person may or may not know." At Level 0, knowledge is equivalent to "the way things are." "Thoughts are distinguished from thinking, but thoughts about things are not distinguished from the way things are; hence, the possibility of false belief is not recognised." "Historically objectification has emerged over the course of many centuries." It has been assumed that individuals must move in locked step through this developmental process in consecutive order. Those of us with an "elder" model of cognition have experienced the highest levels and hold them as a value for cognitive processing. This "elder" model does not suggest a high level of understanding subject matter or skill in working with the knowledge, but it does allow one to take a positive, constructive role in the pursuit of understanding and purposeful activities that promote knowledge-processing skills.

CONCLUSION

In this case study I have tried to show some processes for respectful intercultural learning both for the institutions of the dominant culture and indigenous peoples. While I have provided a personal perspective of the problem of indigenous First Nations recruitment, retention and curriculum, that perspective has been informed by FN and mainstream theory that I trust will provide both a professional orientation to the issues and also permits indigenous entry into the discourse. The constructivist model seems very compatible with the way I was oriented by my elders to FN culture as a "novice/cultural child" of eighteen and fits well with current theory in instructional design I had much to learn in their eyes, and of course I am not finished yet. Their teachings, reflected in the 4 R's of Reverence, Respect, Relevance and Reciprocity, have stood me well over the years, helping to keep me balanced and connected to the community while not constraining my personal and academic development. We have much to learn about cultures interacting in our educational system, but as educational leaders both from the dominant culture and indigenous communities with a mandate for providing equities in education, the problem of programming for indigenous students in local college is a special challenge. I have taken a problem analysis approach and presented the problem in a way that showed some of the educational objectives and strategies from both cultures. "We are all here to stay" and it is time we got on with collaborating on those new spaces we will create together, these new communities of learning. The major strategy is developing a discourse of cooperation in which indigenous peoples can participate more equitably.

NOTES TO CHAPTER 7

1. First Nations populations in British Columbia, Canada, for the most part never signed treaties historically. There is currently a modern-day treaty process in place whereby the government of Canada, British Columbia and First

Nations are negotiating treaties. First Nations members will then ratify these negotiated agreements.
2. Dr Sayers was active on Alberta Treaties 6, 7 and 8 and has also worked on indigenous human rights issues with the UN in Geneva, in recognition of whose unique contribution by a First Nations woman Queens University (Canada) awarded her an honorary degree.
3. In particular, the Hupacasath representatives, the college administration, the attendees, and North Island College coordinator, Mac Newton.
4. This incident happened twenty-five years ago and the scene still motivates me to use it as an example.
5. Bell's "*Reflection Exercise*" (in Bell 1998):
    1. Where were you born and what difference has that location made in your life?
    2. What language or dialects were spoken in your home and how did they affect you?
    3. Where did you grow up, what was your neighbourhood like, and what affect have they had on your assumptions, perceptions, values?
    4. What is your ethnic or racial heritage and what impact has it had on your life?
    5. Was religion important during your upbringing? If yes, how?
    6. Who makes up your family and how do they affect your life?
    7. What traditions are important to your family?
    8. What values are important to your family?
    9. How do members of your family relate to each other?
    10. How is love expressed?
    11. How is your culture expressed in your family?
    12. How does your cultural heritage influence how you perceive and understand others?
    13. What are your values and beliefs and how do they affect your behaviour toward people?
    14. What is your definition of normal?
    15. How do you think about differences in people i.e., are some differences actually deficiencies? If yes, which ones?

    Reading these questions out loud and reflecting particularly on ones own responses to the indigenous or minority learner population is a useful reflective exercise.
6. See web site: http://www.cudenver.edu/~bwilson/hndbkch.html, for the complete article this material is summarised from.
7. A critique of Sweller and Cooper (1985) is that teaching problem–solving may be like teaching babies to talk (Bereiter and Scardamalia, 1992).
8. I think that the *Tomb Raider* computer games that my grandchildren play fit into this category with a lot of others.

REFERENCES

Abi-Nader, J. 1993. Meeting the Needs of Multicultural Classrooms: Family Values and the Motivation of Minority Students. In J.J. O'Hair and S.J. Odell (eds.), *Diversity and Teaching: Teacher Education Yearbook 1*. New York: Harcourt Brace Jovanovich.

Akan, L. 1992. Pimosatamowin in Sikaw Kakeequaywin: walking and talking, a Saulteaux elder's view of native education. *Canadian Journal of Native Education* 19 (2): 191–215.

Apter, M.J. 1982. *The Experience of Motivation: The Theory of Psychological Reversals.* New York: Academic Press.
Apter, M.J. 1989. *Reversal Theory: Motivation, Emotion, and Personality.* New York: Routledge.
Apter, M.J. 1993. Phenomenological Frames and the Paradoxes of Experience. In J.H. Kerr, S. Murgatroyd and M.J. Apter (eds.), *Advances in Reversal Theory.* Amsterdam: Swets and Zeitlinger.
Archibald, J. 1997. Coyote Learns to Make a Storybasket: The Place of First Nations Stories in Education. Unpublished dissertation. Vancouver: Simon Fraser University.
Atleo, E.R. 1989. Grade 12 Enrolments of Status Indians in British Columbia: 1949–1985. Unpublished doctoral dissertation. Vancouver, B.C.: University of British Columbia.
Atleo, E.R.1993. An Examination of Native Education in British Columbia: Kindergarden–Grade 12 Readiness and Self-image and Academic Achievement. Vancouver: Native Brotherhood and Sisterhood of British Columbia.
Atleo, E.R., and M.R. Atleo. 1997. Negotiating Spaces to Live: First Nations Adult Programming. Paper presented at Annual Conference of the Comparative and International Education Society (Western Region), University of Southern California, 14 November 1997.
Atleo, M.R. 1993. The Effects of Social Role Attitudes on the Planning Behavior of First Nations Mothers. Unpublished master's thesis. Vancouver, B.C.: University of British Columbia.
Atleo, M.R. 1998. A Reversal Theory Approach to Adult Learning and Education. Proceedings of the Canadian Association Society for the Study of Adult Education, 29 May 1998, Ottawa, Ontario.
Bell, E.D. 1998. Home page of Leadership Education Course: LEED 7460—School and Community Cultures. Available at: http://150.216.8.1/schofed/leed/7460sylbell.html (accessed 2 November 1998).
Bereiter, C., and M. Scardamalia. 1996. Student-constructed Learning Environment (With On-line Support for the Teacher). OISE CISLE site.
Berry, J.W. 1990. The Psychology of Acculturation. In R.A. Dienstbier and J.J. Berman (eds.), *Cross-cultural Perspectives. Nebraska Symposium on Motivation,* 1989, Vol. 37. Lincoln and London: University of Nebraska Press.
Bracken, C. 1997. *The Potlatch Papers: A Colonial Case History.* Chicago: University of Chicago Press.
Campbell, R.L., and M.H. Bickhard 1986. *Knowing Levels and Developmental Stages. Contributions to Human Development.* Basel: Karger.
Chandler, M. 1997. Continuities of Selfhood in the Face of Radical Developmental and Cultural Change. Presented at symposium Identity Development and Sociocultural Diversity: Cultural and Transcultural Constraints on the Construction of the Self. 27th Annual Symposium of The Jean Piaget Society, 19–21 June 1997, Santa Monica, California.
Chandler, M.J., and C. Lalonde. 1998. Cultural Continuity as a Hedge against Suicide in Canada's First Nations. *Transcultural Psychiatry* Vol 35, m 2, 199–219.
Chrisjohn, R., S. Towson, S., and M. Peters. 1988. Indian Achievement in Schools: Adaptation to Hostile Environments. In J. W. Berry, S. Irvine, and E.B. Hunt (eds.), *Indigenous Cognition: Functioning in Cultural Context.* Dordrecht: Nijhoff.
Cole, M. 1996. *Cultural Psychology: A Once and Future Discipline.* Cambridge, MA: Belknap Press of Harvard University Press.
Elmore, R.F., P.L. Peterson, and S.J. McCarthey. 1996. *Restructuring in the Classroom: Teaching, Learning, and School Organization.* San Francisco: Jossey Bass.

First Nations House of Learning (FNHL). 1998. First Nations Longhouse at University of British Columbia.
Glatthorn, A.A. 1997a. *The Principal as Curriculum Leader.* Thousand Oaks, CA: Corwin.
Glatthorn, A.A. 1997b. Graduate Study and Teacher Effectiveness. E. Carolina University School of Education, Leadership Education web site.
Golla, S. 1987. He Has a Name: History and Social Structure Among the Indians of Western Vancouver Island. Unpublished Ph.D. dissertation. Columbia University.
Government of Canada 1998. Charter of Rights and Freedoms. Available at: http://canada.gc.ca/danadiana/faitc/fa14.html (accessed 3 November 1998).
Gray, J. 1995. *Men Are from Mars and Women Are from Venus.* New York: Basic Books.
Ha-shilt-sa 1998. Adult Education Program at Haa-huu-pay-ak. 7 May 1998.
Hebb, D.O. 1955. Drives and the CNS (Central Nervous System). *Psychological Review* 62: 243–254.
Indian and Northern Affairs Canada (INAC). 1996. Backgrounder: Protocol agreement to establish a common table. Available at: Http://www.inac.gc.ca/news/sept96/9641bk2.html (accessed 17 March 1998).
Indian Association of Alberta. 1970. Policy Paper, a.k.a. "Red Paper." Presented to the Minister of Indian Affairs and Northern Development, Ottawa, Canada.
Institute of Indigenous Governments. 1998. Available at: http://www.indigenous.bc.ca
Joyce, B., and B. Showers. 1995. *Student Achievement through Staff Development: Fundamentals of School Renewal.* 2nd ed. White Plains, NY: Longman.
Katz, L.G. 1991. Pedagogical Issues in Early Childhood Education. In S.L. Kagan (ed.), *The Care and Education of America's Young Children: Obstacles and Opportunities. Ninetieth yearbook of the National Society for the Study of Education.* Chicago: University of Chicago Press.
Kuhn, T.S. 1962. *Structure of Scientific Revolutions.* Chicago: University of Chicago Press.
Lakoff, G., and M. Johnson. 1980. *Metaphors We Live By.* Chicago: University of Chicago Press.
Lather, P. 1991. *Getting Smart: Feminist Research and Pedagogy with/in the Postmodern.* New York: Routledge.
Lightning, W. 1992. Compassionate Mind: Implications of a Text Written by Elder Louise Sunchild. *Canadian Journal of Native Education* 19 (2): 215–252.
McShane, D., and J.W. Berry. 1988. Native North Americans: Indian and Inuit Abilities. In S.H. Irvine and J.W. Berry (eds.), *Human Abilities in Cultural Context.* New York: Cambridge University Press.
Magic-eye. 1998. Magic-eye Stereograms home page. http://www.magiceye.com/3dfun (accessed 3 November 1998).
Malaspina University College. 1998. First Nations Studies Department Home Page. Available at: http://www.mala.bc.ca/www/discover/firstnat/welcome.htm (accessed 3 November 1998).
Meyrowitz, J. 1996. Taking McLuhan and 'Medium Theory' Seriously: Technological Change and the Evolution of Education. In S.T. Kerr (ed.), *Technology and the Future of Schooling: Ninety-fifth Yearbook of the National Society for the Study of Education.* Chicago: University of Chicago Press.
Mezirow, J. 1991a. *Transformative Dimensions of Adult Learning.* San Francisco: Jossey-Bass.

Mezirow, J. 1991b. Transformation Theory and Cultural Context. *Adult Education Quarterly* 41 (3): 180–192.
Mezirow, J. 1992. Transformation Theory: Critique and Confusion. *Adult Education Quarterly* 42 (4): 250–252.
Mezirow, J. 1996. Contemporary Paradigms of Learning. *Adult Education Quarterly* 46 (3): 158–173.
Mezirow, J. 1997. *Transformative Learning in Action: Insights from Practice. An Update on Adult Learning Theory.* New Directions for Adult and Continuing Education No. 57. San Francisco: Jossey-Bass.
Mezirow, J., et al. 1990. *Fostering Critical Reflection in Adulthood: A Guide to Transformative and Emancipatory Learning.* San Francisco: Jossey-Bass.
Miller, J.M. 1996. *Shingwaulk's Vision: A History of Native Residential Schools.* Toronto: CANADA.
More, A. 1987. Native Indian Learning Styles: A Review for Researchers and Teachers. *Journal of American Indian Education* 27 (1): 17–29.
Morrison, D., and A. Collins. 1995. Epistemic Fluency and Constructivist Learning Environments. In B.G. Wilson (ed.), *Constructivist Learning Environments: Case Studies in Instructional Design.* Englewood Cliffs, NJ: Educational Technology Publications.
N. E. Thing Enterprises. 1995. *Magic Eye: A New Bag of Tricks.* Overland Park, Kans.: Andrews and McMeel.
Nuu-chah-nulth Tribal Council. 1996. *Nuu-chah-nulth Residential School Research.* Port Alberni, B.C.: Nuu-chah-nulth Health Board.
Oatley, K. 1996. Inference in Narrative and Science. In D.R. Olson and N. Torrance (eds.), *Modes of Thought: Explorations in Culture and Cognition.* Cambridge: Cambridge University Press.
Ogbu, J.U. 1982. Cultural Discontinuities and Schooling. *Anthropology and Education Quarterly* 13 (4): 290–307.
Ogbu, J.U. 1983. Minority Status and Schooling in Plural Societies. *Comparative Education Review* 27 (2): 168–190.
Ogbu, J.U. 1992. Understanding Cultural Diversity and Learning. *Educational Researcher* 21 (8): 5–14, 24.
Olson, D.R., and N. Torrance (eds.) 1996. *Modes of Thought: Explorations in Culture and Cognition.* London: Cambridge University Press.
Pallas, A. M., G. Natriello, and E.L. McDill 1995. Changing Students/Changing Needs. In E. Flaxman and A.H. Passow (eds.), *Changing Populations Changing Schools: Ninety-fourth Yearbook of the National Society for the Study of Education.* Chicago: University of Chicago Press.
Province of British Columbia. 1998. Ministry of Aboriginal Affairs Home Page. Available at: http://www.aaf.gov.bc.ca/aaf (accessed 3 November 1998).
Renyi, J. 1996. *Teachers Take Charge of their Learning: Transforming Professional Development for Student Success.* Washington, D.C.: National Foundation for the Improvement of Education.
Shulman, L.S. 1987. Knowledge and Teaching: Foundations of the New Reform. *Harvard Educational Review* 57: 1–22.
Schultz, M., and M.J. Hatch 1996. Living with Multiple Paradigms: The Case of Paradigm Interplay in Organizational Culture Studies. *Academy of Management Review* 21 (2): 529–548.
Sigel, I.E. 1990. What Teachers Need to Know about Human Development. In D. Dill et al. (eds.), *What Teachers Need to Know.* San Francisco: Jossey-Bass.
Sproat, G.M. 1868. *Scenes and Studies of Savage Life.* London: Smith, Elder and Co.
Sweller, J. 1989. Cognitive Tchnology: Some Procedures for Facilitating Learning and Problem Solving in Mathematics and Science. *Journal of Educational Psychology* 81 (4): 457–466.

Sweller, J., and P. Chandler. 1994 Why Some Material Is Difficult to Learn. *Cognition and Instruction* 12 (3): 185–233.
Sweller, J., and G.A. Cooper. 1985. the Use of Worked Examples as a Substitute for Problem-Solving in Learning Algebra. *Cognition and Instruction* 2 (1): 59–89.
Tully, J. 1995. *Strange Multiplicity: Constitutionalism in an Age of Diversity.* London: Cambridge University Press.
Turner, M. 1998. website: http://www.wam.umd.edu/~mturn (accessed 3 November 1998).
Vygotsky, L. 1978. *Mind in Society: The Development of Higher Psychological Processes.* Cambridge, MA: Harvard University Press.
Wasley, P.A. 1991. *Teachers Who Lead: The Rhetoric of Reform and the Realities of Practice.* New York: Teachers College Press.
Wilson, B.G. and P. Cole. 1996. Cognitive Teaching Models. In D.H. Jonassen (ed.) *Handbook of Research in Instructional Technology.* New York: Scholastic Press.

8 Notes on the Role of the Teacher in Indigenous School Education[1]

Edmundo Antônio Peggion

In these procedures, it may be noted that strictly speaking we arrive not at pictures of the individual but at pictures of the events in which the individual is involved. This inconsistency disappears when we realise that the term 'personality' refers not to the isolated individual but to the individual in the world. (Bateson 1965 [1936]: 274)

CULTURE AND EDUCATION

It is at the intersection between education and culture that lies the central point in a discussion about the educational processes in which indigenous peoples have recently involved themselves. Both terms carry with them an idea of a set of values and traditions, either internal or external, which need to be considered when working with indigennous peoples. Much has been said about indigenous school education, the experiences and results of programmes which are currently being developed in Brazil, but what is the impact of these processes? By virtue of their novelty, there are few systematic studies that address key structural questions.

Iindigenous school education programmes usually serve to train teachers who will work in schools in indigenous villages. What has been happening is that courses have been run for teachers who belong to either one or a number of indigenous peoples, being supervised by specialists in diverse subject areas, and always having anthropologists and linguists available. The second step of the process, when teachers are in their own communities using the skills acquired in their own training, still has not been the subject of research. Likewise, it is also necessary to locate the place of the teacher, and not just of the school, within indigenous societies.

Today in Brazil, indigenous school education is taking up ever more space in anthropological discussion, less because of a particular interest in the discipline than because of the ever more effective demands of involved populations.

As a function of contact with another society, the school is in itself a new element in indigenous societies. However, this does not in itself mean that education does not exist where there is no school; instead, it is the school institution that does not exist, because it is historically associated with the state and Western society (Durkheim 1976 [1922]: 34–6). In this way, if we think of the school, associated with the state and, in a way, reproducing Western society, how can it fit itself into another society which needs to affirm itself vis-à-vis that same West (cf. Meliá 1989; Silva 1994; Silva & Azevedo 1995)?

As a new element in indigenous societies, the school is given a different meaning from that given by Western society. In some cases, shamans and teachers are placed in the category of "dangerous persons," as both have a relationship with different worlds, the former with the supernatural world and the latter with the "outside" (Gow 1991). To understand the school in these societies, it is necessary to understand its cultural, historical and social context.

Directly linked to forms of social organisation, the traditional education process creates a point of contact which is necessary because of contact with another society. There are new values and codes that need to be appropriated so that the group, faced by a new situation, knows how to place themselves. Thus, indigenous school aims for more than a simple learning of reading, writing and arithmetic:

> If, today, indigenous peoples want schools and literacy, and, at times, ask for this forcefully, it is very probable that for them it would have other purposes—not necessarily educational. (Meliá 1995: 151, my translation)

Based on similar references, this article attempts an analysis of "Projeto Tucum," focusing on its actuation in the region inhabited by the Shavante People, based in Água Boa, Mato Grosso. The observations are the result of my own participation as consultant and lecturer on the programme between 1995 and 1996.

"PROJETO TUCUM"

Indigenous school education began in the colonial period, always with the aim of assimilating indigenous peoples into encompassing society. This political standpoint was still the main model for the education programme until around the 1980s, when, through the action of organised indigenous movements and with the support of non-governmental indigenist support organisations, the picture began to change (Monserrat 1989: 249; Kahn & Franchetto 1994: 6).

According to Kahn and Franchetto (ibid.: 7), there are today two approaches in the field of indigenous school education. The first is the official one, carried out by agencies such as FUNAI (National Indian Foundation—Fundação Nacional do Índio) and state and municipal bureaus, together with religious institutions, which transport "rural school" or bilingual education models into indigenous schools with the intention of translating the Bible. The second approach is that which emerged in the 1980s, through organised non-governmental social movements which, supporting and advising indigenous populations, has been principally stimulating the training of indigenous teachers, giving supervision to the schools and collaborating in the definition of specific curricula.

Nevertheless, due to a closer relationship between the state and non-governmental organisations, the profile of indigenous school education programmes is changing. "Projeto Tucum," for example, develops both approaches mentioned above simultaneously. Prepared in the light of the ideas of the 1988 Constitution, it brings to bear the indigenous peoples' right to an education that is specific and discrete. In this programme there is, concurrently, the involvement of state and municipal education authorities, religious institutions traditionally associated with assimilationist views, along with the participation of a number of organised non-governmental social movements, which originated in the 1980s, as well as the participation of the indigenous populations, all jointly introducing changes in proposals for school education.

"Projeto Tucum" began in 1995 and was planned to end in 1999. It is co-ordinated by the government of the state of Mato Grosso, and works with municipal prefectures, universities, non-governmental organisations and religious missions. The proposed aim is to enable and qualify indigenous teachers, who work or will work in their own communities, to a professional standard.

The proposed curriculum for the trainees foresees the inclusion of elements of indigenous and other cultures, along with the teaching of mother tongue literacy and Portuguese. The intention is to further the development of the student in his or her own cultural universe, as well as allowing a selective and critical appropriation of elements from other societies.

The emergence of a programme of such size, which proposes responses to the demands of the indigenous peoples concerning education, is of fundamental importance. We have, in fact, a paradox; at times, the trainees have been asking for traditional teaching, defined by them as a "white school" (*escola de branco*), while the consultants on the programme have been presenting them with a new model of school education, based on the construction of knowledge. The questions already asked about school in our society are now appearing in indigenous villages. It is possible to find an answer to the suspicions of indigenous teachers in the aspirations of these populations, who are asking to learn a method and a reflection that take Western traditional teaching as their reference point.

These apparently unimportant questions, e.g., the process of learning through systems of observation and repetition, which our society considers to have transcended, would not have been raised had they not already been the norm in indigenous societies. According to Lévi-Strauss (1986: 382), learning occurs partly through the diffuse imitation of adults, and partly, traumatically, during initiation rituals. Command of techniques by all members of a society enables each individual to be creative on his or her own (Lévi-Strauss, ibid.: 383). The training of a teacher creates a new category within these societies, forming hierarchies in the existing relations of collective knowledge. Unlike the shaman, who forms part of the traditional system, the teacher, together with the school, needs firstly to be classified in order to be included in the network of social relations

AN EXAMPLE

One of the regional centres of "Projeto Tucum" is in the town of Água Boa and serves only the Shavante, a people who speak a Jê language and call themselves A'uwe. The descendants of a group made up of Shavante and Xerente, which split in the 19th century (Maybury-Lewis 1984: 40; Lopes da Silva 1992: 365), the Shavante live in a region of the State of Mato Grosso, in a number of villages and indigenous lands. For Maybury-Lewis (1984), who carried out his fieldwork mainly in the 1950s and 1960s, Shavante society consists of unstable conjunctures without any generalised political unity whatsoever.

Shavante have many internal divisions, resulting from their patrilineal social organisation, whereby a man and his male forebears and descendants form a patrilineage, which defends its interests within the group. Each patrilineage thus defined is a faction which, in the general social scheme, is fragmented through marriage. A man, after finally accepting marriage, must live in the house of his wife's father, i.e., uxorilocally. Offspring, moreover, have a close relationship with their parents, support them politically, and are born into a domestic group[2] in which the father is a "stranger" (Maybury-Lewis, ibid.: 145). It is in the domestic group that an important element of factional dichotomy can be seen; the relationship between sister's husband and wife's brother and between inter-generational affines is formally constructed through etiquette, that is, when these groups meet, the one cannot directly approach the other (Maybury-Lewis, ibid.: 150–151). These relationships are always between members of different clans, an important reference for the understanding of Shavante society.

Shavante society is made up of three clans, divided into two moieties. These clans, according to Maybury-Lewis (ibid.: 221), are called *Poredza'ono* (toad-spawn), *Öwawë* (Rio das Mortes) and *Topdató* (circle of the eye). At birth, everyone belongs to his or her father's clan and must marry into the opposing clan. As *Öwawë* and *Topdató* belong to the same group, they may only marry *Poredza'ono*, and the latter only with people of the other two.

Clan definition characterises a division in the society between the individual's group and its opposing group (Maybury-Lewis, ibid.: 222). This division is a basic reference that enables understanding of Shavante society, but it is not the only division to be found.

The Shavante are organised in age-grades arranged hierarchically—birth (*ai'uté*), child (*'watébrémi*), pre-adolescent (*ai'repudu*), adolescent (*wapté*), young adults (*'ritéi'wa*), "sponsor" (*danhohui'wa*), adult (*ïprédu*) and old age (*ïhire*) (Giaccaria 1990: 25). Of these, the main age-sets are called *wapté, 'ritéi'wa* and *danhohui'wa*, the last being the age-set of the "sponsors" of the *wapté* (Giaccaria, ibid.: 25). There are also the age-grades Hötörã, Tirowa, Etepa, Abare'u, Nodzoiu, Anarowa, Tsada'ro and Ai'rere. Members of these age-grades hold relationships which combine hostility between adjacent groups and co-operation between alternate groups (Maybury-Lewis 1984: 213). This results in the formation of two groups, which are active in ritual life. When the *wapté* move to the unmarried men's house, cornerstone of the system, they are introduced into society.

In the unmarried men's house, *hö*, the boy learns to hunt, sing and manipulate elements of the ceremonial universe—learns in fact to be "a good Xavante" (Maybury-Lewis, ibid.: 160–161). It is during this phase of life that the young men initiate a formal friendship with an individual of his own age-grade and belonging to another clan. This relationship, called *ï'amõ*, will last for his whole life (Maybury-Lewis, ibid.: 158).

EDUCATION AND CULTURE

One of Shavante's main concerns during one of the intensive stages of the course was related to the *wapté* age-grade, considered to be a time of learning and understanding and of the creation of a collective spirit in relation to the members of the same age-set. There is, seemingly, a parallel between the *hö*, the unmarried men's house, and the school, as both are spaces of learning. The difference lies in who teaches in each, and in what is taught.

During the beginning of the training course offered by "Projeto Tucum," one of the main problems was the presence of teachers for the whole of the training. This was due to Shavante factions, who can decide to change the teacher even while the course is being run. However, on the part of the leaders there was no decision-making in relation to the individual who would participate in training, but only concerning Shavante society as a whole. Thus, insofar as it altered the political composition of the communities, new names could be put forward to take part in training. Here we can see the effecting of decisions other than simply relating to the training of a teacher. This position—teacher—seems to be part of a large sociological project, which is implicated in categories that are going to extend outside the limits of the social system. The teacher is s/he who makes the transfer of information between two different systems. Given the present circumstances, his or her status, in many cases earning a salary and having a command of Western codes, is raised significantly. However, it should be considered whether this prestige is accorded because the individual is a teacher, or whether s/he is a teacher because s/he was already prestigious as the result of his/her relationships within the group?

Another determining factor in Shavante's training is the relationship between inter-generational affines. When an individual is facing his wife's father, real or classificatory, he must not approach him directly. This behaviour is very important for Shavante in the establishment of attitudes linked to kinship relations. Therefore, during the undertaking of a training course, work groups are organised exclusively by students. In this way uncomfortable situations, such as the meeting of inter-generational affines, are avoided. In such a situation there would be no way of jointly discussing work. As it ended up happening, the alternative found by indigenous teachers was very clear from the point of view of intercultural relations: if you cannot speak with your wife's father, write to him. Far from being banal, this event revealed an appropriate place for writing. When inter-generational affines need to communicate, they can do so formally or through one's daughter or wife. Writing, in this way, is constructed as intermediary, establishing a new type of relationship.[3]

The first stage in the training of indigenous teachers in "Projeto Tucum," undertaken in Água Boa in January 1996, depended on the application of anthropological knowledge (administered by the author of this article). The proposal of the training was to stimulate discussion with teachers in the sense of making a survey of expectations about "Projeto Tucum." Speaking from this perspective, we participated in a discussion about Shavante society. On the second day of training a question was raised regarding the basis on which Shavante society should be discussed, since the teachers were already familiar with it. The second doubt that was expressed was about the way in which anthropology could be taught in village schools. After much discussion, when a council was formed in the middle of the schoolroom, some consensuses were reached regarding objectives. At the moment when fundamental things should have already been defined, based on a curriculum specific to the society, it was considered that such matters should be subject to reconsideration, and the decision about the process was to be taken by village councils.

Thus we can see that the decision over the future of the school lies not only with the teacher, but also with the elders. Today, interest in scholarly knowledge is widespreaed within society. Another question frequently raised during discussions in "Projeto Tucum" concerned the teaching of myths in schoolroom. Usually, supervisors argued that myths should not be recorded in writing, as this would result in "crystallisation," as well as take away their quality as performance. However, as a fundamental theme, it ended up being inevitable that this would appear in indigenous schools. In some cases, elders would go to schools and narrate myths, and in others the teachers would record myths in books and circulate them as collected narratives. As in the case of language, the recorded versions or the adopted style of writing generates a certain discontent as well as heated discussion. New styles are proposed and myths may be recorded again. In general, within this discussion, elders and teachers diverge, the former claiming a traditional right and the latter a right given by the present circumstances. In principle, both agree with the idea of the maintenance of the traditional order. They only differ in the way to proceed.

Both parties represent distinct instances within the same society. The former, a perspective of reproduction of the culture extant before the arrival of effective contact with non-Indians; the latter, a perspective of a larger system, which involves a number of societies.

This new order demands a meticulous choice with regard to the cultural preparation of the arrangement of the school. As Forquin (1993: 14) says:

> The emphasis put on the function of cultural conservation and transmission in education must not prevent us from paying attention to the fact that all education, and in particular all school-type education, always supposes, in truth, a selection from within the culture and a re-elaboration of the contents of the culture destined to be transmitted to new generations (my translation).

Thus, indigenous peoples who have requested schools consider that their social systems need a new element to help them understand another code which is not theirs. The teacher is s/he who selects and re-elaborates the frameworks that result from the interaction between two societies. Significant consequences may follow in the wake of their work.

A marked interest in school education processes, which will probably occur in the future, could transform the school into a central point in society. Moreover, today's teachers will soon be part of the group of mature men of the village council. It remains to be seen whether the selection and re-elaboration of culture made by these individuals will provide the necessary constituents for the construction of a reasonable future for new generations.

NOTES TO CHAPTER 8

1. This article was originally published in *Urucum Jenipapo e Giz: a educação escolar indígena em debate*. Cuiabá: Entrelinhas, 1997. Secretaria de Estado de Educação (State Secretariat of Education)/ Conselho de Educação Escolar Indígena de Mato Grosso—CEI/MT (Mato Grosso Indigenous School Education Council–CEI/MT).
2. A domestic group is ideally composed of a man, his wife, their unmarried sons, their unmarried and married daughters, their daughters' husbands and daughters' offspring.
3. That is, one in which speech and alliance do not clash with each other.

REFERENCES

Bateson, G. 1965 [1936]. *Naven. A survey of the problems suggested by a composite picture of the culture of a New Guinea Tribe drawn from three points of view.* Stanford, Calif.: Stanford University Press.
Durkheim, E. 1967 [1922]. *Educação e Sociologia.* São Paulo: Edições Melhoramentos.
Forquin, J.-C. 1993. *Escola e Cultura. As bases sociais e epistemológicas do conhecimento escolar.* Porto Alegre: Artes Médicas.
Giaccaria, B. 1990. *Ensaios. Pedagogia Xavante. Aprofundamento Antropológico.* Campo Grande: Missão Salesiana de Mato Grosso.
Gow, P. 1991. *Of Mixed Blood: Kinship and History in Peruvian Amazonia.* Oxford: Clarendon Press.
Kahn, M., and B. Franchetto1994. Educação indígena no Brasil: conquistas e desafios. In *Em Aberto. Tema: Educação Escolar Indígena.* Brasília, MEC/Instituto Nacional de Estudos e Pesquisas Educacionais, ano 14, n° 63.
Lévi-Strauss, C. 1986. *Palavras retardatárias sobre a criança criadora. O olhar distanciado.* Lisboa: Edições 70.
Lopes da Silva, A. 1992. Dois séculos e meio de história Xavante. In M. Carneiro da Cunha (org.), *História dos Índios no Brasil.* São Paulo: FAPESP/Secretaria Municipal de Cultura-SP/Companhia das Letras.
Maybury-Lewis, D. 1984 [1967]. *A sociedade Xavante.* Rio de Janeiro: Livraria Francisco Alves.
Meliá, B. 1989. Desafios e tendências na alfabetização em língua indígena. In L. Emiri and R. Monserrat (orgs.) *A conquista da Escrita—Encontros de Educação Indígena.* OPAN. São Paulo: Iluminuras.
Meliá, B. 1995. *Elogio de la langua Guarani.* Asunción: CEPAG.
Monserrat, R. 1989. Conjuntura Atual da Educação Indígena. In L. Emiri and R. Monserrat (orgs.), *A conquista da Escrita—Encontros de Educação Indígena.* OPAN. São Paulo: Iluminuras.
Silva, M. 1994. A conquista da escola: educação escolar e movimento de professores indígenas no Brasil. In *Em Aberto. Tema: Educação Escolar Indígena.* Brasília, MEC/Instituto Nacional de Estudos e Pesquisas Educacionais, ano 14, n° 63.
Silva, M. Ferreira, and M.M. Azevedo 1995. Pensando as escolas dos povos indígenas no Brasil: o movimento dos professores do Amazonas, Roraima e Acre. In A. Lopes da Silva and L. Dioniseti B. Grupioni (orgs.), *A temática Indígena na Escola. Novos subsídios para professores de 1° e 2° graus.* Brasília: MEC/MARI/UNESCO.

9 Disease Versus Genocide
The Debate Over Population
Paula Sherman

Estimates of pre-contact Indigenous populations in the Western Hemisphere have been debated by explorers and scholars since the arrival of Columbus in 1492. There are literally hundreds of studies and texts that deal with the problem of estimating the population of peoples who, in some cases, were decimated by pandemic epidemics brought to the New World by fishermen and traders long before European colonists set ashore on the continent. Bartolome de Las Casas, Alfred Kroeber, Russell Thornton, James Axtell, Frances Jennings, Ward Churchill, Bruce Trigger, Henry F. Dobyns, and Alfred W. Crosby Jr. have all contributed to the discourse, publishing exhausting works on disease and their impacts on Indigenous populations.

Pretences for debating pre-contact population run deeper than simply getting an accurate figure. In truth, it is doubtful that an accurate estimation of all pre-contact Indigenous populations in this hemisphere will ever be discovered. There just is no mechanism available to figure out the true magnitude of the loss from European colonisation. Many Indigenous peoples across the hemisphere lost their lives and communities to epidemics, attacks, and assimilation policies. European colonial policies towards Indigenous peoples were designed for one purpose, to sever Indigenous control over their lands and resources.

Still, regardless of the recent discourse on genocide in the Americas, many scholars continue to play the numbers game. What it boils down to is justification: every time that a historian or anthropologist publishes a study that indicates larger population masses on the continent, another historian or anthropologist on the other side of the debate disputes those findings and releases his or her own study indicating reduced numbers. The lower the numbers become, the easier it is to fabricate justification for what were acts of genocide. As Cherokee scholar Ward Churchill has implied, "the genocide that was committed against Indigenous peoples during the conquest and colonisation of this hemisphere over the past five hundred years has been the most profound event in human history. It has no equal, and falls within the statutes of genocide set by the United Nations" (Churchill 1997).

It is probable that the extermination of Indigenous populations as a result of European conquest of the Western Hemisphere totalled over one hundred million (Dobyns 1989). This magnitude of loss is every bit as great as that of the twelve to fifteen million attributed to Himmler's slaughter mills (Churchill 1997). Acts of genocide are acts of genocide no matter the century or victims. Even in light of the enormous loss, scholars continue to play the numbers game when in reality the population prior to contact makes no difference and scholars should stop wasting time when there are more important historical considerations. There were people here! The argument does not get any simpler than that. It does not matter if the population was over 125 million as proposed by historian Ward Churchill (ibid.), or 8.4 million as indicated by anthropologist James Mooney (Mooney 1928). By focusing so much attention on finding accurate population counts, scholars are missing the larger reality, for the consequences to Indigenous peoples as a result of the European invasion of this continent were the same; acts of genocide are acts of genocide no matter what the population was prior to European colonisation. Focusing on the numbers crunch is by and large a way for Euro-American academia to continue a long-standing tradition of evading its responsibility as scholars to tell the truth about the invasion and settlement of this continent. Putting forth an effort to uncover the magnitude of massacres, taking of lands, destruction of languages and cultural traditions is of vital importance because it would force the United States and Canada to take responsibility for the millions of Indigenous people who died as a result of that invasion.

Why the pretence at historical truth when dealing with Indigenous/ European "encounters?" Academia in both Canada and the United States cannot deal with the past and continually finds ways to whitewash the true history of North America. That is why elementary and secondary textbooks that deal with North American history predominately devote less than a chapter to Native Americans. Lenore A. Stiffarm (1992) argues that 20th-century academics have taught generations of students that only about one million Native Americans resided within the North American vastness in the year 1500, with the supposed basis for this inaccurate estimate resting on the shoulders of James M. Mooney and Alfred Louis Kroeber.

Mooney's work came out first. In his monograph *The Aboriginal Population of America North of Mexico* (1928), Mooney argues for a very low pre-contact population in New England of 25,000 with no explanation other than that they could not have been any greater than the colonists who counted them indicated in the beginning of the 17th century (see Stiffarm 1992). What Mooney failed to take into account was the decimation from disease faced by Native people in the coastal regions from fishermen and traders prior to the major influx of English colonists.

Russell Thornton, in his monumental work *American Indian Holocaust and Survival* (1987), is critical of Mooney's assessment of pre-contact population for the same reason. Mooney made an important mistake in that he ignored the "minor" contact of Europeans and Indigenous peoples prior to his dates of extensive European Contact. Thornton argues that there were significant carrier contacts in virtually every region that resulted in important population losses for Native Americans. In *Indian New England before the Mayflower* (1980), Howard S. Russell puts forward an estimate of at least 60,000 for the three southern New England states and New Hampshire. Adding Maine to the equation would bring the total up to about 75,000 for the region now known as New England. Churchill raises that estimate even higher to just at 90,000 Indigenous peoples in the region in 1600 (see Churchill 1997).

Alfred Kroeber's work was also of vital importance in the debate on population of pre-contact Indigenous peoples. But Kroeber described people he had never really investigated (Kroeber 1966; Churchill 1997). Kroeber emphatically rejected the notion that the nations of North America could be considered capable of so ordering their societies and technologies as to increase their populations beyond a static and sparsely distributed token representation. Kroeber's allotment of one million persons divides into the total area of Canada and the United States (including Alaska) in the ratio of one person per seven square miles. His explanation for this sparsity virtually blamed the condition of savagery, though he must be credited with avoidance of the term itself. He reasoned that Indian societies were characterised by "insane, unending, continuously attritional warfare" and "the absence of all effective political organisation, [and] of the idea of state" (Jennings 1975).

Kroeber's own works show that he disregarded considerable research that went against his own degrading characterisation of Indigenous agriculture and technologies, all pointing towards more complex societies with higher populations (Kroeber 1966).

Many scholars have argued that disease was the real eliminator of Indigenous peoples and that these epidemics were unintended consequences of European contact and settlement on the continent. In a few instances infection may have taken place early on as a result of unintended motivations. But, in thousands of other cases, Europeans realised very early that their presence led to Indigenous deaths. By 1550 at the latest, it was common knowledge that there was a firm correlation between the arrival of explorers, settlers, and military expeditions on the one hand and massive die-offs of Native peoples from pandemic epidemics on the other (Ashburn 1947).

Between 1616 and 1618 a devastating epidemic swept through New England, 90% of the Wampanoag people died as a result. Massachusetts, Pawtucket, and Eastern Abenaki also perished in similar amounts. Literally, dozens of known coastal villages along Massachusetts Bay were abandoned (Churchill 1997). The Pequot people, who had an estimated population of 10,000–13,000, lost between 70 and 90% of their population to smallpox epidemics in 1619 and again in 1634. Some Pequot villages lost 90% of their population to these epidemics. The 1634 epidemics swept through the area just three years before the English attacked their most populous village at Mystic, killing over 600 people.

Churchill (ibid.) argues that the epidemics that swept through New England between 1616 and 1634 came at just the right moment, when the English were feeling very threatened by the presence of over 90,000 Indigenous peoples who were fighting back against encroachments on their lands and cultural traditions. This problem was rectified in 1614 when Captain John Smith materialised on the coastline with a company of Plymouth Company voyagers, shot seven Natives and abducted twenty-seven Patuxet, Wampanoags and Nausets to sell as slaves in the West Indies. Once he appeared, Indigenous people contracted diseases and died in large numbers. Mysteriously, the Indigenous peoples of the region had had prior contact with Europeans for years without disease being spread among the populace.

Whether the onslaught of disease was accidental or used in a form of germ warfare as Churchill (ibid.) suggests, both were caused by the arrival of Europeans and the taking of land and resources that clearly belonged to Indigenous peoples. The fairytales have to cease; reality is not the pleasant bubble-gum version of Indigenous/European relations that has been passed down in myths of "Thanksgiving." The truth is much uglier and equates Columbus, Cortez, Coronado, Mason, Chivington, along with thousands of others with Hitler and Nazi extermination policies. No amount of fumbling with pre-contact population numbers is going to change that fact. Disease was not the only weapon. The Pequots, Narragansetts and millions of other Indigenous peoples were clearly marked for extermination in the competition of European empires for control of the Western Hemisphere.

Applying the United Nations statutes on genocide to the case of the Pequots, Narragansetts and others leaves no doubt that genocide was wilfully committed against them as a means to remove them from their traditional lands and resources and therefore making them available for English exploitation. The leadership of both Plymouth and Massachusetts collaborated with that of the unofficial colony of Connecticut to fabricate a pretext, and then set out on a war of extermination (Churchill, ibid.).

> It was a fearful sight to see them thus frying in the fire and the streams of blood quenching the same, and horrible was the stink and scent thereof; but the victory seemed a sweet sacrifice, and [the English] gave the praise thereof to God, who had wrought so wonderfully for them, thus to enclose their enemies in their hands and give them so speedy a victory over so proud and insulting an enemy. (Mason quoted in Churchill, ibid.:172)

The narrative above is taken from the account of Captain John Mason, who led the attack and ordered the Pequots and their village burned. If what happened to the Pequots does not constitute genocide then how can what happened to the Jews in Nazi Germany be so labelled? There is no difference, genocide is genocide. Underhill, who accompanied Mason and participated in the massacre, defended the killing of women and children with the justification that sometimes the scriptures declared women and children must perish with their parents (Churchill, ibid.).

Once the English had eliminated the Pequots as a threat to English expansion, they moved onto neighbouring Narragansetts in Rhode Island. In June of 1675, three prominent Wampanoags were executed at Plymouth on charges of plotting against the English (Churchill, ibid.). Then, in December of the same year, colonial governments combined once again to remove the Narragansett threat that supposedly stood in their way. They attacked a fortified village located in the Great Swamp with nearly a thousand troops, killing at least ninety-seven warriors and wounding forty-eight others. Up to one thousand women and children were massacred at the Great Swamp in much the same fashion as their Pequot neighbours had been in 1637 (Churchill, ibid.). But, once again, this atrocity was glossed over by historians and anthropologists as a "just war." Thousands of New England Native people were killed, enslaved, or driven into exile during "King Phillip's War" between 1675 and 1676 (Grumet 1995).

For decades, Phillip's head was displayed on a pike atop the brick watchtower of Plymouth's Fort Hill. Phillip's nine-year-old son escaped execution, but was sold into slavery in Bermuda. Leading Wampanoag warriors who surrendered their entire bands to Benjamin Church, who had promised their lives would be spared, were summarily executed amid public enthusiasm, and their followers sold into slavery (Churchill 1997).

By the middle of the 18th century, a large majority of the Native people that remained in the region joined the already growing number of wandering poor. They went from town to town seeking relief from starvation. Having lost their land and resources to European colonization, they had nothing left from which to acquire support.

Nearly a hundred years later the massacres continued. Pennsylvania governor Thomas Penn, when presented with the scalp of a Lenni Lanape leader after the massacre at Kittanning in 1758, actively entertained the idea of having a plaque inscribed with an account of the action and sending the grisly trophy to the British Museum (Churchill, ibid.). A favourite tactic of both the Americans and British during the Revolution was to destroy villages and burn crops late in the season when there would not have been sufficient time to plant and harvest new crops before winter:

> At town after town soldiers spent whole days destroying cornfields and cutting down fruit trees. At the Seneca capital at Genesee the troops burned 128 large houses and systematically burned crops, orchards, and food supplies. Returning to their villages the Seneca found there was not a mouthful of any kind of sustenance left, not even enough to keep a child one day from perishing with hunger. (Calloway, 1995: 51)

Calloway adds further that one Onondaga chief claimed that when the Americans attacked his town,

> they put to death all the women and children, excepting some of the young women, whom they carried away for the use of their soldiers & were afterwards put to death in a more shameful manner. (Calloway, 1995: 53)

The massacres did not stop with the invention of the United States. If anything, they worsened as Americans encroached on Indigenous lands and stole resources. Not even the dead were safe. On March 27, 1814, Andrew Jackson supervised the mutilation of over 800 or more Creek corpses—the bodies of men, women, and children that they had massacred, cutting off their noses to count and preserve a record of the dead, slicing long strips of flesh from their bodies to tan and turn into bridle reins (Stannard 1992). In 1832 Sac and Fox people under the leadership of Black Hawk were attacked by a force of over 1,700 men including future presidents Zachary Taylor and Abraham Lincoln. Over 2,000 Indigenous peoples were killed in this massacre and 500 taken hostage. They escaped, leading the soldiers on a long chase that ended on August 3, 1833, when the survivors, who were exhausted and existing on bark and roots, were surrounded by a force of over 900 men. The Indians, who had remained on the east bank of the river, attempted to surrender, but the troops, frustrated by weeks of fruitless pursuit, stormed their position in an eight-hour frenzy of clubbing, stabbing, shooting and scalping (Axelrod 1993).

The removal policy passed by Jackson in the 1830s caused great loss of life. The Choctaws lost 6,000 out of 40,000; Creeks and Seminoles lost a full 50% of their populations; Cherokees lost 55% of their population alive in 1838 as a direct result of internment and forced exile in Oklahoma (Churchill 1997). Evan Jones, a Baptist missionary who worked among the Cherokee in North Carolina, accompanied his congregation to the stockades and on the forced march.

> The Cherokees are nearly all prisoners. They have been dragged from their houses, and encamped at the forts and military posts, all over the nation. . . . It is a painful sight. The property of many has been taken, and sold before their eyes for almost nothing. The poor captive in a state of distressing agitation, his weeping wife almost frantic with terror, surrounded by a group of crying, terrified children. (Jones quoted in T. Perdue & M.D. Green Perdue 1995: 165)

The carnage continued unabated wherever Indigenous peoples protested American encroachment. The Third Colorado Volunteer Cavalry Regiment was formed and targeted the Cheyenne as mechanism for doing

Disease Versus Genocide 179

away with the Indian problem. William N. Byers commented in favor of this policy in his publications in 1864:

> Eastern humanitarians who believe in the superiority of the Indian race will raise a terrible rible over this policy [of extermination], but it is no time to split hairs nor stand upon delicate compunctions of conscience. Self-preservation demands decisive action against the red devils. (Churchill 1997: 229)

The action called for by Byers happened under the command of John Milton Chivington. Chivington, who had a dorm named after him at the University of Colorado until it was removed in the last decade, stated, " My intention is to kill all Indians I may come across" (Chivington quoted in Churchill 1997: 229) Chivington got his chance when he led an attack force of over 900 men on the sleeping Cheyenne village at Sand Creek in 1861.

> From five hundred to six hundred souls, the majority of which were women and children I did not see a body of a man, women, or child but was scalped, and in many instances their bodies were mutilated in a most horrible manner—men, women, and children's privates cut out, I heard one man say that he had cut out a woman's private parts and had them on exhibition on a stick; I heard another man say that he had cut off the fingers of an Indian to get the rings on the hand. [. . .] I also heard of numerous instances in which men had cut out the private parts of females and stretched them over saddle bows and wore them over hats while riding in the ranks. [. . .] I heard one man say that he had cut a Squaw's heart out and had it stuck on a stick. (Chivington quoted in Churchill, ibid.: 233)

Examples such as this are just a few of the many thousands that exist depicting the genocide that was committed against Indigenous peoples. Those who survived were in some cases removed from their traditional land bases and subjected to new rounds of devastating extermination attempts. The effects of the systematic process of dislocating Indigenous peoples and/or destroying their economic base forced on them conditions designed to bring about their demise as distinct peoples. All were affected, rendered destitute and homeless, harried and harassed relentlessly; the starving and disease-ridden members of the largest mid-Atlantic Indigenous confederation of Pamunkeys, Chickhominies, Naunsemonds, Pappahannocks and Paspaheghs dwindled to no more than 600 in the late 1600s (Beverly 1947). The correlation between such psychological devastation and the inability of the average human to fight off disease is no mystery (Churchill 1997).

Whatever the actual pre-contact population, North American Indigenous populations declined disastrously as a result of European disease and extermination policies. Often overwhelmed by the continuing influx of English colonists, Indigenous peoples were forced to contend with seemingly endless waves of wars and epidemics and were rarely able to replenish their losses. Demoralised by the loss of land and loved ones, many Native peoples seeking conviviality or consolation turned to alcohol. Introduced by Europeans as a mechanism to expand the fur trade, rum was readily available through traders, who by the time of the Pequot War had integrated it firmly into most trade activities. Alcoholism took on the appearance of an epidemic as it devastated entire families and community structures (Grumet 1995). Alcohol continues to ravage many Indigenous communities at the beginning of the 21th century as they try to cope with the generational despair and depression brought on by colonization.

The issues are many and can be traced directly back to the genocide suffered by their ancestors at the hands of Europeans. There have been persistent efforts by scholars such as Francis Parkman and Samuel Drake to classify the massacres of the Pequots, Narragansetts, Cheyenne, Acoma and others as something other than a deliberate plan designed to rid the English of the "Indian" threat once and for all. The Pequot War is a good example of this phenomenon. Scholars refuse to portray the Pequot War as what it was, an act of deliberate extermination, whose survivors were given as slaves to the Narragansett, the Mohegans, and the English. Some of the men were even sold into slavery in the West Indies. All of the Pequot survivors were torn from their traditional land base and had conditions inflicted on them designed to bring about their demise as a people. The English desire to exterminate them was so fierce that in the Treaty of Hartford after the Pequot War the courts at Hartford forbid the use of the name "Pequot" to describe the survivors. There can be no greater example of policies that were designed to exterminate human beings. The survivors of the massacre were forbidden from identifying themselves within their own cultural boundaries. To equate the Pequot War as anything other than genocide is preposterous.

Even with the early availability of data that showed the devastating effects of colonisation on Indigenous peoples, historians and anthropologists continued into the late 20th century to ignore this data in favour of perpetuating the history of America as perceived by men such as Francis Parkman, who shared many of his countrymen's negative stereotypes of Native peoples. Parkman's volumes on *France and England in North America* were influenced by William H. Prescott, who published his work on the *History of the Conquest of Mexico* in 1843. Prescott had many books that chronicled the imperial struggle for control of North America (see Trigger 1986). Many Canadian scholars were in turn influenced by Parkman and shared his view that the contest for the continent was one in which the most advanced society of the time had triumphed over very primitive ones. Generally, the Indigenous people who inhabited the region known now as Canada have been treated by historians as part of the setting for European activities. Little has been done to show the process of colonisation and the connections to the present state of Aboriginal peoples in Canada by non-Native scholars.

Bruce Trigger (ibid.) sees the problem of exclusion descending from men like Parkman who argued that the Indians' power of reason and analysis was inferior to those of Europeans. Parkman characterised Native Americans as savage and uncivilised. He described the Northern Algonkins as inferior in intellectual vigour and moral stability, slow-learning, and incorrigible; the Ojibwas as a ferocious horde and likely to remain so; the Illinois as a corrupt and degenerate race, and the Montagnais as the lowest Algonkin type for whom even cannibalism was not abhorrent. Trigger (ibid.) argues that Parkman's sources reflect the bias in himself as well as the society around him, but 20th-century scholars continued to use him frequently in their analysis of Indigenous peoples.

New France has come away from the colonisation process with a cleaner image than that of the Spanish or English because it successfully played aboriginal peoples both against one another and against competing European powers. Thus, the French have always maintained an air of innocence about their genocidal impact and intent (see Balasi 1992). Algonkin and Iroquois peoples, who had existing conflicts prior to the arrival of the French, saw those feelings of animosity channelled into destructive new wars that were designed to wipe out hundreds of people in one attack. By 1633 some Algonkins and Mohawks sought a compromise and end to the hostilities.

They were prepared to consider intertribal peace in return for exchanging access to European traders, but the English and the French assumed that allies of their European enemies were automatically their enemies as well. European intervention in this negotiation led to thirty years of intermittent Mohawk war against the French and their allies (Trigger 1976). The consequences to Indigenous inhabitants of New France were catastrophic. Algonkin and Iroquois nations lost many people to this new war that had been instigated by French and English desire to control the lands and original inhabitants of North America. The Huron and other Aboriginal peoples were also drawn into the conflict. The Huron alone lost thousands of people to Iroquois raids and were systematically defeated and dispersed throughout the Ottawa Valley by 1649.

France was not innocent of committing acts of genocide any more than the English or Spanish were. In 1730 the Mesquakis were attacked by a force of over 1,400 soldiers, killing about 900, 300 of whom were non-combatants. Far to the south at about the same time, the Chickasaws underwent the same thing at the hands of French-allied Choctaws (Churchill 1997).

The Dutch also perpetrated genocidal acts against the Indigenous peoples at Pavonia. Dutch mercenaries under New Netherlands's governor Willem Kieft had orders to terrorise them into paying tribute:

> About midnight I heard a great shrieking, and I ran to the ramparts of the fort, and looked over to Pavonia. I saw nothing but firing, and

heard the shrieks of the Indians murdered in their sleep [. . .] when it was day the soldiers returned to the fort, having massacred and murdered over 80 Indians, and considering they had done a deed of Roman valour in murdering so many in their sleep; where infants were torn from their mother's breasts, and hacked to pieces in the presence of the parents, and the pieces thrown into the fire and in the water, and other sucklings being bound to small boards, and then cut, stuck, and pierced, and miserably massacred in a manner to move a heart of stone. (Kieft quoted in Jennings 1975: 174)

These sources were readily available to scholars, but they ignored them in favour of the arguments put forth by Parkman, Mooney, Kroeber and others. With this kind of irresponsible historiography, how can children and adults in Canada and the United States possibly understand the socioeconomic issues currently facing Indigenous peoples, if atrocities committed against Native peoples are covered over with claims of savagery, inferiority, or "just wars"? All this fabrication accomplishes is to ensure that Indigenous people remain outside the mainstream of American or Canadian history and at the bottom of the socioeconomic scale.

It all leads back to the representations of Indigenous peoples in past and current works relating to the historiography of colonial America. The debate on pre-contact population is a primary example of whitewashing. Focusing so much scholarly attention on the problem will never produce the results wanted by scholars one way or the other, and removes the responsibility to seek a true understanding of the role Europeans played in the holocaust that was perpetrated against Indigenous peoples over the past five centuries.

Like the atrocities committed against Native people by the English and French, there are hundreds of examples of genocide in colonial Spanish America; yet these remain glossed over in the effort to project lower population levels across the board. Las Casas, who was an eyewitness to many of the early acts of genocide, has been criticised and his accounts of these horrendous acts against the Taino and Arawak peoples tossed aside as unreliable. Columbus is a "protonazi" not only because he symbolises the process of conquest and genocide perpetrated against Indigenous peoples, but because he also bears a personal responsibility of having participated in it (Churchill 1997).

A hemispheric population estimated to have been as great as 125 million was reduced by something over 90%. The people had died in their millions from being hacked apart with axes and swords, burned alive and trampled under horses, hunted as game and fed to dogs, shot, beaten, stabbed, scalped for bounty, hanged on meat-hooks and thrown over the sides of ships at sea, worked to death as slave labourers, intentionally starved and frozen to death during a multitude of forced marches and internments, and, in an unknown number of instances, deliberately infected with epidemic diseases (Stannard 1992). The fact that Columbus is still celebrated in America with his own holiday while the millions who died as a direct result of his policies remain outside the scope of American history is a testament to the pervasiveness of the American myth. It is not bad enough that 90% of 125 million plus were lost in the invasion, or that the remaining Indigenous people in this hemisphere have less than 2% of their original land base and resources, so long as America and Canada can continue to project their nations as shining examples of democracy.

Columbus's programmes reduced the Taino population from as many as eight million in 1492 to three million in 1496. By the 1514 census barely 22,000 survived, with only 200 being recorded in 1542. These losses in population were not simply a factor of pandemic epidemics as has been professed by some historians. The first massive pandemic epidemic actually came ashore in 1513; by then Columbus had already reduced the Taino population by a full 90%. The Spaniards made bets as to who would slit a man in two, or cut off his head at one blow; or they opened up his bowels. They tore the babes from their mother's breasts by their feet and dashed their heads against the rocks. They spitted the bodies of other babies, together with their mothers and all who went before them, on their swords (Stannard, ibid.).

The focus on population in American historiography has become paramount, because to admit that there were over one hundred million Indigenous peoples in the Americas prior to contact is to admit that 96 to 99% were eradicated. Many of those died as a result not of pandemic epidemics but of continual acts of genocide, which reduced their numbers by enormous amounts. As much as several hundred thousand Indigenous peoples died as a result of the Spanish mission systems set up in Florida, California, Arizona and New Mexico between 1690 and 1845. The missions were death-mills in which Indians, often delivered en masse by the military, were allotted an average of seven feet by two feet of living space (Churchill 1997). They worked in the mines six days a week and were provided no more than 1400 calories per day of low nutrient foods. Contrasting this with the calories allotted to African slaves in the same period, there is a remarkable difference in caloric intake with slaves receiving on average 4,200 calories per day. Disease was definitely a factor in the mines, but poor health as a result of overwork and near starvation created the conditions that allowed epidemics to invade the bodies of several hundred thousand Indigenous peoples.

It all comes back to an argument for genocide, with disease an excellent tool for removing populations much quicker than the sword. Failure of past and current scholars to throw out the debate over population in favour of coming to grips with the magnitude of what has transpired in American history is another example of the willingness of scholars to maintain the garbage that has passed up until this point as American history.

The seriousness of the argument cannot be overstated, accepting responsibility for the crimes committed against Indigenous peoples would have implications in international as well as domestic arenas. America and Canada have often projected their countries as the shining example of democracy for the world to follow, when, in reality, both countries have held Indigenous peoples within a rigid system of internal colonialism in which Native Americans have been, and continue to be, subjected to isolation, extermination policies, loss of language and culture due to forced assimilation, destruction of sacred sights, and the highest rates of poverty and suicides in North America.

Indigenous peoples are currently seeking representation in the United Nations as distinct peoples with the right to have their issues heard in an international forum. Many resolutions have come up for ratification in the United Nations regarding the rights of Indigenous peoples. Both Canada and the United States have refused to ratify them all. This is hard to believe in light of their claims to support human rights in an international setting. Canada in fact has the reputation currently of being number one as far as human rights issues are concerned. This is preposterous considering the fact that Aboriginal people in Canada are held in a continual system of apartheid and are still defined in terms of the racist 19th Indian Act.

Until 1985, Aboriginal women had their recognition and that of their children stripped away if they married a non-Native. This was not the case for men who married White women. It was a means for the Canadian government to eradicate Aboriginal people into non-existence. Men do not have the babies, women do; if an Aboriginal man marries a white woman and has children within a few generations the people cease to have high blood quotients and the federal government can then terminate federal responsibilities by claiming they are no longer an Aboriginal nation. Men were not left completely out of the equation, being targeted through enrolment in higher education or on being drafted in the military. Once they left their communities to follow either path they lost their status as Aboriginal people. This pattern of termination of status was instituted throughout both countries. Women were especially vulnerable on both sides of the border and were targeted for sterilisation without their consent by Indian health organisations. In this way thousands of Indigenous people were exterminated before they could even be conceived.

Likewise, the suicide rate of Indigenous peoples in the Western Hemisphere is the highest of any ethnic group. In the western province of Manitoba, the suicide rates of Aboriginal people under thirty-four years old are many times the national average. Saskatchewan statistics show very much the same pattern. On some reserves in Canada, over 80% of deaths were alcohol related (Buckley 1993). Since the highest instances of suicides have been linked to Aboriginal children under the age of sixteen, and they make up the largest portion of the Aboriginal population in Canada, this indicates dire consequences for the future of Aboriginal people if measures are not taken now to stop the depression and despair that many children have to deal with on a daily basis. This despair is a direct result of the conditions that have been forced upon Indigenous peoples. A recent report of reserve housing in Canada states that over 75% fails to meet basic standards of safety and decency; 47% falls below minimum standards, 36% is seriously overcrowded, and 38% lacks water and fixtures (Buckley, ibid.). The pattern is the same across the continent. Indigenous people continue to be at the bottom of the socioeconomic scale while their remaining resources are continually taken by governments and multinational corporations.

These examples are not just current problems that have no relation to the past. The present state of Indigenous peoples in the Americas is directly connected to the conquest and colonisation of this continent. Scholars must comprehend the magnitude of the problem and realise that they are in part responsible for the current and future problems facing Indigenous peoples if they continue to ignore the very real issue of genocide and the problems facing current Native American populations as a result of that genocide.

A striking question for some readers might be what constitutes genocide and how can a 20th century term be used to describe the process of colonisation that started on this continent five hundred years ago. Steven T. Katz looked at the problem in *The Holocaust in Historical Context* (1994) and determined that the neologism "genocide" was coined by Raphael Lemkin to describe what happened to the Jews of Europe during World War II (see Churchill 1997). The problem with Katz's assessment of Lemkin's invention of the term genocide is that he misrepresents Lemkin's description of genocide. Lemkin perceived what was happening to the Jews as part of a much broader genocidal whole in which entire national and ethnic cultures were being destroyed by various means as part of a larger Nazi master plan to impose the larger German national pattern on the whole of Europe. He viewed genocide as a composite of different acts of persecution or destruction, including attacks on political and social institutions, culture, language, national feelings, religion, and the economic existence of the group (Churchill, ibid.).

Article II in the current United Nations Convention defines genocide as the following:

(a) Killing members of the group;
(b) Causing serious bodily or mental harm to members of the group;
(c) Deliberately inflicting on members of the group conditions of life calculated to bring about its physical destruction in whole or in part;
(d) Imposing measures intended to prevent births within the group;
(e) Forcibly transferring children of the group to another group.

During the last five hundred years, Indigenous peoples in the Americas have been subjected to each of the atrocities underlined above. There is no doubt that what happened constitutes what has been termed "genocide." Entire civilisations were eradicated in the Western Hemisphere almost from the outset. By 1800, it has been estimated that upwards of 90% of the Indigenous population of over 100 million or more had been exterminated, and the killing was continuing (Churchill, ibid.).

Once again it comes back to justification for the genocide that has been committed against Indigenous peoples over the past five centuries. Indigenous peoples have died in the millions from this process. Pandemic epidemics were only part of the equation, just as many died from deliberate extermination policies instigated by European powers. These polices have survived into the late 20th century intact in many instances. Suicides among Indigenous peoples go back to the Taino peoples and Columbus. Presently, many young people are being lost to suicides as they give into despair. Indigenous teen suicide rates across North America are 14.4 times the national average (Shkilnyks 1985).

The extermination policy is ongoing. Suicides are only one method; sterilisation and medical experimentation are still being practised on Indigenous peoples. In the mid to late 1980s Inuit children on Alaska's oil-rich North slope were forced to serve as guinea pigs in the "field test" of hepatitis vaccines which had been banned by the World Health Organisation from international distribution because of an assumed link to the transmission of HIV virus. When tribal officials discovered the experimentation on their children, the operation was stopped in Alaska and transferred to other Native American communities to the south (Smith 1992).

Systematically, Indigenous peoples have found their remaining traditional lands destroyed by government and multinational corporations. Reservation lands once considered useless when Indigenous peoples had been isolated there were now found to be rich in uranium and other resources. After a half-century of nuclear power, governments were looking for spots to dump toxic waste material; as it turns out, Indian County has become the favoured location. The U.S. government targeted Native Americans for several reasons: their lands are some of the most isolated in the countries, they are also the most impoverished and, consequently, most politically vulnerable (Churchill 1997).

Desecration has reached the point now where there is no avenue of escape, either for the earth or Indigenous people. More and more Native people are finding their water tables poisoned and their lands filled with hydro dams and uranium mines, all proposed for the betterment of society. Indigenous people have not realised any betterment from this desecration; instead, they have found their societies destroyed for the refinement of the dominant capitalistic society. The James Bay project has already proven itself to be detrimental. It has contaminated the fish, which the Cree people depend on for their nourishment, with methylmercury that leached from the rotting vegetation that was submerged under water from the dam. Also affected by the massive hydro dam at James Bay are the Inuit and Moot peoples, who are fighting to keep their lands from being flooded.

Aside from the destruction of the environment, hydroelectric dams have a devastating effect on the traditional fabric of Indigenous life. After the

Cree of James Bay were relocated, adolescents began to hang out at the mall built by the hydro plant for them. Traditional community life gave way to divisions within the community, driving a wedge between elders, who held the traditional responsibility of passing on community structure to the next generation, and youths that began to hang out in the mall. Roads to the project also bring hunters and plant workers who will further infiltrate and alter the society. The social stress of the community has increased dramatically, leading to increased alcoholism and substance abuse.

The Hanford Nuclear Reservation in Washington state has caused dramatic increases of cancer rates among the Yakima, Colville, Nez Perce, Coeur d' Alene, Spokane, Kalispell, Umatilla, and Klickitat (Indigenous People and the State 1992). Radioactive gases and fluids released between 1944 and 1977 directly affected the fish and wildlife. Eight out of the nine reactors are cooled by the Columbia river that separates Oregon from Washington. This river, which provides Indigenous people with food and economic subsistence, has been contaminated by the Hanford Reservation for more than thirty years.

Mining is another form of destruction Indigenous people fight daily. From Brazil where minerals are extracted from rivers to Montana where strip mining has been used, water is poisoned with chemical substances. The Navaho and Hopi have been contaminated by uranium mining since 1942. Thirteen tons of uranium has been taken from Navaho land alone. More than a thousand open pits have been abandoned with highly radioactive chemicals flowing off from rainfall into water supplies used by the people. Six hundred dwellings on Navaho land are contaminated, leaving the residents subjected to cancer, leukaemia and birth defects (Indigenous People and the State, ibid.).

The Gros Ventre and Assiniboine of Fort Belkap reservation, Montana, are being threatened by the Zortman-Landusky gold mine. If this corporation is allowed to complete the newest phase of development, more than a billion gallons of cyanide solution will be released over the next few years into the local watershed (Indigenous People and the State, ibid.). Likewise, the province of Saskatchewan in Canada has been termed the "Saudi Arabia" of uranium mining, four mines supply fourteen tons of uranium annually. As a result of continually mining uranium in Saskatchewan, the Cree Chipewyan and Metis must live with the half million gallons of untreated waste that went into Lake Wallaston between 1975 and 1977. Radioactive contaminants still leak into the lake from underground water channels (Indigenous People and the State, ibid.).

These examples of environmental destruction of Indigenous lands should come as no surprise given the efforts of Europeans and Euroamericans to bring about the extermination of Indigenous peoples in the past. This is absolute proof that the process is ongoing today. Why is it that at the dawn of the 21st century Indigenous people are still caught in the grip of colonialism? It is quite simple. Indigenous peoples remain outside the scope of humanity because they are considered to be subhuman. What other explanation is there for the total ignorance that existed and still exists on the part of scholars who have examined and reexamined the history of this continent. It is the only explanation for the ongoing obsession with pre-contact population statistics. There were millions of Indigenous inhabitants on the continent at the time of the European invasion. Whether the number was 125 million or 10, there were people here who had a prior claim to all the lands and resources that Europeans stole.

No amount of fudging with the numbers would ever justify what has taken place here over the past five hundred years. Scholars need to come to grips with that basic truth and move on from there. Effort needs to be put into research that is going to force colonising governments to live up to their obligations to Indigenous people, who suffered devastating losses in terms of lives, culture, language, and the environmental destruction of traditional land bases. The first step is to admit to the genocide and stop covering it up. A second step would be to let Indigenous peoples take their place with the rest of the world as full members in the United Nations. Third would be for governments to live up to all the treaty obligations they have with Indigenous peoples. Real steps need to be taken to assure that this Earth is capable of sustaining life for future generations whose livelihood depends on what we are doing now.

Historians have a huge role to play in the future outcome of today's events. Changing the way historiography looks at the contact and colonisation of this hemisphere is paramount if Indigenous peoples are to regain any of the things they lost as a result of five hundred years of domination. Discarding the debate over population in favour of analysing genocide will make it possible to stop future acts of genocide from taking place.

REFERENCES

Ashburn, M.M. 1947. *The Ranks of Death: A Medical History of the Conquest of America.* New York: Coward-McCann.
Axelrod, A. 1993. *Chronicle of the Indian Wars from Colonial Times to Wounded Knee.* New York: Prentice Hall.
Balasi, C.J. 1992. *The Time of the French in the Heart of North America, 1673–1818.* Chicago: Alliance Française.
Beverly, R. 1947. *The History and Present State of Virginia.* Chapel Hill: University of North Carolina Press.
Buckley, H. 1993. *From Wooden Ploughs to Welfare.* Montreal: McGill-Queens University Press.
Calloway, C.G. 1995. *The American Revolution in Indian Country: Crisis and Diversity in Native American Communities.* Boston: Cambridge University Press.
Churchill, W. 1997. *A Little Matter of Genocide: Holocaust and Denial in the Americas, 1492 to the Present.* San Francisco: City Lights Books.

Dobyns, H.F. 1989. *Their Number Become Thinned: Native American Population Dynamics in Eastern North America*. Knoxville: University of Tennessee Press.

Grumet, R.S. 1995. *Historic Contact: Indian People and Colonists in Today's Northeastern United States in the Sixteenth through Eighteenth Centuries*. Norman: University of Oklahoma Press.

Indigenous People and The State 1992. In *World Watch* 75 (United Nations, New York).

Jennings, F. 1975. *The Invasion of America: Indians, Colonialism, and the Cant of Conquest*. Chapel Hill: University of North Carolina Press.

Katz, S.T. 1994. *The Holocaust in Historical Context*. New York: Oxford University Press.

Kroeber, A.L. 1966. Evolution, History, and Culture. In T. Kroeber (ed.), *An Anthropologist Looks at History*. Berkeley: University of California Press.

Mooney, J. 1928. The Aboriginal Population of America North of Mexico. In *Smithsonian Miscellaneous Collections*. Swanton: ed. John R.

Parkman, F. 1983. *France and England in North America*. New York: Library of America.

Perdue, T., and M. Green Perdue. 1995. *The Cherokee Removal: A Brief History With Documents*. Boston: Bedford Books/St. Martin's Press.

Prescott, W.H. 1933. *History of the Conquest of Mexico*. London: E. P. Dutton.

Russell, H.S. 1980. *Indian New England before the Mayflower*. Hanover, N.H.: University Press of New England.

Shkilnyks, A.M. 1985. *A Poison Stronger Than Love: The Destruction of an Ojibwa Community*. New Haven, Conn.: Yale University Press.

Smith, A. 1992. The HIV Correlation to Hepatitis A and B Vaccines. *Warn Newsletter* (Summer).

Stannard, D.E. 1992. *American Holocaust: Columbus and the Conquest of the New World*. New York: Oxford University Press.

Stiffarm, L.A. 1992. The Demography of Native North America: A Question of American Indian Survival. In M.A. Jaimes (ed.), *The State of Native America: Genocide, Colonization, and Resistance*. Boston: South End Press.

Thornton, R. 1987. *American Indian Holocaust and Survival: A Population History Since 1492*. Norman: University of Oklahoma Press.

Trigger, B.G. 1976. *The Children of Aataentsic*. Montreal: McGill-Queens University Press.

Trigger, B.G. 1986. *Natives and Newcomers: Canada's Heroic Age Reconsidered*. Kingston: McGill University Press.

10 Indigenous Peoples, Civil Society and the Environment
The Struggle for Sustainability

Mario Blaser

Foucault (1990: 135–142) contends that since the 18th century a transformation of power has been under way. This started when the exercise of sovereign power began to shift from a "right of death" centred in the exaction of tribute (or in last instance of life) to "a power that exerts a positive influence on life, that endeavours to administer, optimise, and multiply it, subjecting it to precise controls and comprehensive regulations" (Foucault, ibid.: 137). Certainly, this exercise of the sovereign's power is very well encapsulated in the idea of development. Precisely, it has been argued that the term development, understood as transformation that moves towards an ever perfect form, was transferred as a metaphor from the biological order to the social sphere in the 18th century (Esteva 1996: 8). With the term also came the idea of "mastering of nature" now transformed into the mastery of society, a mastery that was endowed in the figure of the sovereign state.

Development has been and is one of the most cherished objectives/justifications/buzz words of the modern state. In the name of economic development entire populations have been relocated out of their ancestral lands, rivers have been diverted, lakes created, and mountains moved. Since the end of World War II, and until recently, nothing could stand in the way of development and nothing was more of a priority than the need for development (Mason 1997: 407–461). This has begun to change in the last few decades. The idea of mastery of nature and society, with its deep roots in the modern dichotomous understanding of nature as separated from society, has given place to what Latour (1993) calls the proliferation of hybrids, Finger (1994: 62) "development spiral," and Beck (1992) "risk society." Aside from the different arguments each of these authors makes, they share the understanding that modern society has brought itself to an unsustainable situation, creating a series of crises (the environmental, representational and political being among the more evident and pervasive) that exceed the capacity of modern institutions to handle them.

These crises are the cause and effect of ongoing transformations to which the idea of development has not been immune. A major result of these transformations is reflected in the creation of "sustainable development" as the new improved successor to the worn-out concept. Made popular mainly by the widely publicised Brundtland Report (WCED 1987: 43), sustainable development is understood as that which "meets the needs of the present without compromising the ability of future generations to meet their own needs." Today, rare is the NGO (non-governmental organisation), agency, government or company involved in some way or other in a development project that does not at least pay lip service to the concept. This wide use is possible due to the highly imprecise meaning of the term. For instance, the needs of some people may not coincide with the needs of others; or worse, to meet the needs of some may mean to compromise the future of others. In this way the wide acceptance of "sustainable development" conceals the inherent conflict of who defines the needs of whom. It conceals a conflict about scales: at what level do we achieve sustainability? At the village level, the nation, the planet (Sachs 1993)? It is from the struggles, in which actors who feel their interests affected engage, that the abstract concept of sustainable development acquires concrete meaning in each particular case.

I mentioned that the shift from plain development to sustainable development has been entangled with ongoing transformations. In this chapter I want to discuss one particular transformation which is very closely associated with the previously mentioned shift. This is the growing importance of Indigenous people, civil society and the environment in defining development's agenda. By means of discussing these interrelated "factors" I will be better prepared to discuss in the final section some tendencies that are becoming visible in this struggle. Thus, in each of the three first sections I will discuss Indigenous people, civil society and the environment, respectively. In the final section I will resume the discussion of "sustainable development" as a site of struggle.

INDIGENOUS PEOPLE

Indigenous people can be singled out as the original victim of development. The idea of development, based in the Western assumption that "the world is objectively knowledgeable and that the knowledge so obtained can be absolutely generalized," has served as the justification to override local (indigenous) way of knowing and doing (Apffel-Marglin & Marglin 1996: 1). Thus, based on this generalised knowledge, the European rulers and settlers saw it as their task to develop Indigenous populations up to their own "cultural level," and at the same time to use the "unproductive" natural resources in Indigenous lands.

Even after decolonisation (including the independence of settlers' colonies from the metropolis, as was the case in the Americas, Australia and New Zealand), the agenda of development has been sustained by the new governing elites. These elites saw it as their patriotic duty to modernise and develop their "backward" countries (Wilmer 1993; Mason 1997). The "greater good for the greater number" was moral justification enough to implement development and remove the obstacles in its way. Indigenous people were considered one such obstacle. In this context the "prior ownership rights and interests of the aboriginal inhabitants are totally ignored as irrelevant by both the state and the invading individuals" (Bodley 1982: 24).

Today, when we hear of a development project being implemented, there are good chances that Indigenous peoples are going to be affected by it. This is usually because for developers an underdeveloped area is one that has not been "properly" integrated within the contemporary logic that rules the world system (the capitalist logic). It is also usually the case that these resources are actually under another regime of use, probably indigenous. Development of "underdeveloped" areas, then, does not look the same from the Indigenous peoples' perspective. For them, the inclusion of their lands and resources, even of their labour force, within the world economic system has meant mostly pain, frustration and alienation (Tanien Ashini 1993: 14–18).

With their ways of knowing labelled as "backward," "primitive," "superstitious," etc., the Indigenous cultures have been put under siege by "educational programmes" to transform them into "never-quite-perfect" replicas of the European educated elites, the only way to be accepted as citizens contributing to the development of the country (Maybury-Lewis 1997). Being under the "custody" of the state, their voicing of problems and abuses has gone unheard in the Westphalian system as internal issues of sovereign states (Wilmer 1993: 2–3). Being deprived of their sovereignty as a people, their lands and resources have been susceptible to seizure by the state or state-authorised agents in the name of the greater good (Clay 1994: 19–30). While it is as true today as yesterday that development is a process that impinges on the core of Indigenous people's possibilities to sustain their own cultures, the political conditions have changed enough in the last few decades as to provide Indigenous people's struggles against "resource colonialism" and top-down development schemes with an improved chance of success (Geddicks 1993). However, these new conditions also entail new risks.

Indigenous people (at least in the Americas) have been resisting conquest, colonization and encroachment since the 15th century by armed struggles, by using the colonisers' legal frameworks, by appealing to international organisations, etc. However, since the 1970s Indigenous people have begun to operate such struggles in a changing scenario that has strengthened their capacities to make things work, if not to their total advantage, then, at least, paraphrasing Scott (1985), to their minimum disadvantage. I identify four mutually reinforcing processes as the background for these improved capacities: the emergence of an international movement of Indigenous people; the increasing recognition of Indigenous peoples' rights to self-determination; the emergence of a loosely connected anti-modernist alliance fuelled by what is perceived as the failures or contradictions of the "modern project"; and the tendency towards the development of new systems of governance below and above the state. The order in which I present them does not imply a chain of causality. Rather, I believe that these processes run parallel and in close connection to each other.

Geopolitics and the push for development after World War II fuelled increasing incursions into Indigenous people's lands (Assies 1994: 32–33). From the 1970s onward, Indigenous people began to organise in wider associations[1] to resist these incursions and defend their livelihoods. Since then, the international Indigenous movement has grown in size and complexity as a network with a varied reach in national governments, international fora and NGOs (Stavenhagen 1994; Assies 1994; Wilmer 1993). International Indigenous movements have as one of their main objectives to assert the right of Indigenous peoples to enjoy self-determination. The way in which particular Indigenous communities may want to exercise this right may vary from different degrees of autonomy within the nation-state to full sovereign independence (Brosted et al. 1985; Assies & Hoekema 1994).

The international Indigenous movement has displayed a stunning variety of strategies to achieve its goals, among them international appeals, litigation, political participation, protest, direct action, networking, use of the media, educational activities and alliances with non-Indigenous groups. Among the more conspicuous allies are some environmentalist movements and, in general, critics of modernisation. However, these alliances have to be addressed with caution. A general discrediting of modernity's ideals may have contributed to a re-appreciation of Indigenous peoples and their cultures as worthy of respect, but we must not forget that certain tendencies or inertia of modernity are still present and, more, that they are dominant. For example, today many of these "critics" of modernity share the widespread belief that Indigenous peoples hold the key to harmonious relations of society with the environment. This belief has spawned a growing interest in Traditional Environmental Knowledge (TEK), though mainly for it to be incorporated into a dominantly modernist managerial framework aimed at sustaining nature because of its value as capital—an idea completely alien to most Indigenous peoples and that, in the last instance, implies just a further domain to be incorporated within the logic of capitalist economics (Escobar 1996: 56–57). At the other end of the spectrum, some "deep" ecologists who revere Indigenous spiritual relations with nature may tend to freeze them as the "Other"—again a very modernist attitude—in an imagined past which has no relation with their current aspirations (Harries-Jones 1993).

To a great extent the critique of modernity is based in the current crisis brought about by the means used to achieve its goals and to fulfil its values. Finger (1994) stresses the point that there are growing doubts about the appropriateness of managing the global environmental problem along the lines of the development spiral[2] of more science, better education and better nation-state politics. As Lash and Urry (1994: 292–293) point out, the usual role of the (welfare) state in organised capitalism, taking care of problems such as health, poverty and the environment, is no longer tenable, at least as originally conceived. On the one hand, the state is too small to deal by itself with problems like global warming and pollution in the oceans that transcend national boundaries. Even the protection of endangered species seems to be "too big" a task for a single state (Princen 1994); thus, the state is being pushed to pass on responsibilities to upward levels of integrated action. On the other hand, it is too big to attend to the nuances of the needs of local populations, who perceive the state as distant and unknowing of the immediate problems. Moreover, the fear, anxiety and insecurity produced by a weakened state and deteriorating living conditions strengthen the tendencies towards ever more circumscribed identity politics (from state citizen to ethnic, religious, sexual and other group ascription), which further weakens the state's power (Finger 1994; Friedman 1996).

In multiple domains "the close links between territoriality and the state are breaking down and thereby posing the question of what constitute the boundaries of communities" (Rosenau 1994: 258). The struggle to define their own boundaries, in which multiple groups and communities are involved, is the context in which Indigenous peoples are pursuing their own struggle. What has changed for them is that now, in a situation of generalised crisis of old structures of governance and of fragmentation of identities, the possibilities for establishing strategic alliances are greater. Under these conditions their own struggles find echoes in other actors' struggles for recognition (Fraser 1995: 68–93). After all, this is what is at the core of Indigenous people's engagement with issues of development, the need for recognition of their own cultures as valid ways of being-in-the-world.

CIVIL SOCIETY

Civil society—the social space in which civic associations understood as "the array of institutions and organizations in and through which individuals or groups can pursue their own projects independently of the direct organization of the state or of economic collectivities such as corporations or trade unions" (Held 1995: 181)—has certainly undergone a major expansion in the last three decades. Indeed, the expansion is such that some scholars speak of a global "associational" revolution (Salomon 1994), of an emergent global civil society (Lipschutz 1992) or, more cautiously, an international civil society (Peterson 1992). This scenario of an expanding civil society has come to play a fundamental role in the emergence of the concept "sustainable development." While, in the past, development was an issue to be treated exclusively by governmental and financial institutions and their cohort of experts, today it is impossible to think of sustainable development without the participation of organisations originating from civil society.

Salomon (1994: 112–115) identifies three sources of pressure to expand what he calls "the voluntary sector." One of the pressures comes from below: people who organise "to improve their conditions or to seek basic rights." Another source of pressure comes from outside: the church, Western private voluntary organisations and official aid agencies who support and promote the formation of local civic associations.[3] The final pressure source is from above: the conservative governments and their policies of reducing government social spending. In general, the three sources point towards a failure of the state to address people's needs. According to Salomon, this failure is the result of the convergence of four crises: the crisis of the welfare state; the crisis of development; the global environmental crisis; the crisis of socialism as a viable politic system. Let me take two of Salomon's crises to illustrate how "sustainable development" has come to be thought closely associated with the expansion of civil society.

Up to the 1970s the environmental crisis and the crisis of development were running closely parallel but relatively separated. As Sachs (1996: 27) points out, the ecocentric and humanistic perspectives about the environment "were foreign to the perceptions of the international development elite." The ecological movements (particularly in Germany, England and North America) in their origins had strong components of preservationism, conservationism and fundamentalism which made them strongly inimical to the idea of development (Bramwell 1989). However, they also contained a strong reliance on the science of ecology that, as Sachs argues, would be the "door" that eventually would allow the marriage of environment and development. The crisis of development, on the other hand, was first perceived as a failure to deliver what it had promised, the economic growth of underdeveloped countries. This failure did not put into question the objective but the means of achieving it. What was singled out as the reason for failure was the top-down approach to development. In this way, by the 1970s, grassroots participation became the new instrument to pursue economic growth (Rahnema 1996).

From the 1970s onward, the up to now separated paths of the environment and development began to merge. Among the first tendencies in this direction was the growing perception that the limits to growth, that had been identified by the Club of Rome report (Meadows et al. 1972), were not "insurmountable barriers [. . .] but discrete obstacles forcing the flow to take a different route" (Sachs 1996: 29). Also, the increasing understanding that the poor were in part responsible for the deforestation and desertification of the world played a role in the "marriage" of development and environment. The Brundtland Report brought this association closer by pointing out that "poverty reduces people's capacity to use resources in a sustainable manner" (WCED 1987: 49). Cast in those terms, the disease (environmental degradation) clearly pointed to its own remedy (development). It can be said that the "wedding" between environment and development took place in the Rio UNCED of 1992. There, the worries of the North about environmental degradation and the worries of the South about continuing development were matched by the sanctification of "sustainable development" as the solution. How to achieve this? By means of the science of ecology that can tell (theoretically at least) how much we can use of a resource to achieve development without harming the environment (Worster 1977).

The role that "civic associations" played in this process was very important. For instance, Finger (1994: 190) notes that the concept of sustainable development was made public for the first time by the International Union for the Conservation of Nature and thereafter enshrined by the Brundtland Report. But more important is the fact that in the framework, based on the Brundtland Report, that prepared the way to Rio, NGOs came to play a fundamental role that, Finger (1994) argues, transformed them and their relations with the emerging environmental and development establishment. As Sachs (1993: xv) puts it,

> [O]nce environmentalism called for new public virtues, now they call for rather better managerial strategies. Once they advocated more democracy and local self-reliance, now they tend to support the global empowerment of governments, corporations and science. Once, they strove for cultural diversity, now they see little choice but to push for a worldwide rationalization of lifestyle.

How had this come about? Certainly, the UNCED process was not the cause, although I agree in part with Finger in the sense that it may have deepened a process already underway. Hajer (1995) has argued that since the Stockholm conference of 1972 a process of institutionalisation of the ecologist movement had been underway. Since when this process of co-optation has been ongoing is not an issue that can be adequately addressed in this chapter. However, it is important to note it, and, also, that from the UNCED onward the role of the NGOs has become more prominent. In the area of development a similar process of co-optation had been underway since the 1970s. The ideas of grassroots participation, empowerment, etc. as a means towards liberation had been used by grassroots activists influenced by the works of Freire (1973) and Fals-Borda (1988), among others. As I mentioned before, to the extent that the development establishment came to recognise the failure of their top-down approach, they became more and more inclined to adopt what until then had been seen as a threat to capitalist development (Rahnema 1996). In this way both development and environment arrived at the UNCED with a strong attachment towards "civic associations" from civil society as instruments of the newly married eco-development establishment.

However, as Finger (1994) has shown, this perspective on the relation between the states (at the international level through the international institutions, and at the national level through ministries, official agencies, etc.) and the NGOs was not necessarily shared by all the NGOs. Thus, following Finger, we can trace a divide between those NGOs that are working more closely within the scheme designed by the state actors and those adopting a more confrontational attitude. The first group includes mainstream environmental NGOs such as WWF, IUCN, the World Resources Institute, etc. The second group includes what Finger call political NGOs such as Environmental Liaison Committee International, Friends of the Earth, the European Environmental Bureau, etc. Working closer to the eco-development establishment, it is logical that the first set of NGOs adopts an acritical stance towards sustainable development, understanding that the only problems to overcome are technical. In other words, they will focus on controlling that the calculations of cost and benefits, environmental impact assessments and environmental regulations meet the standards set by science. The other group, working closer to grassroots constituencies, may adopt more critical stances towards sustainable development, posing the kind of question mentioned in the introduction: sustainability at what scale? Sustainability of what and for whom?

This contradictory role that civic associations play in the developmental agenda points out the fact that civil society is chiefly a place of struggle. Accordingly, one wonders in what sense can one speak of a global civil society? "Global visions are shared by members of a few groups, such as some activists in the peace and ecological movements, but are yet not widespread" (Peterson 1992: 377). It seems that even in these movements global visions are very much an issue of struggle. As Held (1995: 125) describes it, "[T]here is no common global pool of memories; no common global way of thinking; and no universal history in and through which people can unite." However, I will argue that there is an intention, which emanates from both "factions," to create this commonality. In fact, the image of "spaceship earth," the single vessel in which everybody is responsible, etc., is part of a struggle to create this commonality. The effect of this commonality in terms of distribution of "risks" is uncertain as long as the "globalitarian temptation" (Beney 1993) is being contested by a commonality of different localities. I will return to this issue in the final section.

Finger (1994) points that there was a third faction of NGOs represented at the Rio Summit. Less spectacular, but probably more numerous, they were the single-issue NGOs, ranging from "save the turtles" organisations to "stop building the sewage in X." What is interesting is that these single-issue expressions of civil society are spread far beyond environmental worries; they entail mobilisations for justice for particular cases, neighbourhood mobilisations for health services, demonstrations for sexual freedom, etc. All this points again to what I discussed above apropos of identity politics, that their fragmentation creates an unstable scenario whose outcome is uncertain. In spite of how things may appear from the discussion about the two emerging factions in civil society, it is probable that most of civil society's actors are located in this uncharted territory of "single issues" and fragmented identities. I guess that, in a very Gramscian fashion, the outcome will depend on how the "war of positions" (Gramsci

1971: 206–207), to establish hegemonic representations of commonality, proceeds. The struggles in civil society around sustainable development are thus struggles to define what "our common future" means.

THE ENVIRONMENT

In our times there is a generalised perception that after having been silenced for many centuries nature has been given a voice again (see among others Worster 1977; Bramwell 1989; Milton 1993; Grove-White 1993; Harries-Jones et al. 1995). However, "it is crucial to acknowledge how such nature [is] produced, economically, culturally and politically, within different epochs" (Lash & Urry 1994: 295). Given that nature cannot "speak" other than through the translation that human beings make, and with these translations being in no way independent from their conditions of production, nature always "speaks" culture; and in our "global culture," nature has come to speak with a threatening voice. However, I will argue that, while the threat is widely perceived, the voice that is heard differs for variously located actors.

Worster (1977) and Bramwell (1989) have discussed the history and roots of the (late) modern ecologist and environmentalist movement,[4] pointing out that at the basis of their "translation" of nature there is a paradoxical reliance on science. The paradox is that science is perceived simultaneously as the instrument of nature's destruction and as the instrument to diagnose (and for some to cure) the disease. This inbuilt contradiction has a series of consequences for how we hear nature's voice. The mastery of nature based in the "gain of power from techno-economic 'progress' is being increasingly overshadowed by the production of risk"—a risk determined by a technology produced by that same techno-economic progress (Beck 1992: 13). In the face of this contradiction, many "Greens" find themselves attracted either to a religious or spiritual approach to nature (Luhrman 1993), or must rely on science and curtail the contradiction as far as possible (Yearley 1993). The reliance on science in spite of its contradictions opens the door to ever higher doses of science to "cure" the "side effects" of the previous round of medicine, a solution that Finger (1994: 62) calls the "development spiral."

This translation of nature by science has undergone a shift in the last two decades. Nature no longer speaks from the circumscribed locality of the bioregion; nature now talks on a global scale. The voice we hear is the voice of the planet. The sciences of global bio-geo-chemical cycles (Finger, ibid.) have given way to a "global nature," a new "product" which signals new cultural, economic and political tendencies, among which "green globalism" stands out (Lohman 1993; Sachs 1993). Thus, the threatening voice of nature is understood to point out global remedies and global management (Sachs 1993: 18–19). The threats from civilisation in the form of environment's retaliation "only come to consciousness in scientized thought, and cannot be directly related to primary experience. These are [. . .] hazards that employ the language of chemical formulas, biological contexts and medical, diagnostic concepts" (Beck 1992: 52).

Another "language" in which nature is translated is that of aesthetic consumption. Here we can find also a paradox. For Lash and Urry (1994: 296–267), the consumption of goods and services has become the structural basis of Western society. This has enormous effects on the environment. An overwhelming global consumerism makes itself felt in phenomena such as the hole in the ozone layer, global warming, acid rain etc. However, consumerism is also thought to be applicable to solve environmental problems by means of the incorporation of the environmental cost in the products, thus letting the market function as the regulator of environmental stress. In other words, green consumerism is deemed a kind of commitment to environmentally sound practices.[5] There is a further point in respect of consumption as the "translation" of nature's voice. According to Lash and Urry,

> [E]cology in part presupposes a certain kind of consumerism [. . .]. As people reflect upon such consumption they develop not only a duty to consume but also certain rights [to] certain qualities of the environment, of air, water and scenery, and that these extend into the future and to other populations. (Lash & Urry, ibid.: 297)

These authors also point out that the perception of nature and its consumption have undergone transformations connected with globalisation; the main transformation is the conceptual collapse of the difference between nature and culture.

This collapse of the nature/culture dichotomy has, as one of its philosophical consequences, the understanding of nature as a subject and not as an object—a position known as the Gaia hypothesis (Lovelock 1988)—and the understanding of the relation human/nature as a relational total field image, which is the position of deep ecology (Devall & Session 1985). These stances provide a third voice for nature, that of spirituality. In this "translation" nature is apprehensible not through science but through intuitions (Stark 1995: 268). These translations based in "intuitive" understanding of what nature dictates either as right or wrong are expressed not only as value claims, but also as empirical ones. The conflation of empirical and value claims is, according to Beck (1992), one of the central problems the "risk society" must face. The boomerang effect (Beck, ibid.: 37) of the hazards that the agents of modernisation (development) unleash and profit from, strike back at them, thereby creating the "risk society." This "risk society" of reflexive modernity, in contrast with the society of industrial modernity, has to manage and distribute not wealth and goods but hazards and "bads." The global nature of these hazards "bring about 'communities of danger' that ultimately can only be comprised by the United Nations" (ibid.: 47). However, the fact of a real community of danger does not mean that there is a self-conceived community of danger. Such a consciousness collides with the current national-states' egoism and the prevailing interests of different kinds of social organisations, producing a "political vacuum" to address such dangers. The question is whether a solidarity grown out of anxiety can be politically organised and with what result (ibid.: 48–49). For instance, Beck contends that, given that risks are universal and non-specific, one hears or reads about them, which creates feelings of anxiety. Thus, the groups that tend to be afflicted by it are the better educated ones that actively inform themselves with the concomitant result that risk consciousness and activism are more likely to occur where there is no direct pressures to make a living, i.e., among the wealthier people and countries (ibid.: 53).

Now, given the elusive nature of the hazards considered, there is a deep dependency on expert knowledge to define such hazards. In this sense "the affected parties are becoming incompetent in matters of their own affliction" (ibid.: 53). As I mentioned earlier, the problem is that the experts' (scientific) statements on risk are not only empirical ones but also "statements of the type that is how we want to live" (ibid.: 58). This dependency on expert knowledge creates the space for intervention in, and planning and control of, people's life (ibid.: 79). The industrially induced degradation of the environment has set in motion a social and political dynamic that force a reconsideration of the relation between nature and society. In short, this reconsideration implies the end of the antithesis between nature and society. Society can only be understood within nature and nature within society. Environmental problems are not problems of our surroundings but are social problems. In this sense, when the scientist faces his/her object (nature) s/he is dealing with a political object at the same time.

It is interesting to contrast Beck's position on "modernity" with that of Latour (1993), who claims that we have never been modern. Without going into the full details of the argument, modernity, for Latour, has never been achieved because it has always been a delusion based on a false dichotomy: nature/society. By not recognising this delusion, the would-be modernity allowed the proliferation of hybrids (among them Beck's hazards). Latour compares the supposedly modern society with other "amodern" societies and what he finds is a difference in the amount of hybrids allowed. In short, amodern societies have sustained the indifferentiation of nature and society in such a way that what for the "moderns" is nature has always, for them, been political at the same time. Thus, very simplistically stated, the interaction with nature will always be subjected to value claims in a way that unwanted outcomes will usually be visible and prevented. There could not be an empirical claim about nature's state that is not at the same time a political claim about society's state. For example, the adoption of a technology will depend not only on what that technology could "empirically" achieve, but intrinsic to its consideration will be the values embodied in it.

The difference with "modern'" society lies not in that, within it, the adoption of technology does not embody values, but in its denials that there are such values besides the empirical effects of the technology.

By keeping these elements together, amodern cultures have been able to avoid the proliferation of hybrids that weigh so heavily on "modern" society's back. The paradox is that these hybrids, which they have tried so hard to avert, have nevertheless proliferated with the expansion of the West. And here I return to my original point, that environmental threat is perceived differently by differently located people. Beck (1992) describes the particular perception of the environmental threat of the "modern" society (reflexive or otherwise), but his description is also an example of the widespread "modern" misrecognition of other ways to perceive and solve the problems. First, Beck sees the creation of a self-conscious community of danger of the scale of the United Nations as the only possible way to handle risk. As Finger (1994) pointed out and I discussed previously, NGOs are probably filling the vacuum to produce this community. However, this is a struggle, and it is not clear at all that global governance of the kind Beck seems to foresee (one highly reliant on expert knowledge) is the only way out. Secondly, the perception of risk produced by development may be indirect, universal or invisible for "modern" society, but for others, especially those in the rural areas of the Third World (and the Fourth World in all nations), the perception of risk is very direct, particularised and visible. This is because the primary threat for them is the depletion of the material bases for their livelihood, which occurs mainly through the encroachment of the local "commons" by external agents (of development) (Collinson 1997; Taylor 1995).

Thus, it is useful to trace a distinction between what Taylor (1995) denominates popular ecological resistance and radical environmentalism. The latter may probably fit Beck's idea that the "risk society" activist is a wealthy and educated citizen whose involvement with environmental struggles arises from a transformation of consciousness based on the knowledge acquired through expert systems. The prescription of these activists would be an awareness of a global community of danger. Popular ecological resistance, by contrast, is constituted by people for whom the possibilities of survival of their ancestral way of life are severely limited in the short or medium range. The knowledge of their own situation is not only independent of expert systems but also based on their own local knowledge. This knowledge and the actions it prompts confirm that at the basis of many of these movements there is a conflation of nature and society (Taylor 1995: 336; Banuri & Apffel-Marglin 1993; Nandy & Visvanathan 1990). The prescription of these movements is a protection of the local "commons."

It is noticeable that while the conflation of nature and society seems to have reunited all societies at an intellectual level, this commonality sparks such different approaches as to how to deal with the effects of development (or modernisation). Certainly, this is related to the different ways in which risk is perceived. But I would argue that it is also related to the fact that for the "modern" society the conflation of nature and society has occurred only in some peripheral areas.[6] Thus, there is still trust in the capacity of expert systems to manage risks but at the cost of obliterating the possible political effects of such management. The old "modern" blindness is still in action. In this context, the idea that modern society's worries constitute environmental consciousness, and that there is a common risk that we all have to face with the recipes of modern (albeit reflexive) society, moves the focus away from the fact that environmental risk is caused primarily by the rich not the poor. Only with this particular "blindness" can it be stated that the wealthiest 20% of the population living in Europe, North America, Oceania, and Japan, and who utilise roughly 80% of the planet's resources and sinks (Parikh et al. 1991, cited in Banuri 1993: 50–51), are the primary bearers of environmental consciousness. However, it must be recognised that the incipient mistrust of systems of expert knowledge and modernity's goals in general offers the possibility to hear other voices of nature. This brings us back to the prominence that this context has given to Indigenous peoples. Can we learn something from those societies that have always known what we seem to be just beginning to envision, the consequences of thinking society separated from nature? In the next section I will discuss the chances for such a lesson.

SUSTAINABLE DEVELOPMENT: THE STRUGGLE FOR OUR COMMON FUTURE

As I mentioned in my introduction, a common issue stands out among the different factors that impinge on today's development agenda, that is, a conflict over whom and at what level sustainability is defined. This conflict in development's agenda is just one example of a generalised crisis of governance where new structures are being brought into being. To a great extent it can be argued that the crisis of governance is a crisis over the scale at which the emerging political institutions will operate in the future. Will it be local? National? Global? Or all of them at the same time?

This generalised crisis of "turbulence in world politics" (Rosenau 1990) seems characterised by a dynamic that Rosenau (1994: 256) has called "fragmegrative." What he means by this is the interaction of two processes, integration and fragmentation. Fragmegrative dynamics operate in different domains but have a common outcome, the breaking of the links between territoriality and the structure of governance based on the state system. Rosenau (ibid.: 258–269) argues that this dynamic of fragmegration operates in the economic domain by the reorganisation of production and distribution in larger economic units and localised regions; in the political realm by a relocation of authority upwards toward supranational entities, sideways toward transnational organizations and social movements, and downwards

Indigenous Peoples, Civil Society and the Environment

toward subnational groups and communities; and in the social and cultural domain by a reorientation of loyalties and values towards global norms and neighbourhood concerns. Rosenau anticipates the outcome of this fragmegrative dynamic:

> [T]he more pervasive globalizing tendencies become, the less resistant will localizing reactions be to further globalization. In other words, globalization and localization are anticipated to coexist, but with the former setting the context for the latter. (Rosenau, ibid.: 272)

A central "accommodation" at the perceptive level will help in settling the dynamic in the way Rosenau anticipates it. People will come to appreciate multiple loyalties at diverse levels without understanding them as mutually exclusive to the extent that the state efficiency and national identities diminish, but also as the "benefits of the global economy expand and people become increasingly aware of the extent to which their well-being is dependent on events and trends elsewhere in the world" (ibid.: 273). One indicator by which Rosenau finds that globalisation is being favoured is the relatively minimal opposition to the recent surge of interventions by international organisations such as peacekeeping missions and the constraints imposed by the IMF (ibid.: 275). In short, for Rosenau, if the world is "marked more by indeterminacies than by globalizing tendencies, then the future may be less salutary" (ibid.: 276–277). Again the "global solution" appears to be the only possible one.

But how may this global solution to the crisis be put to work? We have seen that, as Beck (1994) argues, there is a certain vacuum of institutions to deal with these framegrative dynamics. In part the answer may come from the evolving governance structures characterised by regimes where state representatives come together to solve specific issues. However, as Hopkins and Puchala (cited in Krasner 1982: 9) point out, understanding regimes to be composed of state actors may be misleading since it is the elites who are the practical actors in international relations. These elites act as epistemic communities who share principles, norms and rules that transcend national boundaries. In this sense, even if NGOs come to play a role in the formation of regimes, as Princen et al. (1994) suggest, they will do so to the extent that they share the principles, rules and norms of the elites that comprise the epistemic community. In fact, that is what can be inferred from Finger's (1994: 210) discussion of what occurred in the UNCED where the NGOs that were nearer to the "evolving structures of governance" were, at the same time, farther from their grassroots constituencies.

Then the question is, what kind of change appears to be underway in terms of emerging structures of governance? The first impression one gets is that these structures are fundamentally trying to handle the upsetting effects that fragmegrative dynamics of globalisation have on capitalism. But as Lash and Urry (1994: 280) indicate, this globalisation (and related practices to handle it) is fundamentally capitalist globalisation since "a hegemonic role is played by the North-Atlantic-rim countries and Japan." The main strategy that seems underway for managing this dynamic is conveyed by the motto "think globally, act locally" (Lash & Urry 1994: 293), which is precisely what Princen et al. (1994) argue that NGOs are helping to do. This strategy tends to stabilise the fragmegrative process by strengthening global structures at the top and deepening fragmented identities at the bottom, while at the same time helping to create the links that keep both processes causally linked. In this context the promises for an enhanced (consumerist) reflexive individualism (Lash & Urry 1994) seem unavoidably to go hand in hand with an enhanced global system of security (Rosenau 1994). However, this view creates a blind spot that allows unwarranted assertions of the kind that Rosenau makes about the meager resistance offered against international institution interventions.

My argument is that this kind of assertion derives from the idea that we are facing processes that, as simple causal "mechanisms," are set in motion and then just follow their own evolving patterns. A completely different perspective appears if we see these processes (fragmegrative, global–local or glocal) as struggles over scales (Swyngedouw 1996). Focusing on the process of "making" the scales instead of beginning from the assumption that global or local exist in themselves and then interact, Swyngedouw (1996:150) argues that "glocalization processes do not proceed uncontested, and social movements organize around a variety of issues to tackle this thorny issue." The "invisibility" of contestation to the evolving structures of governance is part of the struggle. It intensifies the production of "truth effects" in the terms settled by those structures (Gudynas 1993). The globalitarian temptation requires a blindness towards those contestations such as to assert that our problems are global that require global solutions, thereby avoiding discussing the fact that our problems have a local origin which has been globalised (Shiva 1993).

That "glocalization" is a struggle and not simply a process set in motion by obscure forces is evident in the development agenda. It does not matter how many environmental impact assessments are made; or how convincing arguments of greater good are; or even how sustainable the new systems of resources use may appear, for at the bottom lies the question of whose way of life can or cannot be overridden and where are the decisions made. We have seen that so far the hegemonic tendency points towards decision-making at the global level followed by implementation through local level practices: economic decisions on global market strategies direct local tactics; political decisions at the global level of international regimes are progressively enforced through multiple means at the local level of states or communities; and cultural globalisation is achieved through a global culture of consumerism practised through the increasingly fragmented cultural tastes (Harvey 1989; Coombe 1995; Appadurai 1996). Contesting this hegemonic tendency, within which some scholarly prognoses function as self-fulfilled prophecies, are a host of practices at the local level, each seeking to make its own way through.

The multiple cases in which local people resist the integration of their commons within privatised global structures are ubiquitous throughout the third world (see among others Geddicks 1993; Taylor 1995; Peet & Watts 1996; Collinson 1997). As I discussed above, these local tactics are also emerging, through alliances, to dispute how structures of governance will be. If the dominant establishment in ecodevelopment emphasises a strategy of "thinking global and acting local" in order to keep the principles of the capitalist system unchanged (although with new environmentally friendly procedures), these multiple contestations seem to follow the inverse path: think locally and act globally. Such local resistance shows a high degree of dependence on supralocal alliances to succeed. For while the interest and thought are put in the local and immediate problems, the solutions have to be enacted at a global level through networking and support from and with other localities.

While thinking globally and acting locally relies heavily on expert systems and widespread surveillance and control mechanisms which assure that localities follow the dictates of the global structures of governance, thinking local and acting global relies on shared knowledge at the local level, which is then articulated politically, through consensual alliances, with other localities. What chances are there for this counter hegemonic attempt to produce a revolutionary change in the structures of governance? The answer is very uncertain. It will depend very much on the capacity of these alliances to overcome a fundamental problem pointed out by Swyngedouw (1996: 160):

> [It seems] deeply disturbing to find the power of money and homogenizing imperialist culture take control of ever larger scales, while very often the 'politics of resistance' seems to revel in some sort of militant particularism [. . .] in which local loyalties, identity politics, and celebrating the different other(s) attests to an impotence when faced with the call to embrace an emancipatory and empowering politics of scale.

The challenge is to find a common language among the reigning fragmented identities. I believe that the bases for that common language exist in the form of the contemporary collapse (in modern society) of the dichotomy nature/society. As Latour (1993) argues, after taking a long circular path we are back at the point in which we may begin to recognise that the only thing that has made us different from other societies is our blindness to the effects of a dichotomous reality. We may now be able to control the "hybrids," among them the globalitarian temptation, which for some seems almost a natural phenomenon. But now we know that natural phenomena are always social and therefore political. This is what we can relearn from indigenous peoples. I am not arguing that we take them as the exotic models romanticised by some environmentalists. We can learn that trying to be aware of the consequences of our actions, in all dimensions and on a planetary scale, is at least arrogant if not plainly stupid. It is already a complicated business at the local level, never mind at a planetary scale!

Certainly we cannot escape from the consequences of our actions. We thought we could and we rushed for development. This proved wrong. The consequences are catching us up with a vengeance.

Now, in our search for solutions we come across the idea of sustainability, but the dominant tendency is to think it globally and so again the modernist society (reflexively?) overrides these local cultures. There may be a distrust of science and an anti-modernist mood but it seems that the "reflexive" citizens cannot give up their complex of superiority and recognise that these other societies have not just "happened" but that they have made themselves. It can be argued that the organisation and scale of these societies is not the product of a conscious deed, after all even us with our sciences have not been able to master society completely. This argument only holds if we believe that a conscious making of society implies the use of Western rationality, at the basis of which is the nature/society dichotomy. Even if we cannot appreciate that our circular reasoning blinds us to the fact that this very dichotomy is what makes our society hard to master, we may recognise that (and here I use a "scientific" perspective) the hypotheses that mastery of nature will allow the mastery of society (Leiss 1972) have been sustained only by one *ad hoc* modification after other. It is probably time to look for other hypotheses. These Indigenous societies have proved to be relatively successful in controlling their hybrids; why not try their way?

For such societies the evidence of a global "risk society" does not need to be provided by expert-systems. It is evidence enough to find out that what they have for food, shelter or pleasure yesterday, is not longer there today. It is enough to realise that the fish that nurtured them yesterday today make them sick. If we want a globalised world in which sustainability is defined on a planetary scale in order to maintain every atom of the planet integrated within a system that treats it as a capital to be consumed always to the farthest limit that consumers demand and renewal of the resource permits, then we must pay a price. Indigenous societies, with their locally oriented practices, have shown that sustainability at a reduced scale is manageable in terms of democratic participation in decision-making. At a global scale this is doubtful. May we learn these other ways? It is hard to say; there are propitious conditions but strong political wills seem scarce.

NOTES TO CHAPTER 10

1. Here I am referring mainly to the organisation of Indigenous people through explicitly Indigenous agendas, based on Indigenous established goals and for Indigenous people. The expression of Indigenous people's grievances through

political parties has existed (regardless of their effectiveness) previously, especially in countries where Indigenous people are not a minority.
2. Finger (1994: 62) calls "development spiral" the mutual reinforcement that natural and social sciences have as instruments of development: the better nature is mastered the more material resources are there for socio-economic development, which implies better human, political and financial resources to pursue an improved mastery of nature, and so on.
3. Here Salomon seems to be thinking exclusively of Third World and "post-socialist" countries.
4. For this distinction in part I follow Humphreys (1996) in that environmentalists are part of the institutional response of capitalism to the environmental crisis, seeking to solve specific problems. The ecologists embody a more radical stance in which the solution to environmental crisis is sought through the total transformation of society.
5. For a critical assessment of this position, see James (1993).
6. See Lash in the introduction to Beck (1992).

REFERENCES

Apffel-Marglin, F., and S. Marglin (eds.). 1996. *Decolonizing Knowledge: From Development to Dialogue.* Oxford: Clarendon Press.
Appadurai, A. 1996. *Modernity at Large: Cultural Dimensions of Globalization. Public Worlds, Volume 1.* Minneapolis: University of Minnesota Press.
Assies, W. 1994. Self-Determination and the 'New Partnership.' In W. Assies and A. Hoekema (eds.), *Indigenous Peoples' Experiences with Self-Government*, IWGIA Document n°76, Copenhagen.
Assies, W., and A. Hoekema (eds.). 1994 *Indigenous Peoples' Experiences with Self-Government*, IWGIA Document n°. 76, Copenhagen.
Banuri, T. 1993. The Landscape of Diplomatic Conflicts 'Globalism.' In W. Sachs (ed.), *Global Ecology: A New Arena of Political Conflict.* London: Zed Books.
Banuri, T. and F. Apffel-Marglin (eds.) 1993. *Who Will Save the Forests? Resistance, Knowledge and the Environmental Crisis.* London: Zed Books.
Beck, U. 1992. *Risk Society: Towards a New Modernity.* London: Sage
Beney, G. 1993. 'Gaia': The Globalitarian Temptation. In W. Sachs (ed.), *Global Ecology: A New Arena of Political Conflict.* London: Zed Books.
Bodley, J. 1982. *Victims of Progress.* 2nd ed. Menlo Park: Benjamin/Cummings.
Bramwell, A. 1989. *Ecology in the Twentieth Century: A History.* New Haven, Conn.: Yale University Press.
Brosted, J., et al. *1985. Native Power: The Quest for Autonomy and Nationhood of Indigenous Peoples.* Bergen: UNIVERSITETSFORLAGET AS.
Clay, J. 1994. Resource Wars: Nation and State Conflicts of the Twentieth Century. In B. Johnston (ed.), *Who Pays the Price? The Sociocultural Context of Environmental Crisis.* Washington, D.C.: Island Press.
Collinson, H. (ed.). 1997. *Green Guerrillas: Environmental Conflicts and Initiatives in Latin America and the Caribbean.* Montreal: Black Rose Books.
Coombe, R. 1995. The Cultural Life of Things: Anthropological Approaches to Law and Society in Conditions of Globalization. *American University Journal of International Law and Policy* (10) 2: 791–835.
Devall, B., and G. Session 1985. *Deep Ecology: Living as if Nature Mattered.* Salt Lake City: Peregrine Smith.
Escobar, A. 1996. Constructing Nature: Elements for a Poststructural Political Ecology. In R. Pett & M. Watts (eds.), *Liberation Ecologies: Environment, Development and Social Movements.* London and New York: Routledge.

Esteva, G. 1996. Development. In W. Sachs (ed.), *The Development Dictionary: A Guide to Knowledge as Power*. London: Zed Books.

Fals-Borda, O. 1988. *Knowledge and People's Power: Lessons with Peasants in Nicaragua, Mexico, Colombia*. Dehli: Indian Social Institute.

Finger, M. 1994. NGOs and Transformation: Beyond Social Movement Theory/Environmental NGOs in the UNCED Process. In T. Princen and M. Finger (eds.), *Environmental NGOs in World Politics: Linking the Global and the Local*. London: Routledge.

Foucault, M. 1990. *The History of Sexuality: An Introduction Vol. 1*. New York: Vintage.

Fraser, N. 1995. From Redistribution to Recognition? Dilemmas of Justice in a 'Post-Socialist' Age. *New Left Review* 212: 68–93.

Freire, P. 1973. *Education for Critical Consciousness*. New York: Seabury Press.

Friedman, J. 1996. The Implosion of Modernity In M. Shapiro and H. Walker (eds.), *Challenging Boundaries: Global Flows, Territorial Identities*. Minneapolis: University of Minnesota Press.

Geddicks, A. 1993. *The New Resource Wars: Native and Environmental Struggles against Multinational Corporations*. Boston: South End Press.

Gramsci, A. 1971. *Selections from the Prison Notebooks of Antonio Gramsci*. Edited and translated by Q. Hoare, G. Nowell Smith. New York: International Publishers.

Grove-White, R. 1993. Environmentalism: a new moral discourse for technological society? In K. Milton (ed.), *Environmentalism: The View from Anthropology*. London: Routledge.

Gudynas, E. 1993. The Fallacy of Ecomessianism: observations from Latin America. In W. Sachs (ed.), *Global Ecology: A New Arena of Political Conflict*. London: Zed Books.

Hajer, M. 1995. *The Politics of Environmental Discourse: Ecological Modernization and the Policy Process*. Oxford: Oxford University Press.

Harries-Jones, P. 1993. Between Science and Shamanism: The Advocacy of Environmentalism in Toronto. In K. Milton (ed.), *Environmentalism: The View from Anthropology*. London: Routledge.

Harries-Jones, P., A. Rotstein, and P. Timmerman. 1995 A Signal Failure: Ecology and Economy after the Earth Summit. Paper presented at conference Multilateralism and the United Nations System, Costa Rica (December 1995).

Harvey, D. 1989. *The Condition of Postmodernity*. Oxford: Blackwell.

Held, D. 1995. *Democracy and the Global Order: From the Modern State to Cosmopolitan Governance*. Stanford, Calif.: Stanford University Press.

Humphreys, D. 1996. Hegemonic Ideology and the International Tropical Timber Organization. In J. Vogler and M. Imber (eds.), *The Environment and International Relations*. London: Routledge.

James, A. 1993. Eating Green(s): Discourses of Organic Food. In K. Milton (ed.), *Environmentalism: The View from Anthropology*. London: Routledge.

Krasner, S. 1982. Structural Causes and Regime Consequences: Regimes as Intervening Variables. *International Organization* 36 (2): 1–21.

Lash, S., and J. Urry. 1994. *Economies of Signs and Space*. London: Sage.

Latour, B. 1993. *We Have Never Been Modern*. Cambridge, Mass.: Harvard University Press.

Leiss, W. 1972. *The Domination of Nature*. New York: George Braziller.

Lipschutz, R. 1992. Reconstructing World Politics: The Emergence of Global Civil Society. *Millennium: Journal of International Studies* 21 (3): 389–420.

Lohman, L. 1993. Resisting Green Globalism. In W. Sachs (ed.), *Global Ecology: A New Arena of Political Conflict*. London: Zed Books.

Lovelock, J. 1988. *Gaia: A New Look at Life on Earth*. Oxford: Oxford University Press.
Luhrman, T. 1993. The Resurgence of Romanticism: Contemporary Neopaganism, Feminist Spirituality and the Divinity of Nature. In K. Milton (ed.), *Environmentalism: The View from Anthropology*. London: Routledge.
Mason, M. 1997. *Development and Disorder: A History of the Third World Since 1945*. Toronto: Behind the Lines.
Maybury-Lewis, D. 1997. *Indigenous Peoples, Ethnic Groups, and the State*. Boston: Allyn and Bacon.
Meadows, D., et al. 1972. *The Limits to Growth*. New York: Basic Books.
Milton, K. (ed.). 1993 *Environmentalism: The view from Anthropology*. London: Routledge.
Nandy, A. and S. Visvanathan 1990. Modern Medicine and Its Non-Modern Critics: A Study in Discourse. In F. Apffel-Margolin and S. Marglin (eds.), *Dominating Knowledge: Development, Culture and Resistance*. London: Clarendon Press.
Parikh, J., et al. 1991. *Consumption Patterns: The Driving Force of Environmental Stress*. Bombay: IGIDR.
Peet, R., and M. Watts (eds.). 1996. Liberation Ecology: Development, Sustainability, and Environment in an Age of Market Triumphalism. In R. Pett and M. Watts (eds.), *Liberation Ecologies: Environment, Development and Social Movements*. London and New York: Routledge.
Peterson, M. 1992. Transnational Activity, International Society and World Politics. *Millennium: Journal of International Studies* 21 (3):371–388.
Princen, T. 1994. The Ivory Trade Ban: NGOs and International Conservation. In T. Princen & M. Finger (eds.), *Environmental NGOs in World Politics: Linking the Global and the Local*. London: Routledge.
Princen, T., M. Finger, and J. Manno. 1994. Translational Linkages. In T. Princen and M. Finger (eds.), *Environmental NGOs in World Politics: Linking the Global and the Local*. London: Routledge.
Rahnema, M. 1996. Participation. In W. Sachs (ed.), *The Development Dictionary. A Guide to Knowledge as Power*. London: Zed Books.
Rosenau, J. 1990. *Turbulence in World Politics*. Princeton, NJ: Princeton University Press.
Rosenau, J. 1994. New Dimensions of Security: The Interaction of Globalizing and Localizing Dynamics. *Security Dialogue* 25 (3): 255–281.
Sachs, W. (ed.). 1993. *Global Ecology: A New Arena of Political Conflict*. London: Zed Books.
Sachs, W. (ed.). 1996. *The Development Dictionary. A Guide to Knowledge as Power*. London: Zed Books.
Salomon, L. 1994. The Rise of the Nonprofit Sector. *Foreign Affairs* 73 (4): 109–122.
Scott, J. 1985. *Weapons of the Weak: Everyday Forms of Peasant Resistance*. New Haven, Conn.: Yale University Press.
Shiva, V. 1993. The Greening of the Global Reach. In W. Sachs (ed.), *Global Ecology: A New Arena of Political Conflict*. London: Zed Books.
Stark, J. 1995. Postmodern Environmentalism: A Critique of Deep Ecology. In B. Taylor (ed.), *Ecological Resistance Movements: The Global Emergence of Radical and Popular Environmentalism*. Albany: SUNY Press.
Stavenhagen, R. 1994. Indigenous Rights: some conceptual problems. In W. Assies and A. Hoekema (eds.), *Indigenous Peoples's Experiences with Self-Government*. IWGIA Document n°76, Copenhagen.
Swyngedouw, E. 1996. Neither Global nor Local: 'Glocalization' and the Politics of Scale. In K. Cox (ed.), *Spaces of Globalization: Reasserting the Power of the Local*. New York: Guildford.

Tanien Ashini. 1993. We Have Been Pushed to the Edge of a Cliff. In Inter Press Service (ed.), *Story Earth: Natives Voices on the Environment*. San Francisco: Mercury House.
Taylor, B. 1995. *Ecological Resistance Movements: The Global Emergence of Radical and Popular Environmentalism*. Albany: SUNY Press.
Wilmer, F. 1993. *The Indigenous Voice in World Politics*. Newbury Park, CA: Sage.
World Commission on Environment and Development (WCED). 1987 *Our Common Future*. Oxford: Oxford University Press.
Worster, D. 1977. *Nature's Economy: A History of Ecological Ideas*. Cambridge: Cambridge University Press.
Yearley, S. 1993. Standing in for Nature: The Practicalities of Environmental Organizations' Use of Science. In K. Milton (ed.)., *Environmentalism: The View from Anthropology*. London: Routledge.

Contributors

Marlene R. Atleo (ʔeh ʔeh naa tuu kwiss) is the partner of Chief Umeek, thirrd chief of Ahousaht First Nation of the House of Klaaq-ish-peethl, Clayoquot Sound, Vancouver Island, British Columbia, Canada. She is a Director of Umeek Human Resource Development, Inc., a firm addressing cross-cultural issues in education and development through an indigenous Nuu-chah-nulth philosophy and the promotion of literacies for living (textual, psycho-social, computer literacy, institutional, etc.). She is currently an instructor of First Nations courses at the University of British Columbia.

Stephen G. Baines is a lecturer at the Departamento de Antropologia, Universidade de Brasília, 70919–900—Brasília—D.F., Brazil, since 1989, and research scholarship holder at the Brazilian National Research Council (CNPq). M.Phil in Social Anthropology, University of Cambridge, England, 1980; Ph.D. in Social Anthropology, Universidade de Brasília, 1988.

Mario Blaser is an Argentinian-Canadian anthropologist and Assistant Professor at York University, Canada. His current research interest focuses on multiple dimensions of development as a cultural and political practice, particularly as it interacts with Indigenous peoples movements in a globalizing world.

Dr. Jorge Calbucura is a researcher in the Sociology Department, University of Uppsala, Sweden.

Peter d'Errico is Professor of Legal Studies at the University of Massachusetts, Amherst, U.S.A.

Adolfo de Oliveira worked with Indigenous rights for many years as an anthropological advisor to the Federal Attorney-General's Office in Brazil, and as a researcher, since 1994. He has a Ph.D. by the University of St. Andrews, Scotland. He presently works at Mamiravá sustainable development institute in Amazonas State, Brazil

GELIND, or the Group of Study of Indigenous Legislation, is composed of researchers (Claudia Briones, Morita Carrasco, Diego Escolar, Axel Lazzari, Diana Lenton, Juan Manuel Obarrio and Alejandra Siffredi) at the University of Buenos Aires, Faculty of Philosophy and Literature, Institute of Anthropological Sciences (Ethnological and Ethnographical Section) and the National Council of Scientific and Technological Research (CONICET). The group carries out sociocultural research in the Indigenous communities of the Gran Chaco and Pampa-Patagonia regions, Argentina.

Andrew Gray studied social anthropology at the universities of Edinburgh and Oxford. He lived for over three years with the Arakmbut people of the southeastern Peruvian Amazon, on whom he published a trilogy of books (1996–1997, Berghahn Books). Between 1983 and 1989 he was an executive director of the International Work Group for Indigenous Affairs (IWGIA) in Copenhagen, before becoming a consultant researcher for IWGIA and also for the Forest Peoples' Programme of the World Rainforest Movement.

Edmundo Antônio Peggion is a researcher at the Laboratory of Symmetrical Anthropology, University of Rio de Janeiro; and a lecturer at Universidade Estadual Paulista—UNESP, São Paulo, Brazil.

Paula Sherman is a member of the Ardoch Algonquin First Nation located in Ardoch, Ontario, and has a Ph.D. from the University of Connecticut in the Graduate Program in Early American History. Her research interests include the interactions between peoples of the 15th, 16th, and 17th century Atlantic World and how Indigenous peoples fit within the sphere of World System Theory. Currently, she is Professor at Trent University, Ontario, Canada.

James F. Weiner is a Visiting Fellow in the Department of Anthropology, Research School of Pacific and Asian Studies, Australia National University. His research interests include Papua New Guinea; Aboriginal Australia; language, myth, poetry, art; the anthropology of religion; native title; the politics of contemporary indigeneity; indigenous people, mining and the state.

Index

A
Abi-Nader, J. 144
Aboriginal Heritage Protection legislation 80, 82, 83
Aboriginal Legal Rights Movement of South Australia 81
Abraham, H. 97
Addy, Justice 139
Africa 13, 21
Ahmad, I. 117
Ahousaht First Nation 134-7
Akan, L. 142
Alberni Indian Residential School (AIRS) 133, 134-5
Albert, B. 52
Alberta, University of 147-8
alcohol 54, 180, 184, 187
Algonkin 181
Allende, Salvador 70
allotment 37-8, 39, 111
Altabe, R. 122, 126
Amazonia 9, 29, 36, 52, 59
Andrade, L.M.M. de 59
anthropology: Aboriginal studies 92-3, 101; anthropological advocacy 10-11; applied 12-13; economic 24; evolutionary 25, 40; expert witness role 11-12, 18; human rights and 6-7, 39-41, 80; in indigenous education 170; investigation of beliefs 79, 80, 87-90, 96, 100; juridical 18; Ngarrindjeri involvement 81-7, 90-6; political 22, 24; roles of anthropologists 18, 80, 83; social 22-3; views on territory 18-28, 31
Apel, K.O. 5-6, 9
Apffel-Marglin, F. 191, 201
APOINME 1

Appadurai, A. 204
Apter, M.J. 140
Arakmbut, 30-6, 38, 39-40, 41
Archibald, J. 147
Ardrey, R. 22, 26
Argentina: collective property rights 71; Indigenous Fund 122; Law n°23302 122, 123-7, 129-30; limits of the constitutional amendment 9, 122; Mapuche population 65-7; new constitution 126-7; Resolution n°4811 122, 128-30; state of indigenous policy after constitutional amendment and Resolution N°4811 127-30
Ashburn, M.M. 175
Assies, W. 193
Atleo, E.R. 134, 135, 148-9, 152
Atleo, M. 10, 12, 139, 140, 147
Attraction Front *see* FAWA
Australia: decolonisation 191; property rights legislation 71; reservations 37; sovereignty issues 116; *see also* Hindmarsh Island Bridge
Australian Aborigines: Lower Murray populations 84, 85, 86, 90, 93, 96; religion 7, 83-6, 90-5; reservations 37; territories 19, 23, 27; *see also* Hindmarsh Island Bridge, Ngarrindjeri
autonomy: of beliefs 94; concept 7, 80; degrees of 193; denied 115; Inuit 3; dialogical character of indigenous autonomy 3-13; Mapuche 3, 66-7; need for 5
Avery, J. 93
Axelrod, A. 178
Axtell, J. 173
Azevedo, M.M. 166

214 Index

B
Baines, S. 9, 46, 51, 57, 58
Baktaman 94, 95-6
Balandier, G. 4, 20
Balasi, C.J. 181
Bangladesh 18, 38
Banuri, T. 201, 202
Barnes, B. 79, 88
Barrerio, J. 117
Bartelson, J. 113, 117-18
Barth, F. 23, 94, 95
Bartolomé, M. 57
Bateson, G. 165
Beck, U. 190, 198, 199-201, 203
beliefs 79-80; belief, practice, culture 90-5; status of 83; testing of belief 87-90
Bell, E.D. 145-6
Bender, B. 25
Beney, G. 197
Bengoa, J. 68
Bereiter, C. 158
Bergdama 21
Berndt, R. and C. 81, 83-5, 90, 93-4, 101
Berry, J. 141
Beverly, R. 179
Bhaskar, R. 79
Bickhard, M.H. 158
Blackfeet Tribe 109-10
Bloor, D. 79, 88
Boas, F. 19
Bodin, J. 114
Bodley, J. 37, 192
Bolivar, Simon 73
Bolivia 24, 37
Bonfil Batalla, G. 4
boundaries: hardening, 29-36; softening 22-9
Bracken, C. 143
Bramwell, A. 195, 198
Braunstein, J. 122
Brazil: anthropology 10; education 165-71; indigenous territories 37, 71; Northeast and Eastern 1; territorial policy 18; Shavante people 10, 166, 168-9; Yanomami Park 39
Brennan, Justice 98
Briones, C. 8
Brosted, J. 193
Brundtland Report 191, 195, 196
Buchillet, D. 52
Buckley, H. 184-5

Bunyard, P. 39
Byers, William N. 179
Bushmen 21

C
Calbucura, Cacique Juan 66
Calbucura, J. 9
Calha Norte Project 52
Calloway, C.G. 177-8
Camilleri, J. 114-15
Campbell, R.L. 158
Canada: ancestral land 80; anthropologists 11; Charter of Rights and Freedoms 138, 143; collective property rights 71; democracy 183, 184; education 10, 132-4, 150; extermination of Indigenous populations 174, 183; First Nations population 146; human rights issues 184; Indigenous population 175, 180-2; Inuit territory 3; reserves 184-5; sovereignty issues 116; Supreme Court 138; uranium mining 187
cancer rates 187
Cardoso de Oliveira, R. 6, 7, 45, 53
Carpina seminar 1-3
Castaneda, C. 85
Caxias, Duke of 2
Chandler, M. 148
Chandler, P. 153, 154
Chase Smith, R. 29
Cherokee Nation 109, 111, 178
Cheyenne 178-9, 180
Chile: agrarian policy towards Mapuche 9; allotment of land 37; Mapuche rebellions 3; Mapuche reservations 65, 67-9, 73; Mapuche territorial autonomy 66-7; privatisation of Mapuche collective property 69-74
Chirif, A. 29
Chittagong Hill Tracts Commission 38
Chivington, John Milton 176, 179
Chrisjohn, R. 141, 148
Christianity 96-7, 101, 105-6, 114, 116–18
Church, Benjamin 177
Churchill, W. 173-9, 181-3, 185-6
CIDA (Interamerican Committee on Agricultural Development) 68
civic associations 196-7
civil society 194-8
Clarke, P. 83, 96

Clay, J. 192
Club of Rome 195
Coeur d'Alene Tribe 111
Colchester, M. 39
Cole, M. 140, 141
Cole, P. 153
Collins, A. 157
Collinson, H. 201, 205
Colombia 39, 71
colonialism 17-22, 110
Columbus, Christopher 105, 176, 182, 183, 186
conceptual strategies 152-7
Coombe, R. 204
Coronado, Francisco Vázquez de 176
Coronation Hill 101
Cortez, Hernando 176
Costa, Gilberto 46, 48
Crosby, A.W. Jr. 173
cultural: content and processes 139-42; relativism 6, 79; slippage 142-4
Cunningham, M. 4
curriculum 149-50; comparative, 150-1, 151-2; intercultural 150-1

D

Dahl, J. 17
Dal Poz, J. 11
Deere, P. 120
Deloria, V. 4, 18
Denham, M.E. 113-14
d'Errico, P. 9
Devall, B. 199
development 190-1; civil society 194-8; effects on indigenous people 191-4; environment 198-202; sustainable 190-1, 202-6
Dewey, J. 94
dialogy 5
discovery 105-8, 117-18, 120
decolonisation 13-14, 17-22, 28, 35, 40-1, 114
disease 173, 175-6, 179, 183
dispossession 38, 39, 41, 110
Dobyns, H.F. 173, 174
Dorris, M. 108
Drake, S. 180
Durkheim, E. 87, 166

E

earth 21, 24-5, 26, 27
education: aims of Argentinian indigenous law 125-6; aims of colonising states 119; as communicative action 10; conceptual strategies 152-7; cultural content and processes 139-42; culture and 165-6; curriculum 149-50; epistemic strategies 158-9; First Nations case study 132-4; institutional strategies 150; intercultural learning 159; knowledge sets of instructional experts 144-5; multicultural educational leadership 145-6; Nuu-chah-nulth education into culture 134-7; Nuu-chah-nulth educational aspirations 137-8; Nuu-chah-nulth First Nations approaches 138-9; programmatic strategies 150-2; recruitment 146-8; retention 148-9; role of teacher 165-71; shifting paradigms 142-4
Eletronorte 52, 55, 59
Elmore, R.F. 144
encounter 108, 174
Engels, F. 23
environmental issues 186-7, 195-7, 198-202
epistemic strategies 158-9
Escobar, A. 193
Esteva, G. 190
Etcitty, Hastiin Alexander 116
Evans-Pritchard, E.E. 20-1, 24, 79
expert witnesses 11, 12, 18

F

Fals-Borda, O. 196
FAWA (Waimiri-Atroari Attraction Front) 46, 47, 49, 53, 59
FENAMAD (Native Federation of the Madre de Dios) 33-4, 35, 40
Fergie, D. 81, 83, 87, 88, 90
Ferguson, J. 28
Fernández, R. 68
Figueiredo, General 54
Filho, Romero Jucá 56
Finger, M. 190, 193, 194, 196-8, 201, 203
First Nations: conceptual strategies in education 152-7; cultural content and processes 139-42; curriculum 149-50, 159; education 10, 132-4; institutions 132, 150; Nuu-chah-nulth education into culture 134-7; Nuu-chah-nulth

educational aspirations 137-8; Nuu-chah-nulth First Nations approaches 138-9; programmatic strategies 150-2; recruitment of students 146-8, 159; retention of students 148-9, 159; shifting paradigms 142-4
First Nations Health Symposium (1998) 149
First Nations House of Learning (1998) 141, 151
Forquin, J.-C. 171
Fortes, M. 20-1, 24
Foucault, M. 190
Franchetto, B. 166
Fraser, N. 194
Freire, P. 196
Friedman, J. 194
Fujimori, President 35
FUNAI (National Indian Foundation) 1-3, 46-53, 167

G

Gaia hypothesis 199
Gallois, D. 30
Garcia, P. 29, 36
Geddicks, A. 192, 205
Geertz, C. 87, 94-5
GELIND (Group of Study of Indigenous Legislation) 9
Gell, A. 85
Gellner, E. 79
General Allotment Act (1886) 111
genocide 174, 176-83, 185-6, 188
Ghana 21
Giaccaria, B. 169
Glatthorn, A.A. 144, 145
Godelier, M. 23
Goffman, E. 54
Golla, S. 138
Gollan, Bertha 89
Gonzalez, J. 122
Government of Canada (1998) 138, 143
Gramsci, A. 197-8
Gray, A. 9, 17, 18, 39
Gray, J. 143
Green Perdue, M. 178
Grove-White, R. 198
Grumet, R.S. 177, 180
Guatemala 10
Gudynas, E. 204
Guerrero, D. 122
Gupta, A. 28

H

Ha-shilt-sa 147
Haa-huu-pay-ak 147
Hajer, M. 196
Handler, R. 101
Hanford Nuclear Reservation 187
Hanson, A. 79, 87
Harakmbut language 30-1
Harries-Jones, P. 193, 198
Hart, C. 58
Hartford, Treaty of 180
Harvey, D. 204
Hatch, M.J. 142
Hebb, D.O. 140
Held, D. 194, 197
Henriksen, G. 22-3, 39
Hernández, I. 65, 66-7
Hesse, Hermann 137
Hiatt, L. 23
Hidalgo, N. 145
Hillerman, T. 116
Hindmarsh Island Bridge: Royal Commission 81-3, 86, 87-90, 98-9, 100; sacred site claim 80-3
Hinsley, F.H. 113
Hirsch, E. 25, 28
Hobbes, T. 114
Hocart, M. 89
Hoekema, A. 193
Howell, S. 22
Hübner, G. 46
human rights 6-7, 11, 39-41, 184
Hupachasaht 133
Huron 181
Hvalkof, S. 39
hydroelectric schemes 50, 59, 186-7

I

ILO (International Labour Organisation): Agreement n°169 122; Convention (107) 17, 27; Convention (169) 36
IMF (International Monetary Fund) 36, 203
India 38, 39
Indian Reorganization Act (IRA) 111-12
Indigenous People and the State (1992) 187
Indonesia 38
Innu 22-3
institutional strategies 150
integration 1
Intellectual Property Rights 25, 40

International Union for the Conservation of Nature 196
Inuit 3, 186
IPP (Indigenous Peoples Participation Programme) 127-8
Iroquois 181
Iturralde, F. 122
IWGIA (International Work Group for Indigenous Affairs) 37-8, 40

J

Jackson, Andrew 178
Janu'ma 48
Japan 18, 37
Jennings, F. 173, 175, 182, 173
Johnson, M. 142
Johnson v. Macintosh 106-7
Jones, Evan 178
Joyce, B. 145

K

Kahn, M. 166
Kanaky 38
Kariera 19
Kartinyeri, Doreen 80, 87, 91
Katz, L.G. 144
Katz, S.T. 185
Kentehuari, E. 40
Kieft, Willem 181-2
knowledge sets of instructional experts 144-5
Koch-Grünberg, Th. 46
Kolig, E. 93, 101
Korten, D. 28
Krasner, S. 203
Kroeber, A.L. 173, 174, 175, 182
Kuhn, T.S. 142, 143
Kuper, A. 19

L

La Rusic, I. 11, 12, 18
Labbe 68
Lakoff, G. 142
Lalonde, C. 148
land 26, 40, 124
lands 27, 124
landscape 25, 26, 27
Las Casas, Bartolome de 173, 182
Lash, S. 193, 198, 199, 203-4
Lather, P. 140
Latour, B. 190, 200, 205
Law n°23302 122, 123-7, 129-30
Law n°24071 122

Law of Native Communities (Law 22175) 32-3, 35, 36
Law of Private Investment (Land Law, Law 26505) 35-6, 38
laws regulating reservations 69-73
Layton, R. 23, 92
Leach, E.R. 29
Leiss, W. 206
Lemkin, R. 185
Lévi-Strauss, C. 168
Lightning, W. 142
Lincoln, Abraham 178
Lipschuts, A. 68
Lipschutz, R. 194
Lohman, L. 198
Lombardi, M.O. 113-14, 117
Lopes da Silva, A. 10-11, 168
Lovelock, J. 199
Lowie, R. 19
Luhrman, T. 198
Lyttle, C.M. 4

M

McLuhan, M. 150
McShane, D. 141
Maddock, K. 11, 23
Magic-Eye 140
Magnusson, W. 115-16
Maine, H. 20, 26
Mair, L. 21
Malaspina University College Arts-One First Nations 151-2
Malmberg, T. 26
Maori tradition 79
Mapuche 65-6, 73-4; Chilean agrarian policy towards 9; disappearance of reservations 67-8; population 66-7; privatisation of collective property 69-73; rebellions 3; relegation to reservations 67; territorial autonomy 66-7
Marglin, S. 191
Marshall, John 106-7, 109
Marx, Karl 23-4
Marxism, 28
Mason, Captain John 176-7
Mason, M. 190, 191
Mathews, Justice 82, 91, 95
Maya 27
Maybury-Lewis, D. 168, 169, 192
Meadows, D. 195
Meliá, B. 166
Mendlovitz, S.H. 114, 118

218 *Index*

Menem, President 128
Merlan, F. 100
Mexico 4, 73
Meyrowitz, J. 145, 150
Mezirow, J. 144
Miller, J.M. 133, 135
Milton, K. 198
mining 187
Mobil 34
modern society 190, 200-2, 205-6
modernisation 191, 193, 199, 201
modernity 125, 126, 193, 199-200, 202
Mohawk 181
Moksnes, H. 40
Monserrat, R. 166
Mooney, J. 174, 182
Morales, A. 68
More, A. 141
Morgan, L.H. 19, 20, 23, 26
Morphy, H. 23
Morrison, D. 157
multicultural educational leadership 145-6

N
N. E. Thing Enterprises 140
NAFTA (North American Free Trade Agreement) 73
Nagaland 38
Nandy, A. 201
Narragansetts 176, 177, 180
Nash, J. 24
Naskapi 22-3
nature: culture and 199; environmentalist movement 198; role of land 23-4; society and 190, 200-2, 205, 206; spiritual relationship with 193, 198; voices 198-9; Western culture and 80
Navajo (Navaho) 116, 187
Needham, R. 27, 79, 83, 86, 88, 93
New France 181
New Netherlands 181
New Zealand 80, 191
Newcomb, S. 106
Ngarrindjeri: belief, practice, culture 90-6; Christianity 96-7; Heritage Committee, 82; sacred site claim 80-3; testing of belief 87-90; traditional religious life 83-6; "women's business" and the Royal Commission 86-7
NGOs (non-governmental organisations) 8, 191, 196-7, 203

NIA (National Institute for Indian Affairs) 124, 127
Nicaragua 4, 71
NITEP (Native Indian Teachers Education Programme) 141
North Island College 133, 143, 147
Nuer 21
Nunavut 3
Nuu-chah-nulth 132; education into culture 134-7; educational aspirations 137-8; First Nations approaches 138-9
Nuu-chah-nulth Tribal Council (1996) 133, 135

O
Oatley, K. 141
Ogbu, J.U. 141, 143, 149
O'Hanlon, M. 25
Olson, D.R. 141
Ortiz, A. 24
Overing, J. 12
Overing Kaplan, J. 30

P
Pallas, A.M. 144
Papal authority 105-6
Papua New Guinea 85
paradigms, shifting 142-4
Paranapanema Group 50, 52, 54-6
Parikh, J. 202
Parkman, F. 180, 181, 182
Pavonia 181-2
Peet, R. 205
Penn, Thomas 177
Peggion, E. 10
Pequot 175-7, 180
Perdue, T. 178
Peru 24, 29-36, 39, 71
Peters, M. 141, 148
Peterson, M. 194, 197
Piaget, J. 141
Pierce, B. 141
Plant, R. 27
population: decline 179-80; disease 173, 175-6, 179, 183; genocide 174, 176-9, 180, 181-2, 183, 185-6, 188; pre-contact 173, 174-5, 179, 182-3; removal policy 178; suicide rate 184
Posey, D. 25
Prescott, W.H. 180
Princen, T. 194, 203, 204
privatisation 37-8, 69-73

Programa Waimiri-Atroari 50, 55-8, 59
programmatic strategies 150-2
Province of British Columbia (1998) 133

Q
Quechua 27
Quilín, Treaty of 66
Quine, W.V. 79, 83, 94

R
Radcliffe-Brown, A.R. 19-20, 21
Rahnema, M. 195, 196
Ramos, A.R. 52
Ranger, T. 13
Rasmussen, K. 100
recruitment 146-8
refugees 28
Register of Indigenous Communities 123
relativism, cultural 6-7, 79
religion: Australian Aboriginal 7, 82-3, 90-5; belief, practice, culture 90-5; Canadian diversity 138; Christianity 96-7, 101, 105-6, 114, 116–18; freedom of 30, 96, 97-101; Green approach to nature 198; landscape and 27; legal recognition 73, 100-1; missions 167; Ngarrindjeri traditions 83-6; Six Rivers Forest case 97-9; territory and 21, 23-4, 27; testing of belief 87-90, 100
relocation, forced 37, 38
Renyi, J. 145
reservations: alcohol-related deaths 184; allotment of land 37, 38, 39; disappearance of 65, 67-8, 69; environmental issues 186-7; establishment 37, 38, 67; housing standards 185; laws regulating 69-73; Mapuche 65, 66, 67-8; sovereignty issues 109-12
Reserves 34, 50, 52, 55
retention 148-9
reversal theory 140
rights, territorial 29-36, 41
Rio UNCED 195, 196, 197, 203
Ríos, M. 4-5
risk society 190, 199-201, 206
rituals 84, 90
Rivière, P. 47
Rorty, R. 94
Rosenau, J. 194, 202-3, 204

Royal Commission on Hindmarsh Island Bridge 81-3, 86, 87-90, 98-9, 100
Ruiz, L.E.J. 119
Russell, H.S. 175
Ryle, G. 87

S
Sachs, W. 191, 195, 196, 198
Salomon, L. 194-5
Saunders, Cheryl 81, 83
Sayer, Judith 133
Scardamalia, M. 158
Schapera, I. 21
Schultz, M. 142
Scott, J. 192
Segato, R.L. 59
self-determination: concept 54; directed 9, 54; issue 3-4, 9; politics of 3; right to 18, 39, 69, 109, 192-3; sovereignty and 8, 109, 112, 116-20; United States policy 109, 110, 113; the way to 116-20
Sendero Luminoso 32
Session, G. 199
Seven Sisters 91-2
Shapiro, M. 108
Sherman, P. 10
Shiva, V. 204
Shkilnyks, A.M. 186
Showers, B. 145
Shulman, L.S. 144
Sigel, I.E. 144
Silva, M. 57, 166
SINAMOS 33
Six Rivers National Forest 97-9
Skar, S. 27
Smith, A. 186
Smith, C. 100
Smith, Captain John 176
South Africa 21
sovereignty: concept 7, 9, 105, 118; deprived of 192; in federal Indian law 109-13; indigenous assertion of 109; in international law 113-16; issues 4, 10; Mapuche territory 67; self-determination and 8, 109, 112, 116-19; United States law 106, 109-13
space: interethnic contact and 48-9; Waimiri-Atroari concepts 46-8
Sperber, D. 79, 83, 88, 100

Index 219

220 Index

SPI (Serviço de Proteção ao Índio) 46
Sproat, G.M. 143
Stannard, D.E. 178, 183
Stark, J. 199
Stavenhagen, R. 72, 193
Stephens, I. 86
Stiffarm, L.A. 174
Sudan 21
suicides 148, 184, 186
sustainable development 190-1, 202-6
Sutton, P. 91-3, 99
Swazi 21
Sweller, J. 153, 154
Swyngedouw, E. 204, 205

T

Taino population 182, 183, 186
Tallensi 21, 24
Tanien Ashini 192
Taylor, B. 201, 205
Taylor, Zachary 178
teacher, role of 165-71
Temoak Band 112
territory: colonialism and decolonisation 17-22; concept 17, 18-22; hardening boundaries 29-36; importance of territories 37-41; softening boundaries 22-9
Tertullian 89
Tewa 24
Thornton, R. 173, 174-5
Tickner, R. 83
Tindale, N. 81, 83, 85
Titulos de Merced 67, 68, 69
Tonkinson, R. 91
Tordera, P. 68
Torrance, N. 141
Towson, S. 141, 148
tradition: invention of 79; modernity and 125; recognition of 119
Traditional Environmental Knowledge 193
transcultural 12
transmigration 38-9
Trigger, B.G. 173, 180-1
Tucum Project 10, 166-71
Tully, J. 138
Turner, M. 142
Turner, V. 93
Tuzin, D. 94

U

Uluru 92
Underhill, Captain John 177

United Nations: Commission on Human Rights 17; Convention 185; Decade of Indigenous People 108; Declaration on the Rights of Indigenous Peoples 17, 22, 39, 40, 109; Indigenous representation 184; Working Group on Indigenous Populations 17, 39
United States: challenges to indigenous culture 80; federal Indian law 109-13; power over indigenous people 106-8; reservations 37; Senate 113; Six Rivers National Forest case 97-9; Supreme Court, 98-9, 106, 112; territorial policy 18; Tribal College system 150
URACCAN (University of the Autonomous Regions of the Caribbean Coast of Nicaragua) 4
uranium 186, 187
Urquiza, General 66
Urry, J. 193, 198, 199, 203-4

V

Valdivia, Pedro de 66
Varese, S. 45
Velasco, President 32
Visvanatyhan, S. 201
Viveiros de Castro, E. 59
Von Doussa J 83, 95
Vygotsky, L. 141, 157

W

Waimiri-Atroari 45, 58-60; concepts of space 46-8; directed self-determination 9; occupation of Waimiri-Atroari territory 49-53; Programa Waimiri-Atroari 55-8; Waimiri-Atroari Attraction Front 53-5
Walker, R.B.J. 105, 114, 117, 118
Wampanoag 175, 176, 177
wandari, concept of 30-1, 33-4, 36
Wasley, P.A. 145
Watts, M. 205
WCED (World Commission on Environment and Development) 191, 195, 196
Weiner, J. 7-8, 10, 12, 93, 95, 100
Western Shoshone 112-13
Williams, R.A. Jr. 120
Willis, R. 22

Wilmer, F. 191, 192, 193
Wilson, B.G. 153
Wilson, R. 6-7, 11, 27
"women's business": accounts of 86-7, 89-90; Christianity and 97; claim of fabrication 80, 81; custodians 95; dilemma 99-100; existence of 81, 83, 100; Royal Commission and 86-7; Seven Sisters 91
Worster, D. 196, 198

X
Xavante People 10, 166, 168-71

Y
Yanomami Park 39
Yearley, S. 198
Yrigoyen, R. 10

Z
Zapotecos 4

Printed in the USA/Agawam, MA
October 27, 2011

562101.082